FURY TO HELL

KATHRYN SPURLING

FURY TO HELL

NEW
HOLLAND

First published in 2022 by New Holland Publishers
Sydney

Level 1, 178 Fox Valley Road, Wahroonga, NSW 2076, Australia

newhollandpublishers.com

A record of this book is held at the National Library of Australia.

ISBN 9781760794668

Managing Director: Fiona Schultz
Project Editor: Liz Hardy
Designer: Andrew Davies
Production Director: Arlene Gippert
Printed in Australia

10 9 8 7 6 5 4 3 2 1

Keep up with New Holland Publishers:

f NewHollandPublishers
@ @newhollandpublishers

CONTENTS

Introduction   7

Chapter One: 'It was a shock'   9

Chapter Two: 'We were told: "Don't worry about it …"'   17

Chapter Three: 'I don't think there is a tail gunner yet, who isn't scared' 27

Chapter Four: 'You always used to shower and shave and do
      everything before we went'   36

Chapter Five: 'You just weren't anxious to make friendships …
      because they didn't last long enough'   48

Chapter Six: 'I didn't see it, the mid upper gunner didn't see it …'   57

Chapter Seven: 'I'm convinced he could have saved himself …'   66

Chapter Eight: 'You'd move the maggots aside because
      they used to go with your soups'   76

Chapter Nine: 'Für Sie der Krieg ist fertig!' ('For you, the war is finished') 92

Chapter Ten: 'I often wished it were possible to hitch a ride with them' 107

Chapter Eleven: 'It is every POW's duty to try to escape'   116

Chapter Twelve: 'At the back of the mind of any sane POW is fear'   132

Chapter Thirteen: 'I did not expect to be here'   144

Chapter Fourteen: 'We saw the bomber keel over and crash …
      all on board were killed except the tail gunner'   155

Chapter Fifteen: 'Another lousy day …'   169

Chapter Sixteen: 'Men were constantly beaten …   181

Chapter Seventeen: 'We were waiting and waiting for the Yanks …'   194

Chapter Eighteen: 'We didn't realise how precarious our
      situation had been'   203

Chapter Nineteen: 'The most mental and physical deprivation,
      the memory of which I shall carry to my grave'   215

Bibliography   227

Endnotes   233

Acknowledgements   239

INTRODUCTION

They left Australia, the finest of youth – many still teenagers. They believed they were invincible. Imbued with patriotic fervour, they were determined to fight against evil, defend freedom and the British Empire. Seduced by Hollywood's gallant depiction of World War I aviators, and *Biggles* books, they believed there was glamour and safety in joining the Royal Australian Air Force (RAAF). The reality was entirely different. They became Royal Air Force (RAF) Bomber Command fodder in the dangerous skies over Europe. Bomber Command aircrew suffered the highest of casualties. Of the total of 125,000 aircrew, 57,205, or 46 per cent, were killed. A further 8403 were wounded and 9838 were shot out of the fury of the sky into the hell of German POW camps – a total of 60 per cent of all operational airmen. Of the 10,000 Australians who served with RAF Bomber Command, 3486 were killed and 650 died in training accidents, the highest Australian fatality rate of any unit in WWII.

Despite the enormous sacrifice their service did not fit the dominant ANZAC mythology. They were not members of the AIF. Theirs was deemed a cleaner war; they, a privileged section of the Australian military, their duty as bomber crew not real war, not part of the gentleman's code of war, look-them-in-the-eye combat; and at the same time their actions were regarded as indiscriminate and even reckless. Furthermore, they were not fighting a war in the Pacific which threatened their own.

As in the previous world war they knew themselves as 'kriegies' the shortened term of '*Kriegsgefangener*' but, hidden behind the statistics, were the 1476 Australian airmen incarcerated in German lufts and stalags throughout Europe. Subsumed in history because of the inhuman treatment subjected to the estimated 22,376 Australian prisoners of war (POWs) of the Japanese, these POWs received minimal recognition.

Cinematic depictions compounded false impressions and personal post-traumatic stress disorders. Films such as *The Great Escape* romanticised the life in German stalags and lufts. Uniforms were spotless, huts looked more like holiday camps and the heroes showed no signs of starvation or ill-treatment. Similar were television programmes such as *Hogan's Heroes*. This popular six-series sitcom promoted the impression of comfort, comedy, and inept and genial German authorities. Nothing could be further from reality.

When members of the RAAF fell from the sky in the land of the enemy, they were invariably subjected to cruelty by the civilian population while authorities turned away – many were murdered. Those taken into custody received the harshest treatment of all: POWs of Germany in WWII. Their interrogations were vicious as the opposing military attempted to extract information to counter a bombing campaign that took the war directly into occupied territories and the homeland. Unlike other POWs, they were tightly secured behind barbed wire in their own compounds and subjected to the harshest of treatment, should their escape result in them again flying bombers into European skies.

For the men in faded blue battle dress their POW internment was highlighted by courage, and comradeship. It also meant enduring hunger, boredom, deprivation, cruelty, and neglect. Few did not lose 40 percent of their body weight; few did not suffer ongoing illness and depression. Some were killed by their own, caught up in the Allied advance, or the death marches, as POWs were forced by their captors through the harsh winter of 1944–45 to deny their liberation.

They returned to Australia in ignominy. Ignored by the government which had sent them to war, these RAAF ex-POWs were expected to reintegrate into a strange society and reconnect with families who could never understand.

The turbulent journey of Warrant Officer Albert 'Bert' Adrian Stobart (RAAF) illustrates the experience of thousands of others who left Australia to fight a foreign air war. He was ripped from his RAAF 460 Squadron Lancaster bomber only to watch all but one of his close-knit crew perish. For almost two years Stobart barely survived Stalag IVB. He returned a changed man to observe fellow RAAF POWs struggle with anxiety and depression, poor health, and premature death. This is his story and the story of too many others.

CHAPTER ONE

'It was a shock.'

Albert Stobart

Albert 'Bert' Adrian Stobart was born on 11 April 1921 in Sandringham, Victoria, to John and Beatrice. Initially hoteliers in the gentle green English countryside, his parents migrated across the world to the strong colours of Australia. The family moved to the Melbourne suburb of St Kilda and then Brighton. They were a devout Protestant family, regular churchgoers. Bert, the youngest of seven children, attended Sunday School and was a member of the church choir and school.

The Great Depression bit in 1929 with the collapse of the share market. Australia's export income plummeted resulting in a national economic crisis. Thousands of Australians struggled to find work and many more, shelter and food. Unemployment rose to 32 per cent by 1932 and charities struggled to feed the destitute and starving. The Stobart family was fortunate. John Stobart was an electrical engineer and not only worked for a contractor but also for the British Australian Tobacco Company (WD & HO Wills). It seemed money could always be found for tobacco and cigarettes even during a depression, so the nicotine addiction kept John in work and the Stobart family in relative comfort. The innocence of youth shielded Bert from understanding the grief and deprivation suffered by people around the world: 'Whilst we were brought up in hard times, we were never badly off.'

As the worst of the Depression eased, for Australian adolescents this remained an uncomplicated era, with simple pleasures. Neighbourhood children played cricket and football and a host of other games on streets – clearing away makeshift wickets and goalposts should the occasional motor vehicle crawl down their road. They came home when they were hungry. Families ate dinner together before moving to the living room to listen to the radio or read books. Comics were poured over by Bert and his siblings and with three older brothers and three older sisters he fared well in hand-me-downs and well-thumbed reading material.

His education commenced at Sandringham State School, then Elsternwick and then St Kilda Park School. Secondary schooling was at the prestigious Melbourne

Grammar between 1936 and 1938. This generation of white Australians revered Great Britain. On Monday mornings students saluted the flag at school assembly and recited 'Honour the King'. Anzac Day and the Armistice on 11 November were solemnly observed. At Grammar, the services were highlighted by guest Old Melburnians who had served in World War One (WWI). 'We thought they were such old men, but they were only about 25 – that was old to us.' Bert proved his sporting prowess at Melbourne Grammar achieving house colours and making the first rugby union XVIII and second cricket XI. Being the youngest of seven encouraged a restlessness; academics did not appeal and he left school with a Merit Certificate having not sat his Intermediate examinations.

Noel (Stobart).

In 1938 he was a junior salesman with Stott & Hoare, Melbourne, selling office equipment, on a salary of 30/– a week. The employment was rather boring, but life was good, the golden beach and rolling surf were but a short distance away and a large family meant there were few dull moments. He was already keen on a girl he had known from school – her name was Noel, in keeping with her Christmas Day birth.

It was 3 September 1939 when Australian Prime Minister, Robert Menzies, sombrely announced in a national radio broadcast that because Britain had declared war on Germany, so too was Australia at war. The Stobarts were at the Dickens Street Church of England church that Sunday and returned from listening to a sermon extolling peace and goodwill to an announcement that the gates of hell were about to open. 'It was a shock,' Bert remembered as he observed his parents' faces. They had weathered the Great War in England and the memories remained vivid. They understood its dark depths and far-reaching claws; they had four sons, all military service age, who had no such memory. As Bert Stobart attempted to conceal his excitement, little did he realise that for him it would mean the descent into hell, firstly in the European air war and then struggling to survive a German POW camp.

Bert joined the militia in 1939 initially because it paid 8/– a day. Employers were required to allow their workers time off for training and that meant 56/– a week, more than his salary. His brothers were in the militia before him. He liked the idea of the military comradeship and the occasional camp, though at indoctrination a sergeant looked him squarely in the eye and said, 'I hope you make a better soldier than your brothers did.'

He trained as gun crew, on 18-pounders and howitzers, not exactly up-to-date artillery, but after WWI and the war to end all wars, successive Australian governments saw few votes and little need in money spent on military equipment. Australia wasn't ready for war, nor was Britain, nor Europe. Germany, under National Socialist German Workers' Party (NAZI) dictator Adolf Hitler, had undertaken rearmament in violation of the Treaty of Versailles, while world leaders watched and procrastinated.

In January 1940, as a member of the militia 2nd field artillery, Bert was in camp at Seymour, Victoria, for three months. Members of the regular army at the nearby Puckapunyal training establishment, did not hesitate to show their derision, referring to members of the militia as 'chocolate soldiers', or 'choccos', a harsh jibe meaning part-time volunteers weren't real soldiers, and would quickly melt in the heat of battle. It was a bad summer in bushfire-prone Victoria and much of his militia time was spent fighting fires with nothing more than a potato sack. Between the jibes, heat, the crowded tents, the willy willies that blasted bodies with dust when tent flaps were rolled up to counter the heat, and 160 days in khaki, Bert had been dissuaded from joining the Australian Army and fighting a ground war.

Australian Government demilitarisation after WWI, compounded by myopic faith in the protection of Britain meant Australia's navy and army were diminished. Attitudes within the Australian Defence Force (ADF) hierarchy meant the Royal Australian Air Force (RAAF) had suffered worst. The air force was not part of the exalted and common interpretation of the Anzac legend, which extolled the virtues of Australians splashing ashore, rifles raised, on Turkey's Gallipoli beach, or defying German machine guns entrenched on the Western Front. These military leaders were yet to be stunned and edified by the strategic configuration which would dominate war between 1939 and 1945, when the battle in the skies proved devastating and decisive.

German forces demonstrated the effectiveness of 'Blitzkrieg' (lightning war) in the invasion of Poland. This offensive warfare, deploying mobile manoeuvrable forces including armoured tanks, with air support, resulted in rapid victory while minimising the loss of soldiers and artillery. The Luftwaffe (German Air Force) was pivotal and its strength, obvious. By 1935 Germany was equal in first-line air power with Britain, but the English were slow to react. British industry could manufacture aircraft rapidly but there was a desperate need for aircrew.

It was decided that the British Dominions could supply the Royal Air Force (RAF) with personnel as they had soldiers, in WWI. On 26 October 1939, the United Kingdom finalised a training scheme and in December 1939, the Empire Air Training Scheme (EATS) was initiated. Australia's commitment was to supply

10,478 aircrew every year. Given the depleted state of the RAAF the assignment was herculean.

The RAAF was underprepared. Australia had trained only 50 pilots per year for Australian service, or deployment in Britain with the RAF. There were very few Australian-based training establishments and fewer instructors. A meagre collection of Hawker Demons, Ansons and Seagulls were the only aircraft – none of which were suitable for frontline service. Volunteers with a higher level of education commonly required of army or navy recruits were urgently wanted, men who could master the sophisticated equipment coming online and the skills required to take it into the skies and survive. Time and patience were needed but by 1940 there was little of both; the RAAF was very much running to catch up.

The Anzac legend may have been fundamental to Australian culture, but there was glamour and mystique attached to flying. Swashbuckling heroes, with white scarves streaming behind them as they piloted flimsy aircraft in World War I air battles, featured prominently in fiction and cinema. At war's end they stunned regional crowds below with their acrobatics and offered joy rides. For those unable to afford that luxury there were always *Biggles* books, cinema matinees featuring *The Adventures of Tailspin Tommy*, and constructing model planes out of balsa wood and glue while the imagination played. Two WWI veterans, Paul McGinness and Hudson Fysh, dreamed of taking passengers into Australian skies and beyond. On 16 November 1920 they registered Queensland and Northern Territory Aerial Services Limited (QANTAS). Not only did this pioneer internal air travel but in 1935 services between Brisbane and Singapore commenced. QANTAS aircraft proved vital at the commencement of yet another war in Europe.

The RAAF appeared to offer a more glamorous, cleaner, safer war. By 1940 cinema newsreels highlighted the heroics of spitfire pilots while typically downplaying the brutal cost in lives. Within the first six months of WWII being declared, an estimated 100,000 Australian volunteered to enlist in the Australian Defence Force (ADF). Around 68,000 of these applied to join the RAAF, 11,500 as aircrew[1]. RAAF recruiters were totally overwhelmed, and volunteers were told to wait months, which invariably extended into another year. Some tired of the delay and enlisted in the Royal Australian Navy (RAN) and 2nd Australian Imperial Force. Bert was determined to wait. He had tasted army training in the militia and decided it was not for him, he just wanted to fly. RAAF pilot candidates required a 110 minimum intelligence quota, better than average eye-muscle coordination, reaction speed and night vision.[2] His enlistment paper was submitted in July 1940 when he was 19 years and four months. His call-up finally came on 20 June 1941 at 20 and two months, with the added excitement of being categorised 'Aircrew V (Pilot)'.

RAAF Course 16 through 4ITS, Victor Harbour. Albert Stobart is sitting in the front row, second from right (AWM).

Britain was urgently asking for 300 pilots, 2000 observers and 3300 gunner/ wireless operators.[3] With more twin-engine bombers going into service there was a greater need for gunners. Bert only got as far as Melbourne's Spencer Street Station when RAAF authorities admitted that they had selected too many pilots. With too many 'Aircrew (P)', authorities simply started at 'A' and stopped down the line when they figured they had enough. It was a disappointment for Bert whose name started with 'S', and who had hoped his militia gunnery experience might ensure he remained in the RAAF. If there was scrutiny of the obsolete guns he practised on, he might still be cut from the program until more instructors were found. He held his breath and was classified 'Aircrew V (G)'.

Aircraftsman Albert Stobart became a member of RAAF Course 16 through the Initial Training School (ITS) at South Australia's Victor Harbour. The four-week course included lectures in aerodynamics, meteorology and navigation. Inoculations against every disease known to man were pumped into arms, sometime both arms at the same time, and then recruits harshly sent on a cross-country run. Bert had little difficulty in the physical side of service life: the marching, parades, and physical exercise under the ever-watchful eyes and loud, colourful language of drill instructors. The theory component proved insurmountable. He had trouble with Morse code, those dots and dashes seemed to blend together in an unholy mess. His training was extended to another month. Bert quickly acquired the nickname 'Stoppy' due to the Australian preference of either shortening or lengthening names, whichever seemed easier. It seemed rather appropriate given his lack of speed with Morse.

Not considered suited for the theory-based navigator stream, Bert was designated Wireless Operator/Air Gunner (WOP) and posted to the RAAF's No. 1 Wireless Air Gunners School (1 WAGS) at Ballarat, Victoria. The Ballarat Airport, 7 kilometres from the city centre, was opened in 1914 and 1 WAGS was established there in 1940.[4] By May 1945 some 5025 had graduated through the school. Bert 'Stoppy' Stobart was not one of these.

Ahead was seven months of radio theory and electrical science – and a Morse code operating efficiency of 18 words a minute in code and plain language. Learning to operate wireless equipment to send to and receive from Wackett aircraft was also required. For Bert it meant another delay – seven months more study, more dreaded Morse code; he was unsettled. Melbourne Grammar acquaintance Alexander 'Donny' Douglas Finlayson (408569) was as unhappy at enduring wireless operator training as Bert. They both fronted the commanding officer and requested to be streamed as air gunners. This they believed meant not only no more theory and intrusive Morse dots and dashes, but a faster track to war.

Instructors agreed Stobart and Finlayson were unlikely to ever sew on the WOP insignia. However, there was no early escape from 1 WAGS Ballarat. Gunnery training was not undertaken at Ballarat due to the close proximity of a populated area. Neither would they be sent ahead to Evans Head, New South Wales, but were ordered to remain until their WOP course passed out. It was less than ideal for the impatient gunners and they spent weeks transporting stores, driving ambulances, and counting down the days. The frustration increased when, in December 1941, Japanese forces attacked Pearl Harbor, and Australia was forced to fight wars in Europe and in the Pacific. Unsullied by the horrors of conflict, Bert was busting to get into the action. There was even more need for pilots, if only he was at the Service Flying School, but this was thwarted by red tape.

On 4 May 1942 Bert and his class departed for Evans Head and No. 1 Air Gunners and Bombing Air Gunners School (BAGS). He could not have been happier and was enthusiastic for the next training regime to learn air-to-ground and air-to-air gunnery. Bert thrived on the practical and had little difficulty in learning how to assemble, disassemble, service guns, load magazines, and set an aircraft gun in position. Learning aircraft recognition and how the Frazer-Nash turret worked seemed to take him closer to the enemy. Examinations and oral tests on tactics, turret handling, range procedure, and the correction of machine-gun malfunctions while blindfolded all made sense to Bert.

It was good to feel the metal trigger beneath his fingers and the power of the weapon, to know this was what they would soon be using against the enemy. In his urgency, Bert didn't appreciate how rudimentary the training was. Countless

Gunnery training on Australian obsolete equipment (AWM).

hours were spent on a Vickers GO gun, a gas-operated gun with the rounds on the top – an ordinary ring and bead sight – round after round. The only aircraft available were the old Fairey Battles – best known for causing high crew fatalities. An ungainly medium bomber with an open-back cockpit, it could only offer ground target practice, or at a drogue pulled behind another aircraft; 'easy because the drogue was pulled straight and level so not hard to hit', remembered Bert. As there was no interrupter gear fitted to the Fairy Battles, great care had to be exercised when shooting at a moving target, to avoid shooting themselves down. In an average flight of an hour, 300 rounds could be expended. To complete the course trainees had to fire off 2000 rounds. Bombing training was carried out by dropping 8 x 11½ lb (5.2 kg) practice smoke bombs in circular sand targets set in the Australian bush.

After graduation, wireless operators/air gunners (WOP) took different routes, for further training in Australia and Canada; to the north of Australia for the nation's defence; to the Middle East; and, to the United Kingdom. Bert was done with training and being recategorised Air Gunner meant the likelihood of operations sooner rather than later. During 1939–40 the RAAF qualified a mere 143 aircrew. Bert graduated on 29 May 1942 – one of 191 air gunners qualified during 1941–42, one of 5322 RAAF aircrew.[5] It was a proud moment to sew on his one wing insignia with the letters AG, and Sergeant (Sgt) stripes.

He had his mind and heart set on defending England and joining Bomber Command. This posting materialised and he returned to Melbourne on leave. It was here Bert saw his first United States military personnel. 'They looked like they had just stepped out of a tailor's shop, beautifully coloured brown jackets, light-coloured trousers.' It was hard not to admire the streamlined uniforms of Americans; but not the ribbons emblazoned on their chests when they had yet to see combat.

Embarkation date loomed, and RAAF personnel were encouraged to write wills and 'put their affairs in order'. This included allotting two shillings a day from their salary to next-of-kin. RAAF sergeants were paid 15/6d per day, 2/– per day

Noel and Bert after he joined the RAAF (Stobart).

more than RAF sergeants, so it was considered tactful to ensure parity while serving with the RAF.

There was too little time, too much to say, but no way to say it. The family attempted to look nonchalant but caring. In his wallet Bert carried a photo of Noel, a statuesque dark-haired girl with a lovely smile. He had met her when she was a 15-year-old student at Merton Hall, and he was at Melbourne Grammar. They liked each other immediately and knew they would marry as soon as they were old enough – the war delayed that plan. Bert asked his mother if she could accompany Noel to the jeweller to select an engagement ring.

No-one could foresee the terror and trauma that lay ahead. Australian aircrew destined for RAF Bomber Command would face a horrific war in the night skies over Europe and suffer the highest fatality rate of any single Australian defence force contingent in WWII. The final goodbyes as the train pulled out from Melbourne's Spencer Street station were difficult, his father's 'Goodbye son' attempted with bravado, his mother's face not so stoic, and Noel's tears proved a lasting memory.

CHAPTER TWO

'We were told: "Don't worry about it, ops are on tonight,
you'll get accommodation tomorrow night".'

F/S Albert Stobart (RAAF)

The euphoria took a hit when Bert boarded his transport for England on
24 August 1942. A cruise liner would have been nice, but an old WWI coal burner
with hammocks for 900 aircrew? 'It was a shocker,' were the only words Sgt Stobart
could muster. At least the RAN cruiser escort was comforting. The danger in the
Indian Ocean from German raiders loomed. The RAN had suffered a terrible loss
on 19 November 1941 when the light cruiser HMAS *Sydney II* disappeared with
its entire crew of 645, following a fierce battle off the Western Australian coast
with the German raider *Kormoran*.

The coal burner crawled around South Africa with stops at the ports of Durban
and Cape Town, exotic destinations for a generation raised in the shadow of WWI
and the Depression. Bert's contingent visited the South African capital shortly after
Australian Imperial Force (AIF) troops, whose exploits were less than favourable
to their nation's prestige. 'They couldn't believe that we were Australians. They
thought we were a different nationality altogether from our behaviour.' Stories
relayed by the locals were embarrassing, but one brought a smile to Bert's face.
Australian soldiers had lifted a Volkswagen car up the main Cape Town post office
steps, placed stamps all over it and scrawled the message that the car was to be
returned to Germany.

The voyage was frustratingly slow as his transport inched its way up towards
England. There was the suggestion that if everyone rowed it could be faster than
the engines. The threat of German U-boats to all Allied shipping was omnipresent.
At Cape Town, Bert had encountered a Melbourne Grammar school friend,
also aircrew. His transport had been torpedoed; fortunately, most on board had
survived. Being on possibly the slowest ship in the Atlantic did little to alleviate
nervousness. It seemed to take forever, and the sight of the English coastline was
an immense relief. Barrage balloons covered the sky to prevent attack on shipping
from the air – an introduction to a nation under siege.

There were many emotions. Bert was finally in the land of his parents, the motherland. He hoped there was time to visit places they spoke of nostalgically and relatives he had yet to meet. Signs of conflict were clearly evident in the coastal town of Bournemouth, where Australian aircrew were initially billeted. This once vibrant seaside resort had been filled with the laughter of children frolicking in the calm water as their parents relaxed on the beach. Now there was no laughter. Due to the threat of air raid, English children had been evacuated from the large cities and coast to host families in the countryside. The Blitz, the strategic bombing campaign conducted by the Luftwaffe against London and other English centres between September 1940 and May 1941, had killed an estimated 32,000 citizens, injured three times that many, and destroyed millions of homes. In Bournemouth, the sand on which holidaymakers had regaled, was now covered by barbed wire and concrete. The grey weather reflected the sombre mood of war-torn Britain.

At the Personnel Reception Centre, aircrew were billeted in the comfortable Bathhill Court flats, six-storeys high – a skyscraper for Australians. 'Lovely apartments, hot and cold water, everything,' wrote Bert. How he later reflected on the luxury of these days, whilst enduring other European accommodation. The Bournemouth townsfolk were welcoming and referred to these boys dressed in blue as 'you bronzed Australians'. The majority were aged, their children and grandchildren having joined the war effort.

Once the aircrew daily lectures were concluded the Australians took advantage of the English pubs and the afternoon tea dance, where the remaining youthful female dance partners could be found. The amenities and catering for Australian aircrew awaiting advanced training were run efficiently by Canadians. The Australians couldn't understand why the Canadian commanding officer complained about conditions and, 'the rotten, crook food'. He was even less popular when he addressed them with, 'It's a hell of a war but it's better than no war at all.' It seemed a ludicrous statement to these unseasoned volunteers, but one they reflected on differently post-1945.

There were opportunities to board trains and explore. London was a first destination. Walking around landmark buildings such as Westminster Abbey, Big Ben, and Buckingham Palace, so prominent in school textbooks, was thrilling. The shattered homes, commercial areas and bomb craters were sobering. The white cliffs of Dover, the stuff of songs, none more famous than that sung by Vera Lynn, were now festooned by ugly early-warning radar masts. Battle dress and anti-gas equipment were issued, and with news from Occupational Training Units (OTU) that RAAF acquaintances from previous courses had been killed, the war had become very real.

Bert was sent for additional gunnery training in Wales in January 1943. Everything was so different to the elementary training received in Australia. The weapons were the latest, more precise, more powerful. He kept watching the posting lists as some of his Bournemouth contingent had already left; why not him? Perhaps it had something again to do with being down the alphabet – when would it be his turn? Finally, on 2 March 1943, Sgt Albert Stobart was sent to Litchfield, Staffordshire, England, and the RAF 27 Occupational Training Unit.

Litchfield was steeped in history. Mesolithic, Roman, Anglo-Saxon relics, remnants of the Viking invasion; the three-spired Litchfield Cathedral built between 1195 and 1249 which witnessed the worst of the Reformation, the worst and best of the Industrial Revolution. Here he was, this Aussie bloke from Brighton, Victoria, surrounded by centuries of history, sent to defend against another foreign invasion. Bert sent the obligatory postcards home, but his mind was on the most important part of his RAAF career: 'crewing up'.

In a large room at RAF Litchfield, hundreds gathered – uniforms of various blue hues, different national crests on their caps and shoulders, and insignias on their chests. Bert knew a few of the air gunners but that was all. A senior officer gave a speech underlining the importance of what they were about to undertake. Crews needed a pilot, navigator, a wireless operator, a bomb aimer and two air gunners for the first conversion on Wellington medium bombers. When they converted to Lancaster heavy bombers, a flight engineer joined. The effectiveness and safety of a crew depended on the right choices and how well they became a cohesive unit.

Rumours were rife about different aircrew, about their competency, their manner, their leadership. Bert had his mind set on a particular pilot who came with a solid reputation. Unfortunately, it was not up to him – the pilot was the captain of the crew and the individual who chose. The favoured pilot moved in a different direction and as Bert dropped his head, another pilot approached. He introduced himself as Robert 'sometimes called Robin' McPhan, an Australian. He too had been doing his homework and believed Bert was a valuable gunner. There was little time to think, less time to debate. You needed to make the decision then and there and hope for the best. Bert agreed to join McPhan's crew as the rear gunner. He later discovered that the pilot and crew he had initially wished to join were killed on their first operation. It was not the last time he was touched by fate.

The world was moving faster and men needed to become acquainted quickly sharing the tight confines of an aircraft, blending as a unit, knowing they were only as strong as their weakest link. Bert was Albert Adrian Stobart and it was humorous that as he met these men whose fate was to be decided together, that there seemed to be a competition as to who had the longest name. Their captain

The Vickers Wellington medium bomber (Norris).

was Robert Barr McPhan RAAF (4143788) aged 30 from the small NSW Central Coast settlement of Kanwal, 50 kilometres south of Newcastle. The bomb aimer was Sydneysider, John Andrew Spence, RAAF (421135), 31. The mid-upper gunner was Ian 'Jock' Bruce Hilton (RAF) and Robert Leslie Freeman (RAF) from Epwell, Oxfordshire, 22, was the wireless operator. So far, another Englishman, their navigator, Sgt Michael 'Simmo' John Christopher Simpson (RAF) aged 28, from Teddington, Middlesex, led the competition for the longest name. They were an interesting mixture of accents, ages, and personalities. They now needed to master their individual skills and duties as quickly as possible. Failure to do so meant either the crew received additional training or an individual was removed from the crew and reverted for further muster training. Connecting as a crew meant it was imperative to remain together and the shame and delay of the latter was too embarrassing to consider.

After basic familiarisation with the Vickers Wellington medium bomber, their lives were dominated by circuits and bumps – take-offs and landings – and simulated emergencies. Instructors were aircrew who had completed a tour of duty. These men with their well-worn uniforms sporting a Distinguished Flying Cross (DFC) or Distinguished Flying Medal (DFM) ribbon were easily admired; they had not only completed 30 operations but lived.

McPhan had to pilot the twin-engine aircraft, but it was an easy plane to fly, its two 965 HP Bristol Pegasus engines capable of a top speed of 250 miles per hour (402 km/h). Part of his skill set was coping with engine failure – flying on one engine and making single-engine approaches and overshoots. Blind flying competency had to be acquired. The loss of the airspeed indicator was a distinct concern and there was a small margin above stalling speed when landing. The Wellington was squat and low to the ground, with large propellers that swung in a wide arc close to the pilot's window. McPhan needed to remember not to ever lean out too far.

Left, Robert McPhan and on the right, John Spence (Spence family).

Freeman had to acquire a proficiency in air-to-ground wireless communications and Bert was very pleased Freeman was the one responsible for Morse code. Besides maintaining radio contact with England, with the master bomber and others in the bomber stream, Freeman needed to locate enemy aircraft by means of different forms of electronic equipment and to assist the observer with triangulation 'fixes' to aid navigation. He was already ahead of RAAF wireless operators, whose Australian training had not included British signals organisations, wavebands and codes.

Simpson, the navigator, sat at a small table behind McPhan. Like Freeman, being English trained he was totally acclimatised to the weather and current equipment. Australian navigators suffered from a lack of experience on British technology, such as the Dalton computer, and little practical familiarity on distant reading or astro-compasses. Simpson had to become efficient in navigation and the radio navigation system, GEE, to guide the bomber to the target and safely home.

John Spence had some catching up on the same equipment, as well as acquiring a quiet confident tone. On the approach to the target the bomb aimer guided the aircraft until the bombs had been dropped. If the bomb sight was fed the right numbers for course, speed, altitude and wind direction this could be accurate. Spence

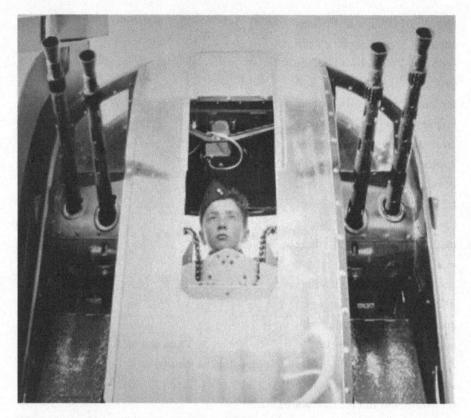

Rear gunner turret Wellington bomber (AWM).

was also the front gunner, of the two Browning 303 machine guns positioned above the bomb sight. His position was normally noisy, cramped and very uncomfortable, as he lay on his belly in the lowest position on the target approach, but his word 'bombs gone' were the most welcome during an operation.

Hilton, the mid-upper gunner, sat in a turret above the bomb-cargo compartment. His transparent perspex cupola in which were mounted two Browning 303 machine guns, offered an uninterrupted view of the length of the bomber and above. Unlike the RAF trained Hilton, Bert needed to adapt and learn quickly. There were different atmospheric conditions: softer colours, mist, grey, rain, and then snow.

If there was an exposed position on a bomber it was here, in the rear turret, and not for the faint-hearted or weak stomached. The rear turret followed all the aircraft movements, pivoting rapidly on its centre of gravity horizontally and sideways. There had been no training on modern turrets in Australia and bomber weaponry was more complex. Now, finally, he was moving in the right direction, even if it was backwards – the last to leave and the last to get away. Circuits and bumps were tough. There was an appreciation for the pilot wrestling with the controls but for the rear gunner who had to wait for the bump, it was 'a bloody side worse ... I have the rotating surface joint moulded in my skull after one bad one', described one rear gunner.[6]

It was March 1943. For Bert, so many months training since enlistment in June 1941 had given rise to doubts that he should have enlisted in the navy or even the army, because he would have been in the thick of battle long ago. Now, sitting alone in the Wellington's rear turret, he knew this was where he was meant to be. Strapped to a chair by a lap belt – him and four guns, two and two under each other, that fired 1300 rounds a minute – a sight mounted in a turret resembling a mirror with a circle and a dot. The surrounding perspex canopy offered 180-degree vision.

His biggest enemy during the first months of 1943 was not fighters but the cold. Until the crew was operational there were no fur-lined or heated flying suits. In an attempt to stave off the biting chill, Bert wore every piece of clothing he had and several pairs of socks. The early winter snow had been novel; flying in a bomber's rear seat in the worst of the British winter meant snow was no longer quaint and there were only thoughts of the Australian summer, white beaches and shimmering surf.

Cross-country flights, day and night, the length and breadth of England, Scotland and Wales, sometimes as long as six-and-a-half hours. The bombing range off the Welsh coast was visited frequently. At night all external and internal lights were switched off, the only exception being the navigator's table light. It took around 30 minutes for the eyes to adjust to night vision. Internal lights if needed were red. For Bert in the rear turret the synchronised camera, mounted mid-turret, allowed instructors to review gunnery accuracy on imagined fighters.

There were few idle hours. When English weather hampered flight training there was more training on the ground. For gunners, a turret set up on a frame and powered by a petrol motor driving a hydraulic pump allowed them to train their sights on any aircraft, and even birds. Additional effort and time were needed to maintain physical fitness, and for machine gun range drill. Lectures on aircraft recognition assumed greater importance and Bert sat in many a darkened room as slides were flashed onto a screen and he identified enemy fighters.

For the crew there was increased familiarity with parachutes. The rear gunner and pilot wore similar harnesses, strapped around the base of the body so that it was sat upon in flight. Other crew wore parachutes that clipped onto shoulder and chest straps. Commonly their parachutes were not worn during flights but stored on the fuselage next to them. The crew underwent numerous parachute and water

A Lancaster flight engineer (AWM).

escape drills. Bert hoped he never needed to leave his aircraft under the silk canopy of any parachute.

By January 1943, the Allies were achieving victories. On the Eastern Front a Soviet counteroffensive in November 1942 ended the Battle of Stalingrad, one of the fiercest and bloodiest of the European war, with the last German soldiers surrendering on 31 January 1943. By February, German forces had retreated from North Africa. There was a new urgency within RAF Bomber Command to push further into occupied territory and more frequently, to hasten the Allied advance. The enemy's ability to manufacture and rearm could only be destroyed by the bombing campaign.

The OTU course lasted 14 weeks but a crew was not permitted to leave Litchfield until each member had completed a set of standardised exercises and attained the specified proficiency. The dangers inherent in accomplishing these were clear; no-one graduated OTU without becoming fully aware of the peril, as trainee crews crashed and disappeared with alarming regularity. This was not only due to crew inexperience, but better aircraft were kept for operations and training units needed to make do with older, less dependable bombers. Between 1939 and 1945, 5237 were killed undertaking their operational training and 3113 were injured. The McPhan crew worked well as a unit and graduated after three months and one day, on 3 June 1943, to 1656 Conversion Unit and Lancaster bombers.

The Avro Lancaster was a four-engine heavy bomber powered by Rolls-Royce Merlin piston engines enabling a maximum speed of 280 miles per hour (450 km/h). The 'Lanc', as it was popularly referred to, could fly at a ceiling of 24,500 feet (7500 m). A long, unobstructed bomb bay allowed for a 14,000-pound (6350 kg) bomb load and the largest bombs used by the RAF.

A flight engineer joined, and he proved a poor fit. Flight engineers were introduced into bomber command in 1942 with the advent of heavy four-engine bombers. The flight engineer liaised closely with the ground crew on the service of the bomber. In flight they were required to control the aircraft mechanical, electrical, hydraulic and fuel systems and assist the pilot with take-off and landing. The position was demanding as they not only required a thorough technical understanding, but lightning speed in an emergency. In the event of an engine fire the fuel supply had to be immediately cut and the propeller feathered. The right quantity and fuel–air mixture to the engines needed to be maintained. Miscalculation resulted in lower performance, lower speed and descent. During an operation it could also result in flames from the exhaust pipes making the bomber a luminous target for enemy fighters.

In late 1942 and early 1943, flight engineers were commonly re-mustered ground crew, not aviators. The McPhan crew's flight engineer turned out to be one of these. 'He was a terribly nervous bloke, who panicked.' On the first circuits and landings he was air sick. One night his fuel calculations proved radically incorrect causing a near tragedy. It was mutually decided that a return to ground crew was the safest option for the entire crew. Fortunately, the next flight engineer to join was a vast improvement. The 27-year-old Scot, from Cumnock, Ayrshire, was not only a nice bloke who enjoyed flying but he took out the title for the longest name. Sergeant Thomas Oswald Steele McCulloch (RAF 984102) was warmly welcomed.

Their training took on a new urgency. The demand for aircraft was great and for aircrew even greater. On 3 July 1943, the newly promoted Flight Sergeant

(F/S) Albert Stobart and his crew, were posted to RAAF 460 Squadron, based at RAF Binbrook, Lincolnshire. On the day they arrived they were told there was no aircrew accommodation available – quarters were full. The statement that followed was delivered with alarming calmness: 'Don't worry about it, ops are on tonight, you'll get accommodation tomorrow night.'

CHAPTER THREE

'I don't think there is a tail gunner yet, who isn't scared.'
Flying Officer (F/O) Clifford Timothy O'Riordan (RAAF)

The blunt statement, 'Don't worry about it, ops are on tonight, you'll get accommodation tomorrow night,' was correct. On 3 July 1943, a large raid was conducted against Cologne, Germany. Squadron 460 Lancaster, W844 and crew: Pilot Officer Clifford Edwards (411885), 31, South Como, WA; F/S Lancelott James Frazer (420653), 20, of Gosford, NSW; Flying Officer Walter Frank Spier (421093), 21, of Sydney; F/S Cyril Francis Joseph Truscott (22378), 23, born in Emmaville, NSW; and three RAF crew, Sgt Alan Edwin Tytherleigh (1624946), 19, of Cambridgeshire; Sgt William John Rees (1317610), 20, from Glamorgan; and Sgt Charles Young (1074494), 30, from Aberdeenshire did not return.

Their fate was not known: had the bomber exploded in mid-air? Had they plummeted into the North Sea? In time, the names of W844 crew were engraved on the Air Force Memorial, Runnymede, Surrey, overlooking the River Thames, joining 20,268 others who had no known grave. In July 1943, their belongings were quickly boxed and stored – bed linen washed, a quick tidy up and there was now room for the next crew, Bert Stobart's. It was a little crowded in the hut because Edwards and Spier had been commissioned officers and therefore billeted separately from non-commissioned aircrew. Within RAF squadrons officers and non-commissioned officers did not live, drink, or socialise together. The McPhan crew were pleased that all being sergeants and flight sergeants they were not yet separated by rank; it was good to be together, and having to salute your own crew members seemed strange. Flying Officer Ray Kelly (431104) believed:

> This attitude was intolerable, especially in aircrew ... The permanent service types could not understand the Australians' non-compliance with established protocol.[7]

There was comfort in being attached to an Australian squadron, even if this was more in name than reality. In October 1939, Australia had agreed to recruit and train, through the Empire Air Training Scheme (EATS), 10,478 aircrew every year for the British air war against Germany and Italy. Initial discussion was that the bulk of aircrew would serve with RAAF squadrons in keeping with Article XV of the EATS, which permitted the establishment of national squadrons within the RAF order of battle. This was to give Australian aircrew a sense of pride and solidarity and for the Australian Government and its Air Board to maintain some official control.

Whereas the Canadian Government created 15 distinctive Canadian squadrons within Bomber Command and ensured some autonomy for its national air force, the Australian Government and RAAF formed eight: 455, 458, 460, 462, 463, 464, 466 and 467, but chose not to assert the same degree of control.[8] Many of the crews attached were not Australian, and Australian aircrew were commonly posted to RAF squadrons, often the only Australian in a crew, and who referred to themselves as 'the odd bods'.

RAAF squadrons 460 and 466 had the highest proportion of Australians and members regaled the noses of their bombers with Australian emblems and caricatures. For Bert Stobart, 'It didn't mean that we were all Australians, but at least we were, an Australian squadron.' With two Englishmen and a Scot in his own, it was just good, to see more Aussie uniforms than he had since leaving home and, it was better than the alternative. His Grammar School mate and fellow Morse code dropout from Ballarat days, F/S 'Donny' Finlayson (408569) was attached to RAF 199 Squadron and although Donny had another Aussie, F/S Frank Gee (412129) in his crew, they were stuck flying Stirling bombers. Some boasted the four-engine Stirling was very manoeuvrable in the air, but it was slower and had a lower operational altitude and range than Lancasters.

RAAF 460 was created at RAF station Molesworth, Cambridgeshire, on 15 November 1941 and equipped with Wellington bombers. It was relocated to RAF station, Breighton, Yorkshire, in 1942 and then RAF Binbrook, Lincolnshire in May 1943 where its maximum strength ran to 30 aircrews, around 210 airmen with a further 800 air force support men and women. The village of Binbrook lay in a valley close to the fishing port of Grimsby, the airfield on top of the Lincolnshire Wolds. In summer it resembled the chocolate box English image, but the weather tested the Australians. Observer Arthur Hoyle wrote:

Most of the time cloud hung low, it often rained and sometimes snowstorms blew in from the north … It was cold and forbidding.[9]

For members of 460 the centre of the village was the larger of two pubs, The Marquis of Granby, but this too became haunted by the youthful faces that came and never returned.

During WWII, RAAF 460 Squadron would fly 6264 operations and 1019 of its airmen were killed. Bert needed to temper his excitement as he arrived up the hill and saw the long line of camouflaged buildings. Finally, he could begin operations, but his chosen wartime service was one of the most dangerous. During 1942, 33 crews from 460 Squadron had been killed in operations and another three in accidents. By the time Bert and his crew arrived on 3 July 1943, 17 crews had already been lost that year. They had taken the beds of crew killed the night of their arrival.

A bomber returned pockmarked with bullet holes. The pilot's ankles and feet were badly injured, the navigator was dead. Bert observed, 'the upper and rear turrets looked like they had been sprayed with red paint'. This was the new reality.

You couldn't let it affect you, your crew needed to have complete confidence in you, so you just had to handle it, get on with it, and keep believing it is not going to happen to me.

Two days later, the McPhan crew undertook their first frontline flight. It was 'gardening', the innocuous name given to the laying of mines, 'vegetables', from the air. 'Sprog crews' – first operation crews – were commonly set 'gardening' or the dropping of propaganda leaflets – 'nickels'. On 6 July, 18 Lancasters, four Stirling, and 24 Wellingtons were sent to France. Pinpoint accuracy was needed to drop the five mines, otherwise it could jeopardise Allied shipping. The McPhan Lancaster cruised down the River Garonne towards the mouth, where German ships were known to harbour. The required altitude was just 3000 feet (914 m). Suspended in his perspex bubble, Bert had a wonderful view. There was a flash of memory, of happy days spent at Brighton Beach, hot summer days, salt and surf, of meat pies and ice cream. The guns resting against his arms and legs rudely reminded Bert he was a long way from carefree days basking on an Australian beach. The first operation was unsuccessful; after six hours his crew returned with the full load of mines, unable to ensure a precise drop. The following operations needed to be more successful and for Bert there could be no opportunity to reminiscence on simple pleasures. On 8 July, the target was Cologne.

During 1943 air raids escalated as Bomber Command entered the third phase of the campaign, concentrating on three major targets, known as the Battle of Ruhr, the Battle of Hamburg and the Battle of Berlin. The rich deposits of coal within the Ruhr Valley enabled large-scale manufacturing. Between March and the second

Pilot and skipper, F/S 'Robin' McPhan (Spence family).

last week in July 1943, Düsseldorf, Dortmund, Essen, Duisburg, Bochum and Wuppertal were subjected to concentrated bombing. The campaign then moved to Hamburg, with 92 bombers not returning. From November 1943 to March 1944, an estimated 9105 bombers attacked Berlin with 539 crews not returning. Bert Stobart's crew began their air attacks as the Battle of the Ruhr was concluding and the attacks against Hamburg commenced; 1943 was a terrible year.

Aircrew referred to the Ruhr Valley as 'Happy Valley' because it was anything but. Flight Lieutenant (F/L) Douglas Glasson (411695) had the dangerous task of attacking the Ruhr nine times.

> The Germans were 90 per cent certain that the Ruhr would be a target – they virtually knew we were coming … they would concentrate their fighter and ground forces … flak and searchlights were concentrated as the defences overlapped in a number of areas.[10]

The German Kammhuber Line, established in 1942, consisted of an early warning chain of radar stations, each just 20 miles (32 km) apart. Extending from France through Belgium, Germany, the Netherlands and Denmark, the system allowed early detection of British aircraft and for Luftwaffe fighters to be unleashed with deadly force. By the end of 1943 it was estimated that there were 1500 German fighters defending the western European skies. Some 900,000 men manned the highly efficient 88 mm dual purpose anti-aircraft (flak) guns from the French and Dutch coasts to Berlin. As Bert sat in the briefing room on 8 July he watched as the faces of the experienced crews paled when the target and course were revealed: 'Happy Valley', yet again.

The pre-flight activity was hectic; preparing for the real thing was way more intense. It could have been due to nerves, or ensuring everything was done and you were suited up completely, but Bert couldn't remember eating prior to this first raid. His stomach was in a bit of a tangle; he needed to get this right. Somehow, they were delivered to their bomber; somehow, they managed to take up their positions. Bert knew his lack of assuredness was shared by each member of his crew.

Robin McPhan had initially the greatest responsibility. Bert wondered if having a mature pilot of 31 years of age wasn't a bad thing. Just taxiing the Lancaster in traffic was busy enough; getting the Lancaster with a full bomb load into the night sky the next trial – after that, the responsibilities were shared.

Cologne had already been heavily bombed. On 30–31 May 1942, the city was subjected to the first 1000-bomber raid. By the end of the war, over 34,700 long tons of bombs had been dropped and an estimated 20,000 citizens killed. Bert became fascinated by the bomber stream, 282 aircraft heading for Cologne. Sitting in the rear turret awarded the best view of the lights and dark shapes, but he reminded himself that some of the dark shapes may not be friendly. Suddenly the sky lit up.

Flashes … you could see the flak bursting around you, black stuff, big black puffs of smoke, shell fragments, bits and pieces of shrapnel, flying through the air, like shotguns, but much more concentrated.

The closer they flew to Cologne the more concentrated the flak. Fire below yet icing above. The rear turret of one bomber froze up crossing the English Channel and was rendered useless but the crew decided to proceed.

A bomber below caught fire and plummeted to earth. Bert felt caught between an action movie and a horror show. He again checked his guns. Another aircraft exploded in mid-air.

You can't help thinking how lucky you are, you're not getting hit. You could see it, you wouldn't hear it in a lot of cases, you know it was just the black stuff bursting around you.

On the run up to the target the silhouettes of other bombers, in even closer proximity, then:

> *A big flash in the sky and you know that it's one of yours, that the anti-aircraft fire has hit the bomber with his bomb load on … a full bomb load, you can imagine what that would be like.*

It wasn't great after all, having the best view in the aircraft. Crews reported the 'glow of fires' and 'impressive explosions'.11 Bert needed to push every thought away and concentrate; otherwise, he wouldn't be doing his crew justice and, 'all that sort of thing … you can't let anybody down … everybody thinks the same'.

And then he saw it, 'the first time I have met a night fighter. We were right over our target'.12 The cloud cover was heavy but there were gaps and the fire glow outlined a fighter. All those days sitting in a darkened room recognising shapes flashed on a screen. The fighter flew level before banking towards them and Bert shouted in the intercom 'prepare – go'. McPhan skidded the Lancaster around and the fighter disappeared. The rear gunner of another Lancaster accounted for a night fighter but only after his mid-upper gunner was seriously wounded. The McPhan Lancaster returned with a few holes. For its crew this was their first attack, and they were already changed men –only 28 operations needed to complete a tour.

The nerves had barely settled before the next day's briefing. They were to bomb Gelsenkirchen, located in one of Germany's largest coal-mining and coking districts, with adjacent heavy manufacturing and synthetic oil refinery. The bomber stream consisted of 422 aircraft and flak was heavy over the target. One Squadron 460 bomber was blown upside down twice by shell, and while struggling to regain control and height the pilot realised he was flying upside down.

On the return journey Simmo's voice was on the intercom asking for a star shot. To obtain a navigational shot at the stars to plot the position of the aircraft meant McPhan needed to fly the Lanc level and at the same height. It was never a popular request. No sooner had Simpson attained his position than they were coned in dazzling light. First the blue master light and then 12 other searchlights came straight at them. What followed was a barrage of anti-aircraft fire, and Bert knew fighters would not be far behind – like moths to light. McPhan dived the Lancaster straight down the light and turned sharply.

They crossed the Dutch coast at a mere 8000 feet (2438 m). 'We were lucky the good old aircraft got home.' Upon landing, shrapnel was discovered in three of the four engines. Simmo was asked not to ask for a star shot again. The adventure was told in the mess together with, 'I think we were doing about 340 miles an hour

Being coned by searchlights was a terrifying experience (Stooke).[269]

down the light', or, more. They were fortunate, because 11 aircraft from the night operation did not return.

The Battle of Hamburg was code named 'Operation Gomorrah'. Bert Stobart was raised in a religious family, he went to Sunday school, Sunday church services. He was familiar with the Old Testament. Sodom and Gomorrah were ancient cities near the Dead Sea that were destroyed by God as punishment for the vice, depravity and wickedness of their inhabitants. Doubtless the bombing campaign would be hell for everyone involved, those above and those below. The campaign lasted eight days and seven nights, beginning on 24 July 1943 when 791 aircraft dropped 2300 tons of incendiary bombs causing fire which still burned three days later.

Hamburg was not only a large industrial centre, particularly for metal refining, but the biggest port, with 110 miles of docks, the Blohm and Voss shipyards, and German submarine pens. On 24 July 12 British aircraft were shot down. RAF authorities believed the raid had been a success, due to the new radar-jamming device called 'Window'. 'Window' was 4-kilogram bundles of thin strips of metal-coated paper which, when released from the aircraft, would scatter and float down

Bombers Moon, painting by Alan Moore (AWM).

causing radar echoes, effectively jamming German radar screens and disrupting the scramble of night fighters.

F/S Keith Arnold Skidmore (421759) and F/S Gerald Alan Rourke (420322) were the only Australians in their crew, both gunners, Skidmore in the mid-upper turret and Rourke in the tail. Skidmore was responsible for releasing 'Window' from the fuselage flare chute, but was unlucky to still have a close encounter with a fighter.

> *A fighter attacked. I think I was shaking so much that the bullets couldn't hit me! I think the fighter made three attacks ... the bullets ripped right along the fuselage. I did see one of the crew hit.*[13]

His flying suit was on fire. Rourke emerged from the tail turret to grab his parachute and indicated for Skidmore to follow. As Rourke attempted to bale his legs became caught in his turret and there was no escape. With the aircraft aflame and disintegrating around him, for Skidmore time seemed to stand still.

> *My mum and a bloke I believed to be Jesus Christ came into the plane. Each took one of my hands and they walked me down to the centre of the plane and told me to lie down, which I did.*[14]

The next he knew he was falling, his face and hands burnt, but he managed to feel his parachute not on his chest but above his head: Skidmore pulled the ripcord.

The parallels between his experience and that of Bert Stobart would be discussed when they met months later in Germany.

The McPhan crew was part of the 24–25 July attack described as 'the heaviest raid of the war' thus far. There was thick cloud over the North Sea but as they reached the European landmass the cloud began to break up. Unlike the blokes down the front of the Lancaster who preferred cloudless nights, Bert preferred the opposite; it meant fewer night fighters and those that did manage to scramble were easier to see.

Bomber Command intended to attack Hamburg again on the night of 25–26 July 1943, but fires from the raid the night before hung over the city reducing visibility. The attack was switched to Essen, the target the Krupp factories, the premier German armaments manufacturer in WWI and WWII. The McPhan crew was one of 600 which effectively stopped further production at Krupp. Squadron 460 Lancaster W4987 skippered by F/S Lionel Christensen (415100) limped back to England having been hit from above by bomb fragments. During the emergency landing the Lancaster behaved erratically, nosed down into the runway and burst into flames. The crew survived with only minor injuries.

On 27 July Bert Stobart moved into the briefing room with none of the enthusiasm he had just weeks before. Participating in attacks on Cologne, Gelsenkirchen, Hamburg and Essen had been testing. They were due for a week's leave by the end of the month and he planned to get as far as away from the base as he could. The curtain was pulled back and his lips tightened: the red cotton thread snaked across the map of Europe to Hamburg – bugger! A night force of 787 aircraft were released on Hamburg. An estimated 2313 tons of bombs, mainly incendiaries, a record for one target, were dropped on an area of just 2 miles by 1 mile. The United States Eight Army Air Force had bombed Hamburg that day.

Due to unseasonably dry conditions it caused a deadly vortex of fire. The inferno with winds up to 150 miles per hour (240 km/h) and temperatures of 1470° Fahrenheit (800° Celsius) lasted three hours and killed an estimated 40,000 people. The firestorm below left a lasting effect on those above. One bomb aimer commented how even the water in the docks glowed red with reflections of the fires around.[15] It was difficult to comprehend why orders were received from high command to attack Hamburg again with 787 aircraft on the night of 29 July. Operation Gomorrah proved as hellish as the name implied. 'You knew what was happening, but you didn't stop, you had to think of them as an enemy.' Man's cruelty to man, the mind could not be allowed to dwell, it needed to fixate on the 'us or them', that this had to be done to finish the war. The personal justification proved harder to accept in later years.

CHAPTER FOUR

'You always used to shower and shave and do everything before we went.
I suppose in case we didn't get one for a long time.'

F/S Bert Stobart (RAAF)

If Bert Stobart needed encouragement to weather the storm, within 460 Squadron there were some legendary tail gunners, none more so than F/S Roberts Christian Dunstan (419018) and Flying Officer (F/O) Clifford Timothy O'Riordan (403397). Dunstan had enlisted in the Australian Army in 1940. He was attached to 2nd Battalion 8th Field Artillery Company and sailed for the Middle East. In January 1941, a shell splinter tore into his right leg and doctors needed to amputate. Only then was it learnt Dunstan was just 18.

Discharged from the army he entered the RAAF recruiting office to apply

for aircrew. Initially dismissed as being foolhardy, Dunstan persisted, arguing that he could fulfil duties that did not require two legs. Given his gunnery training the RAAF relented. By May 1943, he was attached to 460. Dunstan used crutches to get to his aircraft and then crawled through the fuselage to reach the rear turret. He was undeterred by the unlikelihood of his escaping a damaged bomber, and completed a full tour of 30 operations, the day before his 21st birthday.

F/S Roberts Christian Dunstan (AWM).

Tail gunners were known as the wild men of aircrew, but this description was not appropriate when speaking of O'Riordan. Bert knew him by reputation and introduced himself to the gunnery leader at the first opportunity. Born in Sydney, O'Riordan was educated at St Ignatius College Riverview and University of Sydney. By 1936, he had a law degree and was a barrister operating from chambers in Phillip Street, Sydney. He was a King's Counsel when he enlisted in the RAAF on 6 January 1941. There had been an ambition of becoming a pilot, but his age was against him – 31 was deemed too old to begin pilot training – and gunnery was the shortest route to war.

The following year, attached to several RAF squadrons, O'Riordan was the tail gunner in most of the major raids in a variety of aircraft. Gradually his English crew were rested, and he accepted a posting to RAAF 460. O'Riordan had long held the view that, 'Dominion airmen are regarded with some suspicion by the RAF,' so he welcomed the change. An entirely different work ethic was found: 'The atmosphere is grand. The work is done but no bull.'[16] He was surprised with the efficiency, pride, and personal interest ground crew took in their aircraft and crew and couldn't help but be impressed by how 'fiercely democratic' the Australians were. O'Riordan was soon acting as counsel for Australian aircrew facing court martial for being 'too fierce' and 'too democratic'.[17]

To the inexperienced Bert Stobart, O'Riordan personified bravery and equanimity. Bert was, however, unaware of the thoughts and emotions O'Riordan divulged in the privacy of his personal journal. Meeting a gunner in the sergeants' mess who was returning to Australia due to air sickness, he wrote,: 'Met this type before, scared stiff and looking for excuses'; but at the same time expressing his own fear.

> I don't think there's a tail gunner yet, who isn't scared each time he crawls into that turret and the doors are closed behind him … whose nerves fail after being shot at a few times.[18]

Surprised at meeting a rear gunner wearing a Distinguished Flying Medal (DFM) ribbon, O'Riordan admitted, 'I don't think many last long enough to get it.' His depression deepened when he was recalled to duty from a well-earned two weeks' leave and trip to London. O'Riordan admitted that he was drinking a lot more alcohol, probably too much. His journal was increasingly sprinkled with mention of aircrew killed, 'Ten blokes wiped out … Nowadays, chaps are going daily.'[19] He felt the rear gunner strain of 'looking for jerries in the night'.[20] A practising Roman Catholic he kept religious symbols on his body and thanked God 'after each touchdown'.

On an operation to bomb Essen his bomber was coned by searchlights and anti-aircraft fire and a flak ship found their range. The crew barely made it home – Australian aircrew mates did not. His friend F/S Kenneth Aird (403415) and crew, 'crashed and burnt … Only a fortnight ago I said so long to Ken', it made life even more difficult, 'when you see intimate friends like him go'.[21] Another mate crashed, broke a hip and his leg was amputated. All of a sudden, 'four or five of your cobbers have gone'. On his next operation, another near miss, and O'Riordan confided, 'I am more certain than ever that someone is looking after me.'[22]

Australian aircrew were increasingly concerned about the situation back home, knowing that their country and loved ones were seriously under attack from Japanese forces. Each piece of news of the slightest Allied advance in the Pacific was welcome. The comment voiced frequently by Australian aircrew stuck in England was, 'I'd like to be in a large bomber stationed in the Far East.'[23] Exacerbating concern was that little news and rhetoric within Britain alluded to the war in the Pacific. Prime Minister Churchill was renowned for his stirring speeches but, wrote O'Riordan, 'his speech spent nine-tenths on the German situation, and as an afterthought mentioned Japan'.[24]

There was no escaping the war. Days off found aircrew gathered near and far and news that someone else was not returning to his family in Australia. O'Riordan crossed paths with aircrew who were convalescing from bullet and shrapnel wounds. The journal entries became more abbreviated. One operation after another, one near miss after another. O'Riordan was appointed gunnery leader as early as August 1942 and this only increased his responsibility. His next entry: 'Eighteen chaps in two nights is a lot. Can't seem to realise that they are gone for keeps.' He began drawing crosses above names. By September 1942, his hut had lost seven and he scrawled, 'certainly no future in this business'.[25] He mourned for men who would stand out in any crowd. The calm exterior had to be maintained but there was little to say when approached by youthful, inexperienced rear gunners like Bert Stobart.

The irony of this war was inescapable. From an affluent family and profession, O'Riordan had travelled overseas prior to the war. In Germany he had enjoyed drinking with locals in a wine house, enthralled by the magnificence of Cologne Cathedral. Five years later he and his crew were ordered to bomb Cologne. 'War is a horrible thing.'[26] O'Riordan was not enjoying this tour of Germany. The names of targets covered the map, each seemingly as dangerous as the last. More crew members were stood down for medical conditions – there was no shame in that, they had flown too many raids, seen too much and had too much expected of them. O'Riordan admitted he was struggling with his own nerves; the constant surges of adrenaline followed by the unsettling nothing. He received news that his best mate, fellow Aussie, F/S James Grant Crockett (403393), and crew had been shot down over Holland with no survivors. The same month he observed a fire near the airfield and discovered it was the bomber of another mate. 'I was only talking to him at breakfast this morning.' Now doing circuits and bumps again with new learner crews, being a 'spare gunner', did nothing for O'Riordan's confidence.

On 29–30 July 1943, Bert Stobart's crew did not fly but 777 aircraft were sent to bomb Hamburg again and 28 did not return, including, 460 Squadron Lancaster ED525. The pilot was Australian Flying Officer (F/O) Allan James Johnson (402507); the wireless operator was WO Reginald Maxwell Burcher, RAAF, (411440); WO Derrick George Scruton (RAF) was the navigator; and RAF Sgt Frederick Sydney Ralph responsible for the bomb aimer duties. The mid-upper gunner was WO Pax Lloyd Evan Jones RAAF, (402508); and F/O Clifford Timothy O'Riordan (403397), was the rear gunner. If the most experienced crews in the squadron could be killed, what then were the odds against a crew with just eight operations surviving?

Six days leave every six weeks was greatly anticipated and Australian aircrew were grateful for the scheme whereby British families welcomed them into their homes. It was what was missed most – that sense of home, of family. For British aircrew they could return to their own houses, their lives, but Australians were very much a long way from theirs. It was a relief to get far away from the base and all talk of bombers, guns and targets.

Bert was invited into the home of an English vicar; his religious parents would approve. It was a classic English cottage in Cornwall and the reverend was a very cordial host. In the evening he drove Bert and his 460 Squadron off-sider to the local pub and collected them later at a pre-arranged time. They appreciated that it wasn't proper, for the vicar's car to be parked outside the local hostelry. The home and guest bedrooms felt luxurious after base quarters. The airmen were encouraged to sleep late at which time breakfast was delivered. Bert thought it only gracious to attend the clergyman's church on Sunday and take up the collection.

He returned from leave to learn of the terrible raid on 2–3 August, another on Hamburg. The meteorology forecast had been gravely wrong. Instead of following a storm front, the bomber force had flown only halfway over the North Sea when they flew straight into cumulonimbus cloud. Thunder, lightning and extremely violent air currents created havoc. Australian Rear Gunner F/S Bernard William McCosker (413009) of RAAF 466 Squadron amused his skipper by calling over the intercom:

If this lightning doesn't stop playing round the turret I'm getting out. There's not room for two of us in here.[27]

Looking to the rear turret (Spurling).

That was the only amusement. Static electricity ripped down wings with propellers discs of light. 'It was a most devastating experience ... the noise was fantastic, everything metal in the cockpit glowed from the St Elmo's fire.'[28] In the midst of everything, turrets and windshields iced up. From normally stoic aircrew, words like 'terrifying', 'shocking', 'we got a thrashing', were relayed to intelligence officers from crews fortunate enough to return.[29]

It was now 9 August 1943 and Bert felt rested after his days at Cornwall. The McPhan name was written on the operations board. Aircraft were dispersed around the airfield in case of air attack. Bert's crew were transported to the bomber they were to fly that night, hoping it was a dependable, well-maintained aircraft, one they were comfortable with. The superstitions were already established. Their successful operations had been on Lancaster ED421s. Tonight, they were to fly ED986, destination as yet unknown. Each crew member checked his duty space thoroughly. Adjustments were near impossible during the operation, mainly due to the cumbersome gauntlets and gloves worn as protection against the intense cold.

In a stooped position, Bert moved down the metal fuselage and into the turret. With ground power connected, he rotated the turret sharply in every direction, then cocked and fired each gun to ensure perfect working order. Any glitch he needed to refer to ground crew immediately. Crew reported to McPhan that all systems were working perfectly, and they left for lunch.

The afternoon was occupied by section briefings and Bert and Jock Hilton made their way to gunnery. The target was not disclosed, but the gunners were warned of the type and likely number of enemy fighters they may encounter that night. Experience told them how long and difficult the night's operation was likely to be, but this conjecture, they kept to themselves.

The rest of the afternoon was their own. A doze in the sun, if there was any, the quietness of your own bed and space. Invariably it was important to write to

RAF briefing (AWM).

loved ones. If the worst happened, there was also that letter in the bottom drawer titled: 'If I don't return'. This expressed gratitude for the life lived and attempted to assure family that you had died doing your duty – as if such words could offer relief from the enormity of the grief. If the wait and silence of the afternoon proved unsettling the sergeants' mess offered conversation and laughter from tall tales and exaggerated exploits.

There was a hushed atmosphere in the main briefing room as the briefing officer pulled away the curtain to reveal the red thread stretching from England into the nether regions of Europe. The target, Mannheim, to attack Germany's oil infrastructure, Mannheim Motorenwerke, naval armament factories, and BASF, a large chemical plant that encompassed 3 miles of Rhine River frontage. The lengthening summer daylight enabled a longer reach for Bomber Command, and for aircrew that meant more time in the air. The now practised routine was in place. 'You always used to shower and shave and do everything before we went. I suppose in case we didn't get one for a long time.'

The silence deepened as aircrew collected flying gear, including the inflatable life jacket, affectionately referred to as a 'Mae West' after the well-endowed Hollywood actress. Escape parcels were distributed containing photos for false passports, several documents, a razor and ointment, pills to make ditch water drinkable, maps and a compass. Bert was provided with an electrically heated inner flying suit,

Bombload for a Lancaster (Stobart).

slippers and gloves, plus an outer flying suit, gauntlets and boots – all greatly appreciated when flying at 20,000 feet in his exposed turret and temperatures of between –20 and –30 degrees Fahrenheit (–29 and –34°C).

In the crew room they methodically climbed into their gear while the medical officer did his rounds handing out 'wakey wakey pills' – caffeine pills – to those who believed they may have difficulty staying awake during the eight-hour flight. Bert preferred not to take them. He had no trouble staying awake down the far end, pivoting in his turret this way and that, desperately hoping he missed nothing that came at them through the darkness. He also knew that should you take the pills, and the operation was cancelled at the last moment, it was impossible to get to sleep that night. The normal option then was 'to get on the grog'.

Transport collected aircrew and deposited them at their aircraft. Not a lot was said during the short trip; not a lot could be said. The emotions were complicated. There was the knowledge that your involvement in the raid was necessary, this was what the training had been for, and there was pride in the undertaking only other aircrew could appreciate. There was also the presence of the disquieting feeling of how good it would be not to board the truck at all. Some crews undertook strange routines to quieten the superstitions and stress. A common one was to stand in a line by the runway, open flies and allow urine to stream as far as a man was capable.

They climbed into the Lancaster with only Jock Hilton and Bert turning right. The next minutes each man ran through his pre-flight check and via the intercom reported to Robin McPhan, that this was completed. Bert knew the ground crew had been thorough, but he cleaned his perspex canopy again, no marks or specks to confuse the eyes and brain. The waiting was always worse than the doing; the nerves were always better when totally occupied. The waiting meant the mind wandered, back to stories heard in mess, unsettling tales of near misses, those who survived, and those who did not. The mind wandered to home.

Nothing much to say before yet another operation (http://ww2today.com/faq).

*You'd think about your people at home. I'd often think when we were taking off,
I'd be going off to the target, when my girlfriend would be going to work.*

There was that quick calculation timewise, Australia was ten hours behind. Bert
'would work it out', how his parents, 'would be going about their daily housework',
and Noel was travelling to her job. By the time their day was finished 'we'll be going
over Germany'.

Bert prayed he remained with the same crew. This was only their ninth
operation, but the trust was already there. It could happen at any time for a crew
to lose a member, commonly for medical reasons, and that was disconcerting. You
needed to have complete familiarity and trust in others to endure this war in the
air. He knew of Australian aircrew who were now spare crew – aircrew without a
crew – then attached to another crew for one or a couple of operations. That was
a horrible scenario.

F/O Robert Milne (422616) was a bomb aimer (BA) who had completed 19
'ops' when his regular pilot was grounded, and his crew made 'spare bods'. You had

no say in which crew you were attached to. Milne found himself added to a RAAF 463 Squadron crew. They attended the pre-flight and the briefing when at the last minute the regular BA arrived with a clearance to fly. The adrenaline was slow to dissipate as he returned to the crew room, took off his gear, and settled back in his quarters. That crew did not return.

Milne was then attached to the crew of Pilot Officer (P/O) Cyril Borsht (426416). This was a good crew, made up of five Aussies and two Englishmen. Milne completed seven successful operations with them. The original BA then returned and Milne lost his seat. It was a pity as he had bonded well with them. On the next operation the Borsht crew was shot down, the engineer was killed, one evaded capture and the remainder of the crew became POWs. It made Milne think.

F/S Robin McPhan sat in the warm cockpit, the cold night air blowing through the open side window. The taking off part was dangerous as the 'Lanc' laboured to lift from the airfield with a full bomb load. He waited for their turn to roll onto the runway from the taxi perimeter. The Merlin engines throbbed loudly and vibrated in their own urgency. McCulloch watched the engine temperatures rise; idling at length was never good. The Aldis light turned green. The two men in the cockpit concentrated on the gauges: cockpit check, fuel full, flaps 15, pitch fine,

brakes and mixture rich. It was not unknown for a Lancaster to run out of airfield if a less experienced pilot failed to put down 15 degrees flap or incurred a mechanical fault at the critical point of take-off. The result was terrible, bomber and crew obliterated in a wall of flame as the bombload and fuel ignited. The throttle was pushed fully out, and the McPhan-skippered bomber lumbered down the runway.

Bert felt the tail tilt upwards and hoped the disappearing view of the airfield wasn't, the last. There was expelling of held breath and looks between crew

460 Lancaster mid-upper turret, F/O Henry Erb, RAAF, DFC (AWM).

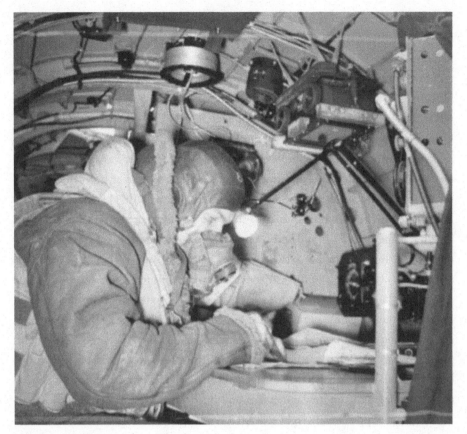

Navigator (AWM).

at the front end: dangerous bit over, now the next dangerous bit. Their pilot eased the aircraft up to 7000 feet (2134 m) for the first leg of the outward journey. Over the English Channel both gunners let off a couple of rounds to ensure guns were working. The Lancaster climbed to 10,000 feet (3048 m) and oxygen masks were strapped to faces. Finally, cruising height of 20,000 feet (6096 m). The Lancaster bounced a little as it met with turbulence. As the Dutch coast approached Bert was on full alert constantly rotating the turret up and down, left and right. Other bombers joined the stream, 500 in total, from every part of England. It was no time to get philosophical, but all this, all these men, were flying to destroy.

Jock Hilton's voice came over the intercom 'Bank port! Bomb bay doors open above.' In the mid-upper turret Hilton could see the length of the bomber and above, but not below. McPhan made a rapid course change as another bomber crossed their path – either a damn new pilot or a lousy navigator. It would be a bloody shame to be taken out by your own, not uncommon when the skies were crowded. Large raids were dangerous as bombers from various bases came together.

Inexperienced pilots and navigators who didn't make the correct course changes flew into the flight paths of others, as could pilots executing evasive action to avoid flak or fighters. It was, however, comforting to feel turbulence in the slipstream of another bomber because 'you knew you weren't by yourselves'.

Bursts from the anti-aircraft batteries buffeted the aircraft. The ominous black wall of spent anti-aircraft shells. Bright searchlights probed, sweeping back and forth. The night sky was lit up by vapour trails, lines of dancing lights. Green tracers snaked towards British aircraft. Watching from ground level it was a light show like no other; at altitude it meant attack. Bert swivelled his turret but could see no menacing shapes. Suddenly a bomber was starkly silhouetted in bright searchlight. Bert waited for the aircraft to dive, to shift course, but more tracers and a swiftly moving shape opened fire. The bomber erupted into flames. White parachutes burst open; Bert counted 'one, two, three … four, only four.' If they survived, they were POWs for the rest of the war – not an enviable future.

Closeted away at his navigator's desk, Michael 'Simmo' Simpson saw none of the drama outside: 'Fifteen minutes to target skipper.' McPhan took the bomber's altitude down to 14,000 feet. Pathfinder aircraft had marked the target with colour and the target was already alight. BA John Spence took over: 'Master switch on, bombs fused.' McPhan needed to keep the Lanc level, but targets were always different, depending on how much flak, and the heat from explosions below.

'Left, left skipper steady, right steady … bombs gone. Bomb doors closed.' Great words those. From his position Bert watched bombs fall and the resulting inferno.

Bomb aimer John Spence (Spence family).

The Lancaster lifted now its cargo had been expelled and McPhan took it higher still, as they turned for home. For some of the crew their main responsibility was over; for Bert, the searchlights continued to probe, the flak was still heavy and enemy fighters ever a threat. In 1944 the British developed and installed electronic equipment named 'Fishpound', a fighter warning device mounted on the belly of a bomber. But this was 1943.

CHAPTER FIVE

'You just weren't anxious to make friendships ... because they didn't last long enough.'

F/S Bert Stobart (RAAF).

They had survived the attack on Mannheim. There were celebratory drinks for the rear gunner who shot down a fighter on his first operation. Another Australian was asked to shout a round of beer when he related that he had spent his honeymoon in Mannheim and there had been a street collection for the Luftwaffe. 'I contributed to it then, but I wondered what they thought of our contribution last night.'[30]

Bert Stobart could not remember hoping for bad weather when he was home: he wished the sun always shone, bathing the Melbourne suburbs in bright light. Here in England, it was different – bad weather meant no flying. Only the crazy wanted to bomb every night. The sane were those who preferred bad weather, just enough to take the edge off the nerves, refresh the senses, and then you were ready to try to finish this bloody war.

The operations board on 10 August 1943 did not list the McPhan crew. Lancaster ED986 was to be flown by Squadron Leader (Sqn Ldr) Carl Richard Kelaher (267504) and ED421 was under maintenance. The target was Nuremberg. There were always mixed feelings: the need to get on with your job; being part of the stream; but relief as well. The following morning, they were told the flak had been particularly violent and of the 653 aircraft 16 crews were missing. ED986 flown by Squadron Leader Kelaher barely made it back to England. Kelaher had commenced his RAAF Point Cook cadetship in 1936, one of only 43 chosen from more than 1000 applicants. His experience was legendary in 460, and to get his damaged aircraft and crew back across the English Channel added to the legend.

Less than a month later Kelaher and his crew of three Australians and three RAF were shot down by a night fighter and killed.[31] The odds against completing one tour deteriorated as Bomber Command ventured further into Germany. Aircrew asked themselves: what were the ingredients for survival? Because clearly, with the death of Kelaher and crew, experience was no longer the reliable ingredient.

'Maximum effort tonight', was jargon learnt quickly by aircrew and never comfortable to hear. There were no easy targets, just dangerous and more dangerous, but 'maximum effort' meant the latter: a big raid on a major city with as many bombers as 460 and other squadrons could get in the air at one time. The most 460 could mobilise was 26 if all aircraft and aircrew were combat ready. With a maximum raid, two or three crews could be expected not to return. The mind couldn't help but do the maths.

> To finish a tour, you needed 30 trips, what are your chances when you lose one or two a night, of completing 30 trips? Doesn't work out, does it? ... You would only have to be there a night or two before you realised the chances of making it through weren't great.

Enormous strength of character was needed knowing that each time you flew, you were defying the odds. Luck was unfathomable, fate was fickle. 'If the bullet had your name on it, there was nothing you could do about it', was the only way RAAF Halifax bomber wireless operator, F/O Maxwell Norris (426900) made sense of it.[32] For Australian 460 pilot, WO Gordon Stooke (409332) the reality was, 'We came to accept mates getting the chop.'[33] Bert Stobart struggled. 'With so much death around ... you take it on board, but you couldn't let it affect you.' The consequence for aircrew being unwilling to fly was omnipresent and dramatic. 'You'd get the LMF [Lacking Moral Fibre] discharge.' In front of his squadron the airman was stripped of his rank and mustering and dismissed with a harsh dishonourable discharge.

Answering the telephone the morning after an operation was best avoided. People rang to speak to an airman and were told simply: 'He didn't come back last night.' The words 'He was killed' were never used because it was best for relatives and mates to hope the airman evaded capture or was a POW. Neither was the word 'killed' used amongst aircrew, it was, 'Oh, so and so didn't come back' or, 'Oh, he's gone for a Burton!' Bass's Burton Ale was established in 1876. It was easier to soften the reality by believing aircrew had gone to the pub for an ale than depict them blown to pieces. The other reaction was as innocuous: 'Oh that was a bit of bad luck.' Bert was aware it all came down to 'luck or fate or whatever you called it' but that number 30 stayed in the mind. A tour of 30 operations meant you were released to a training unit or could even go home.

It was 22 August and at a late hour in the evening when night operations were announced, and the board included the name McPhan. Geography had never been one of Bert's favourite subjects at school and now this geography lesson was even less popular. The new name to be familiar with was Leverkusen – known for its

Terrible losses. Of the 12 aircrew, identified in this RAAF 460 squadron photo, eight were killed (AWM).[270]

chemical factory, which was to be bombed by 462 aircraft. The weather en route was good until they reached the Belgium port city of Antwerp, when cloud increased. The target was obscured, making precise bombing difficult, but it also meant that anti-aircraft artillery could not cone bombers, and discharged a less accurate blind barrage. A half moon over the return journey saw attacks from night fighters. The official bomber account reported, 'Not a very satisfactory raid, as cloud obscured the target. All aircraft returned safely.' Sqn 460 aircrew believed any raid was satisfactory if they all returned. The following night proved disastrous: 57 aircrews did not, including one from 460.

On 23 August 1943 there was heightened tension on the base. Ground crews were working at a frenetic pace – that night was a 'maximum effort against a major target'. Main briefing was scheduled for 1700 and the briefing room was full when the 460 Commanding Officer, Wing Commander Charles 'Chad' Ernest Martin RAAF (402059), strode onto the platform with the Flying Officer Control, the Intelligence Officer, the Meteorological Officer and other section officers. Aircrew rose and Martin gestured for them to sit. As the scraping of platform seats subsided the doors were closed and secured by armed military police. Martin spoke: 'Gentlemen the target for tonight is Berlin.' Expletives were murmured as the wall map of Europe was uncovered. Pins and coloured cord showed the rendezvous point for the bomber stream, the course across the Dutch coast, the approach to the target and the route for return. Martin waited until there was silence and continued.

460 Sqn briefing with strained smiles for the camera (AWM).

He did not need to accentuate how important this attack was, on German morale as well as physical damage to the capital city of the enemy: this was appreciated by everyone in that room, as were the dangers.

'Berlin'. The name kept echoing in his head as he followed his crew up the Lancaster ladder and turned right. So hard to believe – a force of 727 given the task of bombing Germany's capital. Their Lancaster EE132 had been loaded with one 4000-pound bomb, one 1000-pound bomb and 13 cans of incendiaries. Bert crawled along the metal tunnel, climbing over metal spars, into his turret, and strapped himself in. There was no room for a parachute and sitting on one proved annoying and distracting – gunners preferred the hard surface of their seat. If needed, Bert had to bring the turret into the centre and forward, open the door, extract himself into the aircraft, collect his parachute, strap it on, and finally exit the bomber. Time was needed. If the turret or door jammed, and another crew member was alive, they needed to release any malfunction. This was just another reason the life of a rear gunner was the most precarious.

The 460 airfield was crowded with 24 Lancasters jockeying for position. There were to be a total of 115 Bomber Command Lancasters in this attack. Only 107 managed to take off, with six aborting due to technical problems. Eight Lancasters would not return. McPhan was aware mosquito aircraft (Pathfinders) were to drop red and green route markers and red over the target. He and Simpson needed to ensure they rendezvoused with the bomber stream at the set position and crossed the enemy coast at an altitude between 20,000 and 23,000 feet. After bombing, height could be maintained at a lower altitude to gain speed while crossing the northern German coast. Freeman knew the night's radio frequency was 'Darky'. Hinlock was instructed that at precisely 0340 he was to disperse the bundles of windows from the Lancaster. Spence had been briefed at the precise latitude and longitude to release the bomb load. Bert just needed to be vigilant and for his guns to be fully loaded. There was not a great deal known of the Berlin defences, but German protection would be understandably forceful.

The bomber stream consisted of 710 Stirling, Halifax and Lancaster bombers from 460, 100, 101, 109 and 12 squadrons, and 17 Mosquitos from Binbrok, Ludford, Elsham, Hemswell, and Lindholme. The battle order 'was to fly south of and beyond the city for 20 mls (32k) before turning in a north-westerly direction' according to 460 BA, Jim Munro.[34] The sky was jammed and both Jock Hilton and Bert needed to be alert as McPhan and other pilots began to weave and change altitude to avoid enemy detection.

The weather was good and visibility excellent as they approached the target. Bert looked below at the heart of Germany – hard to believe. It was a concentrated attack, heavy explosions and fires billowed to over 15,000 feet. Official reports cited 'the whole of Berlin Southeast' was obliterated. Aircrew were surprised at the comparative lightness of the flak; they had expected their adversary to do everything to protect the capital. Then the true ferocity of the defences was realised. Twenty belts of searchlights inside and on the capital's outskirts were cooperating with fighters. Bombers streaked across the beams as quickly as they could, but it was impossible to avoid the 'swarms of fighters'.

Gunners needed to 'get inside the mind of the German pilot', to try to imagine which was the best way for an attack and, react. A bomber could turn very sharply but 'the fighter would still shoot at you, but he couldn't follow you all the way around'. Tacticians who sat in the comfort of an office, decided German fighters would not approach from below. Their reasoning was that a fighter pilot couldn't risk being caught up in the explosion of a fully loaded bomber – aircrew discovered otherwise.

The familiar drumming of the Lancaster engines was almost relaxing – and then he saw it. For aircraft recognition, the instructor had flashed a head-on view of a Ju88 fighter on the screen for a split second and shouted, 'Come on boys, what is it? Quick – your life depends on it!' That exclamation reverberated in his head as Bert yelled into the intercom: 'Alert, enemy ahead.' He had never shot at a night

Bombers about to join the stream (Pearson).

fighter before and realised in the excitement he had called it wrong – the fighter was ahead of him, not the aircraft.

The fighter was manoeuvring rapidly for the best attack. Bert shouted: 'Enemy at the side, at starboard! Bank!'. McPhan made a rapid course change and both gunners fired. The fighter broke off his attack. Bert didn't know if it was he or Hilton, who hollered into the intercom – McPhan's congratulations were enough. The Lancaster's Browning guns firing 1300 rounds a minute formed a cone of fire, but the bullets were still small compared to the larger cannon fire of fighters. Both gunners had been in good position to fire, and this proved enough to drive the fighter off to find a less vigilant crew. There was no anger or dislike held against these members of the Luftwaffe, 'They were doing their job, trying to protect their people and country', you just had to keep doing yours. More fighters appeared. Bert could even make out the shape of a pilot who had his navigation lights on hoping to draw fire before executing his own attack. It was a deadly game.

A bomber on the port side exploded.

You say: 'Oh some poor bugger has been hit' … you don't weep … You block it out, not let it get to you.

The adrenaline coursed and might need to reignite. 'Fight and flight' became an often-used phrase in generations to come, but never was it more true in the rear turret of a bomber. Precariously suspended in a glasshouse in space, a sudden course change, nose down, the tail gunner rocketed upwards. Vomiting, 'going for the big spit', was not uncommon. Bert needed to concentrate, stay alert, look after his own; but there was always that sick feeling as he watched another aircraft and those within disintegrate and plummet downwards in flames.

As the Lancaster taxied down the runway and the engines became silent, the body took time to relax and then fatigue seeped into every muscle fibre. After an operation the tail gunner was normally the last out of the aircraft. The guns needed to be unloaded, the turret centred, the intercom disconnected, doors needed to be unlocked and locked. Stiff legs and arms were unresponsive when crawling along the fuselage in the dim light of early day, in bulky clothing, tugging a parachute as every projection grasped at you. Hands were cramped from working guns and even though gauntlets were worn for most of the operation, grease and gun powder had seeped into pores. Next it was debriefing by intelligence officers. There were maps and photos to comment on. What did you see? How heavy were the flak batteries? Where were they situated? How many fighters were scrambled? and Did you witness British aircraft hit? It was never, 'Which crew were hit?' but, 'Which aircraft?' Bomber aircrew had been told early in the war that they needed to return the aircraft, aircraft were more valuable than lives; but with casualties rising dramatically, aircrew wondered if this was still true.

After debriefing breakfast was supremely welcome. Despite severe food restrictions elsewhere, crews were entitled to generous meals, particularly a breakfast of bacon and eggs – a luxury in war-torn Britain. Few could argue it was not well-deserved after an eight-hour operation. There was no return to the airfield to wait for others – sleep was desperately needed. Rarely did airmen manage even six hours sleep before the routine commenced; another day and another night. When they woke it was impossible not to notice the empty beds in your hut, and at lunch, 'they'd tell you who didn't come back'. Good news was that a crew had made an emergency landing elsewhere and would be back later in the day. Crew members stayed close and didn't trade life stories with new airman.

> You just weren't anxious to make friendships, it was safer that way because they didn't last long enough on the squadron to get to know them.

While undergoing the next operation briefing, ground staff secreted away belongings and another crew moved theirs in. You didn't speak of those who had filled the beds before them. A great deal went unsaid: the statistics against completing a full tour; the high probability that after the next operation, their beds, or yours, would be empty and belongings secreted away.

Debrief (AWM).

Media headline announced: 'Last night's attack on Berlin was twice as heavy as any that the capital has ever had.' For Londoners who had felt the wrath of German bombers it may have brought some consolation. An opposite sentiment was experienced by the families of the missing British aircrew after the 23–24 August attack on Berlin. Of the Lancasters, 20 did not return; 25 of the 251 Halifax bombers were shot down as were 17 of the 124 Stirling – in total 298 aircrew were killed and 117 became POWs.[35] This included the families of 460 crew ED421 skippered by Australian F/S Alexis Townsend Richards (413796). Richards survived the crash and became a German POW, as did fellow Australians, F/S Kevin Gay (413574) and F/S James Clarence Munro (412175). The RAAF's F/S James Geoffrey Collins (404749) and F/S John Marsh (414359) and RAF Sgts William Armstrong Finlay (1686496) and Thomas Smale (1812351) were killed. It was another example of the profound nature of survival and death, and with the demise of their favourite aircraft, ED986 and now ED421, how precarious their own lives were.

The following night, 27–28 August, Bert Stobart and his crew were part of a 674 aircraft attack on Nuremberg. Bomber Command reported that many fires were started as a result of the bombing and these merged to burn a large area. Crews were subjected to heavy flak and a concentrated attack from fighters. One rear gunner who had participated in 54 operations and had bombed every German target of importance said he had never seen so many fighters before. Thirty-three British aircraft and crews did not return. The McPhan crew were nearly number 34: 'It happened so quickly.'

CHAPTER SIX

'I didn't see it, the mid-upper gunner didn't see it, nobody on the aircraft saw it.'

F/S Bert Stobart (RAAF)

Occasionally Americans arrived destined for squadrons of massive Superfortress bombers.

The Brits weren't renowned for making their aeroplanes comfortable they built their bombers to do the job, to cut down on other weight and carry more bombs. American bombers offered more comfort.

The statement was said with a tinge of jealousy. The Superfortress was indeed better fitted out inside but unsuitable for night flying as the engines released too much exhaust and light. The Australians preferred the notion that navigation was not the forte of Americans and therefore, 'The Yanks couldn't find their way home at night'.[36]

Bomber Command 'maximum effort' raids intensified to obliterate industry, military resistance and German morale. More and more British aircrew fell from the skies. Losses of 10 to 20 per cent were becoming conservative. By 1943 around 75 per cent of aircrew shot down had completed fewer than half their 30 operational tour and those remaining on active service, struggled with the cruel randomness.

Crashed British aircraft had revealed technology and the development of German counter measures. A web of sophisticated radar installations ensured few British aircraft could cross the English Channel without being noticed. German night fighters were fitted with radar tracking devices to find their targets.

Bert walked back to his quarters with an overwhelming desire to write to Noel. He had just observed what was left of a Lancaster shot up over Germany. The pilot had done a magnificent job to return at all but there was nothing much left of the rear gunner – another young Australian who would never see his family or country again. There was also a poem titled 'Maximum Effort' circulating in the sergeants' mess. The first paragraph alone was memorable.

My Airforce days were often bright and gay
But there were days of sadness and dismay.
I'd get to know the crews that used the Mess
And get involved with some, I must confess.
I'd say farewell to some familiar face
But sometimes they would not return to Base.
They'd take off in the prime of life to do
A job which would beat folk like me and you.
Young boys cut down in the prime of life,
Some hadn't had the time to take a wife.
Some of them managed to stay alive.
They'd take off on another bombing raid
They'd have to face another night of hell.[37]

With the latest photo of his fiancée propped up on the small table he pulled the cap off his fountain pen and allowed the ink to flow. Her likeness was in stark contrast with the wrecked bodies he had just witnessed. He offered the usual information about the crew, who were his brothers, and how much they depended on each

other. He had written so much of these six airmen; Noel was intimate with their foibles and strengths and yet was unlikely to meet only the Australians until after the war. Bert penned of how he looked forward to their being married and of the house they could build in Melbourne, not far from the beach they both enjoyed. He did not mention that tonight, he was to bomb Nuremberg.

The McPhan crew had missed the first operation against Nuremberg. On 27 August they were to fly in the 674 aircraft attack. Nuremberg was an important target. Two Siemens plants produced

Noel (Stobart).

electric motors, pumps, generators, dynamos, searchlight transformers, complete searchlights, electro-motors and other electrical equipment and other factories made ammunition, chemicals, and aircraft components. The city was crucial not just for its manufacturing, but because the Nazi party had made Nuremberg its spiritual centre. Newsreels of mass gatherings praying on the shrill words of a charismatic leader had been witnessed around the world. Nuremberg, consequently, was pivotal to the morale of the enemy.

Lancaster rear gunner (AWM).

Bert felt the familiar bump as the Lancaster left the airfield and watched as the strip disappeared. Passing over the Channel, he tested his guns and settled back into his seat. The mind drifted. The face of Noel, with her wonderful smile, the last words they struggled to get out before their hands fell apart. His mum's cooking; yep, he could really do with some of her meatloaf, or lamb roast. They were surely thinking of him but could never understand the life he was leading.

Bert thought of the letter he had just written and how he never told the truth. How could he write of the things he had seen, of a very damaged aircraft being dragged off an airfield with the blood and gore of the crew plainly in view – what was left of someone's son or husband, being hosed out of a rear gun turret. He didn't write the truth, just about the fun stuff, the shenanigans his mates got up to; his last leave in that pleasant part of England, with the welcoming host, or about the weather – always the weather, the cold wind, the snow, so few sunny days as enjoyed back home. 'This is sortie number 10; I have 20 to go.' Bert chastised himself and hauled his attention back to the inky blackness. The 27–28 August attack on Nuremberg was considered a victory with accurate bombing leading to extensive fires. Flak was heavy and a tremendous force of night fighters met the bomber stream as they left the target. Thirty-three British crews did not return. The McPhan crew never reached Nuremberg.

It happened so quickly. There was a shuddering and ripping as another bomber was suddenly 'weaving across the top of us'. Bert watched as a section of the starboard fin sheared off. McPhan's voice on the intercom asking what was going on, he could feel a change in his rudder bar and a different pressure at his feet. The skipper asked his gunners if they were okay.

He was checking to see if I was still there because he thought the turret might have been knocked off ... how could another aircraft cut across the top of you and so quickly?

The voice of Hilton on the intercom, sounding a little stressed. The mid-upper gunner had been lucky to still have his head – there was some new air-conditioning in his turret in the form of a hole in the perspex cover. Hilton had seen a flash and ducked. Had he been facing the other way the result would have been deadly. McPhan on the intercom again asked his gunners for damage reports. Bert and Jock agreed that some of the camouflage and paint was gone as they could see 'silverwork', but not the full extent of superstructure damage.

They had been blameless but colliding with a fully loaded bomber was not recommended, and had the guilty aircraft been a fraction or two lower, two crews would not have survived the explosion. McPhan was unhappy with his controls, and with the wireless aerials wiped off, communication was scratchy. The crew conferred and the decision was made to abort. Simpson calculated they were around 30 miles (48 km) inside the French coast. As McPhan swung the bomber back over water they jettisoned their bombs and the decision was to land at the closest English mainland airfield, Tangmere. As they manoeuvred over the Channel, McPhan called for Spence to check the bomb bay. 'We still had the cookie!' Frantically Spence manually released the 4000 pounder (1800 kg).

Tangmere, on the West Sussex coast, was home to a fighter squadron that had played an important role during the Battle of Britain. Unsure of wireless contact, the crew hoped their being friend not foe was recognised. McPhan called to his crew 'I've just got to go in.' There was great relief as the Lancaster settled down on tarmac. Freeman had continued to transmit and according to base staff, 'We could hear you, but you couldn't hear us.'

Fighter pilots and their support staff were accorded the public glamour and glory denied those in Bomber Command, but they appreciated the risks their partners in blue were taking in the night skies over Europe. The welcome was generous. Examination of the Lancaster proved that the decision to abort had been justified and it was expected nearly a week was needed for repairs. They were

F/S Frank Gee (left) and F/S Alexander Douglas 'Donny' Finlayson (AWM).

ordered to remain at Tangmere until they could fly the bomber back to Binbrook and the ensuing days proved unexpectedly enjoyable. A visit by a Lancaster was not common and great interest was shown in the aircraft and its crew was feted. 'We lived off base and just enjoyed ourselves.' As they farewelled Tangmere they performed a fly past and, 'a bit of a shoot up for them, showing them what a Lancaster could do'. It wasn't in keeping with RAF protocol, but it felt good.

Returning on 1 September to Binbrook their high spirits were dampened by the news that they had missed a major attack on Berlin the night before and of the 621 aircraft taking part, 47 were shot down, including a 460 Squadron Lancaster ED986 which they had crewed in the past. P/O James Douglas Hocking (411910) had been the captain on this occasion. The other Australians killed were P/O Leslie Jack Haymes (415082); P/O Harold Frederick Symons (415364); F/S Trevor John Jones (411699); and F/S William Hugh Fitzgerald (414014). It was learnt later that RAAF F/S William Ralph Ingram (413199) and RAF Sgt J. J. Wood (1985821) were POWs. Bert was well acquainted with the gunners. He had helped celebrate the 21st birthday of Jones that month. Fitzgerald from Charleville, Queensland, had enlisted at 18 and had died at 20. They were buried in a Berlin cemetery.

News then came that his mate F/S Alexander Douglas Finlayson was also dead. 'Donny' and Bert were former Melbourne Grammar School students. They

10 Minutes to Take-off (Stobart).

rekindled a friendship at Ballarat and had disobeyed RAAF WOP/AG procedural training, to avoid the dreaded Morse code. Donny had crewed up with fellow Aussie, F/S Frank Ernest Gee in RAF 199 Squadron, and was shot down during the 31 August attack on Berlin. Bert had shared many a beer with Donny and a love of gunnery. He needed to acknowledge that Jones, Fitzgerald and Donny had simply 'gone for a Burtons', and 'it' was not going to happen to him. But with each operation this was harder to believe.

The McPhan crew was listed to fly on the night of 3–4 September – target, Berlin. The official Bomber Command record cited in relation to Berlin that:

> *It was the target every aircrew member wanted to see in his logbook for the prestige that name gave it, but it also caused the greatest surge of fear.*[38]

It was difficult for Bert to be as resolute as he had been months before, particularly with the deaths of gunner mates just two days earlier. Bert went through the well-practised routine. He looked at the brand-new uniform he had purchased, ready for his next leave, and tidied his bed space. At the last minute he pocketed the black and white photo of him and Noel and left for dispersal.

By previous operations this was a small raid of 320 aircraft, of which 316 were

Lancasters. Bomber Command hierarchy reported that the 3–4 September 1943 attack was very successful.

> With 1,000 tons of high explosive and incendiaries dropped in 20 minutes, the concentration was as intense as in any attack this year. It brought Bomber Command's total tonnage for the first eight months of 1943 to over 100,000 tons dropped.[39]

Of the 320 crews despatched 21 did not return including three RAAF 460 Squadron crews.

There was still twilight when the crew of EE132 were dropped off at the Lancaster. They were aware that this was operation number 11. The Flight Commander of the 460 flight was the legendary Squadron Leader Carl Kelaher and his aircraft was already in the air. Bert checked his watch and 2000 was fast approaching. He listened to Spence confirm with their skipper that the bomb load – 1 x 4000 lb bomb, 48 x 30 lb and 690 x 4 lb incendiaries – was aboard and not yet fused. Freeman acknowledge their call sign was AR, and 'Simmo' instructed Robin McPhan on the crossing course.

Bert's guns spat out a practice round and below the sea was luminous as the moon rose.

It looked bloody cold and unwelcoming and Bert hoped that he never had cause to put into practice the ocean ditching regime they had trained for. A couple of airmen in the mess were sporting Goldfish Club badges, a club founded in November 1942 by the chief draughtsman of the world's largest manufacturer of air-sea rescue equipment. After hearing the stories of aircrew who had survived a sea ditching and owed their lives to a 'Mae West' or the rubber dinghy, his company agreed to fund survivor badges with a white-winged goldfish flying over blue waves. Although the RAF did not sanction the wearing of the badge, morale took precedent. It was a club Bert had no desire to join.

They still had a long way to fly and EE132 had just crossed the Dutch coast at 17,000 feet (5182 m) in the vicinity of Scheveningen, when their world disintegrated. 'I didn't see it, the mid-upper gunner didn't see it, nobody on the aircraft saw it.' The starboard engines burst into flames, which spread rapidly along the wing. The Lancaster began a downward spiral. They had been shot from below by an ME110 night fighter with an upward firing cannon, piloted by Unteroffizier Johann Kurz.[40]

McPhan's garbled voice came on the intercom asking, 'Who's hit?' before communication dropped out. In the advent of the intercom dropping out, a light with 'P' displayed above each crew member, indicating the need to leave the aircraft. The light lit up and Bert centred his turret, crawled into the main fuselage, and grabbed his parachute. An injured Hilton was trying to extract himself. With difficulty Bert hauled himself up and freed Jock from the turret. As they began to slide down the fuselage Bert assisted the other gunner to harness his parachute. 'We were downhill, running at this stage, you know with the flames coming out.' Bert realised the Lancaster had lost a lot of altitude and was likely down to around 10,000 feet (3048 m). He kicked out the rear door and watched Hilton fall through the opening. Bert paused; he curiously felt no panic. 'Should I go up and see what the rest of them were doing, if everything was right up front?' He climbed as far as the main spar and was struggling to get over it. Something clicked in his brain. 'I thought "Oh well, we'll probably see them on the ground ... I gotta get out".'

The drill practised was to kneel, carefully somersault out of the aircraft, count slowly to seven – or was that ten? – to clear the bomber, and when on one's back, place an arm over the parachute enabling the elastic bands to pull the wrapping away, and the spring to eject and release the canopy. That was the drill. Bert released his grip from the main spar, fell down the fuselage and out of the Lancaster. He only just cleared the fin and pulled the ripcord. There was a tremendous jerk and horrifying sound of stitches being torn on the heavy leather straps. 'Christ, let them hold,' shot through his brain. The ground came up too quickly. There was no time to complete those instructions that went something like, taking the initial landing on relaxed legs, pulling yourself into a ball, and rolling to the left or right as preferred. Bert released his parachute harness too soon, landed with a terrific thud and knocked himself out.

He wasn't sure how long he was unconscious. Struggling to his feet, his parachute was nowhere in sight and he realised he had likely suffered a concussion. He felt decidedly ill. There was no bomber, no other crew, and his confused brain could make no sense of what had happened. 'Had he been told to bale out? If so, where was everyone? Was he in Holland?' Bert began to wander and entered a school. A child came up to him. 'I was a bit silly, I gave him my aircraft brevvy, Anzac list, my gunner's badge and escape money.' Bert had no idea what he was doing. 'I felt so sick.' The next hours remained a blur. He thought a Dutch policeman took him to his home. 'That's when I vomited, and I think he put me to bed'. When he awoke the uniforms were easily recognisable and the German soldiers were none too gentle as they bundled Bert into a car. He still felt squeamish and thought:

This will be good, I'm bound to be sick, and I'll puke all over them. But I didn't, I didn't puke, maybe it was just as well, I would have got belted.

Bert had seen the Lancaster flying level but on fire. 'I thought I would see some of the crew, but I didn't.' On 3 September 1943 Lancaster EE132 had exploded on impact, 3280 feet (1000 m) behind the farm Zwijnenburg, near the village of Benschop, 24 miles (39 km) south of Amsterdam, the Netherlands.

The same night, RAAF 460 Lancaster W4988 was caught in the Berlin searchlights and attacked by a Ju88 night fighter. The Australian captain, F/O Francis Archibald Randall (413896) ordered his crew to bale out and fellow Australian, BA, P/O Lindsay Grafton Greenaway (403601) did so. Randall regained some control and the Lancaster limped towards Denmark before another engine gave out and the order to bale was reissued. The parachute of the Australian navigator F/S Norman James Conway (413829) did not open, and he was killed. Greenaway became a German POW, the RAF flight engineer, Sergeant A. H. Jones evaded capture and the remaining crew were interned briefly in Sweden and returned to England the following month. Randall was killed later the same year.

The official war record reported that the two crews were the '269th and 270th of 594', from 460 Squadron which did not return, and 'the 5018th and 5019th crews shot down'.[41] Also killed during the 3–4 September attack on Berlin, was the 460 Flight Commander, RAAF Squadron Leader Carl Richard Kelaher and crew. The statistics were stark and clinical, unable to relay the true waste.

On 8 September, the commanding officer of 460 wrote to the families of the men who flew in the McPhan crew. The language was identical in each letter. He regretted to inform them that the official designation was 'missing' but that there was the possibility crew may be prisoners of war. Personal effects were to be safely stored and returned.

> *Your son carried out his duties in a very keen and conscientious manner, and his loss will all the more deeply, be felt in the Squadron.*[42]

Later, hope was lost for all but two families. The body of F/S Robert Barr McPhan was buried in Amersfoort, Holland. The remains of F/S John Andrew Spence, F/S Michael John Christopher Simpson, Sgts Robert Leslie Freeman and Thomas Oswald Steele McCulloch, being too difficult to identify, had been buried in two graves in the same Dutch cemetery.

CHAPTER SEVEN

'I'm convinced he could have saved himself ...
makes you think about fate.'

F/S Bert Stobart (RAAF)

Too many thoughts, all confused, not helped by his throbbing head. When Bert muttered nonsensically to interrogators, he could do little else. 'I thought it was all a dream, I thought it's not happening.' He was in a small room in a jail of some kind. Standing over him was a German officer and another in civilian clothes. There were many questions about what his crew was attacking and from where, the specifications of his Lancaster. Bert had originally dreamed of being a pilot, but it appeared that when these Germans learned he was a tail gunner, they lost a lot of interest, 'it seemed rear gunners were considered the least smart, the least interesting to question'.

The German officer spoke perfect English and as the atmosphere relaxed, he proceeded to complain about his English wife. They had lived in England but when the war started, he returned to Germany 'to fight for the fatherland'. He referred to his wife as a 'bitch' because she did not wish to accompany her husband and was divorcing him. Bert could well understand why; he would want to divorce this bloke too, but it was best not to voice that thought. Why was Bert fighting for England? 'You're all the way from Australia, you shouldn't be here in the first place, you're just wasting your time.' Bert replied it was his duty because Australia was part of the British Empire. A guard asked Bert if he had a 'Player's cigarette' because it had been a long time since he had smoked a 'decent cigarette'. Bert mumbled an apology, 'I don't smoke.' The whole experience was weird: 'With all this going on I thought to myself, "This is a bloody dream".'

His mind was still not functioning well. At least this meant playing dumb was not at all difficult. All Bert wanted was to have a good lie down. He was bundled on a train with two other British airmen and at another stop the same questions were asked. Bert offered his rank and serial number. The Germans proceeded to tell him that a large number, of aircraft had been shot down and that the British could not sustain such losses before losing the war. There was no disagreeing.

Stalag IVB (Stobart).

He was bundled back onto the train. Much repeated by his captors was the phrase: 'For you the war is over'. It took some thinking about, that statement; Bert figured they were right and wondered what the future held.

As the train passed through Cologne the guards pulled up the blinds so the airmen could appreciate how much damage they had caused Germany.

> I thought to myself, 'We didn't do too much damage to the cathedral', but then the train sort of took a turn and I could see the sunlight, through the whole cathedral, it was only a matter of walls standing up. It was well and truly battered.

The feelings were mixed, as the remainder of Cologne came into view. This was what the operations he had flown intended, this was what success looked like, but! Bert couldn't remember the last time he had eaten and that routine prior to take-off, which included shower, shave and meal, was more appreciated. Transport changed and this time any semblance of a passenger train vanished. Clearly the interrogation and casual atmosphere had concluded and he was pushed into a railway cattle truck with 50 others. 'We were all jammed in together tight.' For five days they remained as the carriage rattled along. There was not enough room to sit, let alone lie down, so they endured as best they could. With no toilet facilities,

From the main gun guard house (AWM).

every so often, the train stopped so the prisoners could alight to relieve themselves beside the tracks – armed guards omnipresent. The prisoner of war experience was already proving horrible.

The journey ended at Mühlberg, a large German town beside the river Elbe. The bedraggled columns of mainly British airmen, moved, rather than marched from the station, were already ghostly images of their previous proud and alert selves. Citizens emerged and hurled abuse and, if close enough, punches. Bert had little comprehension of the German language, but the anger was irrefutable. He had never really thought about being a POW, but as the column of the newest POWs arrived at their destination, Stalag IVB looked exactly as could be expected, 'Like a dirty big cage.' There was high wire netting and guard houses with German soldiers and heavy machine guns. The heavy wooden and wire gates were swung open and German guards awaited. Behind the second gate and barriers, men in British uniforms gathered and watched as their latest companions passed into the confines of this very different world.

There were separate compounds holding long barrack-styled buildings. If you could ignore the wire and armed enemy, it resembled military bases frequented during RAAF training. The atmosphere was, however, decidedly different.

Areas were wired off and in different sections, each with their own barriers and surrounded by the high exterior fence topped with curled barbed wire.

There were solemn welcoming greetings from awaiting POWs, and senior RAF and RAAF officers introduced themselves briefly before each of the new

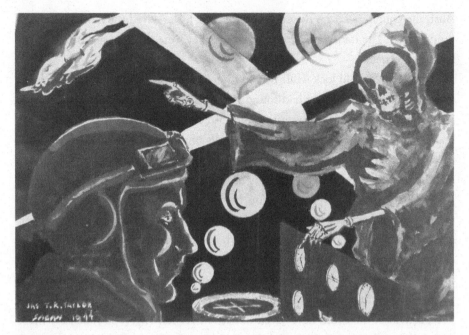

The Nightmare of Bomber Crew, painting by Jas. T. R. Taylor (Kingsford-Smith).[271]

arrivals were handed over to different hut representatives. An airman in a scruffy uniform escorted Bert into a hut, introducing him to those assembled inside. A bunk space had been made available for him. It was all rather overwhelming, and Bert was acutely aware his demeanour was subdued, certainly not his typical happy and friendly self. When later required to escort new arrivals to their quarters, he realised just how typical his demeanour had been.

He was trying to listen to the voice of his escort and comprehend the advice and information, but it was difficult. He was handed a cup of piping hot tea which he downed far too eagerly and coughed as his throat burned. Food was pushed into his hand and this was consumed as eagerly. He was led to the ablution area. Bert was moving as if he was disconnected from reality. The shower and shave and clean clothes were most welcome before he was told to stretch out on his bunk and sleep. He was exhausted but the dreams, flashes of something worse, accorded him little respite. He was falling, there was smoke, flame, no other parachutes, no Lancaster.

Bert awoke with a start, his new clothes wet with sweat. He had no idea how long he had been out for. A face, the welcome, friendly face of Jock Hilton, his mid-upper gunner – the man he had helped strap into a parachute. 'I thought you were dead,' Jock declared rather loudly. A smile came to Bert's face, 'I thought the same.' Jock looked worse for wear, a few bandaged bits and pieces. He had just arrived, and when informed of Bert's presence insisted he must see him. The Scotsman and

Australian gunners sat on the edge of the bunk. Jock relayed the news Bert didn't want to hear. The Lancaster had crashed, and they were the only survivors of their band of brothers.

The Germans told Jock while he was receiving some medical assistance that his crew had been killed. They had found Bert's discarded flying helmet and Robin McPhan's unmarked body was found some 302 feet (92 m) from the wreckage. The bodies of the remaining crew were found badly mutilated in the forward section of the Lancaster. Someone had jettisoned the bomb load but with a heavy fuel load and the fire, the bomber exploded as it came to ground.

McPhan, as did all pilots, sat on his clipped harness and parachute. This meant he could exit the bomber quickly, unlike others who had to strap on their parachutes. Bert and Jock wondered if the bomber was too low for the crew to bale out, or perhaps Spence, Freeman, Simpson and McCulloch were wounded and in no condition to do so. Robin McPhan must have attempted to crash land the Lancaster thinking, 'he could set it down and probably get the whole lot out'. They were, 'convinced he could have saved himself'. Bert felt anger: so much for those desk jockeys who said German fighters could not fire from below, that there were no upward directed guns; that was clearly nonsense.

Jock was assisted to his own hut and Bert spent time alone attempting to process what he now knew. It wasn't easy to think of these men on whom he had depended, and with whom he had bonded, being dead. It had been necessary to convince himself that death could not come to his crew, just so he could board that transport, which took him each darkening night to the airfield. They had preferred each other's company off duty, listened to each other's family news, approved the latest photographs from home. Bert thought of those photos, of the happy smiles in grainy black and white photos of them together and those they shared with each other. British relatives of RAF crew had adopted the Australians as family. Robin McPhan had spoken of a nurse he had met and how they considered themselves engaged, even if he had as yet to tell his parents. Bert thought of Heather Spence. BA, John Spence, 'was the old man of the crew' at 31. He and Heather had watched a son die in 1939. How would she now survive the grief of losing her husband and raising their remaining son, Bob, alone?

Hut members had respected his need for isolation, but now they needed to return to their own spaces and begin to lead Bert into his new existence.

Stalag IVB was a large camp covering around 74 acres (30 ha). It had been opened in September 1939 to hold 17,000 Polish soldiers captured in the September 1939 German offensive. The Poles were transferred to other camps when in May 1940 French soldiers came following the Battle of France. By 1941 Australian soldiers

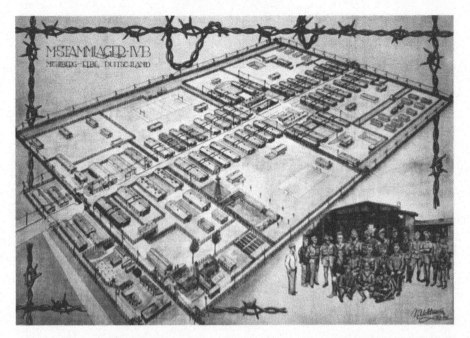

Stalag IVB painted by N. Uchlmann, 15/3/43, featuring the different nationalities incarcerated (Stobart).

captured with the fall of Greece arrived, and later Russian POWs as the Soviet Union was invaded. More frequently British aircrew were incarcerated.

The British compound included a transit compound. Each of the two compounds contained four wooden huts with paper-rubber tarred material roofs. Floors were brick. Each hut was 120 feet long and 30 feet wide (37 m x 9 m), with a bed space for 218, although rarely did they billet fewer than 300. The fortunate had bunks, the less fortunate slept on tables and forms (platform seats). Four 25-watt bulbs lit each hut. Bribing guards improved the lighting.

Two brick stoves provided heat and internees attached hotplates to cook their food. The fuel for heating and cooking was practically nil and too rare to keep the fires burning. The German kitchen supplied the POWs with soup once a day and hot water for drinks. Eating facilities were basic and with no issue of knives, forks, spoons, plates, or cups, these needed to be constructed out of anything.

Broken windows were not mended so the cardboard from Red Cross boxes was utilised – nothing was ever wasted. The water supply at best was spasmodic and washing was only possible when the kitchen was not in use or at night. The washroom, which divided the huts into two, contained 20 taps, but few were serviceable. Lavatories were brick buildings housing cesspools, straddled by long wooden planks. The latrine in the hut washroom was to be used only at night and in dire need.

Stalag IVB hut interior.

In June 1941, the International Red Cross had been permitted to inspect the camp. The report was favourable, but German authorities had been careful to ensure the appearance resembled a holiday camp. Australian army sergeant Robert Young, of Sydney, had been captured in Greece and was in Stalag IVB suffering from 'congestion on the lungs'. Young assured the Red Cross that he had 'no complaints', but Young had.[43] He was unhappy with the disparity between the lives of French POWs and the rest. French POWs were housed in a better part of the camp, and he had been entertained watching French officers arrive with subordinates carting luggage, lots of luggage. They enjoyed a much more comfortable existence and appeared barely guarded. It was a conclusion made by other POWs, and they could never understand why.

As Stalag Luft IVB evolved into a larger camp with POWs from many nationalities, the disparity became more and more evident. Two compounds housed aircrew. These and the Russian compound were surrounded by the highest security measures. Other camps holding French, Serbs, Poles and other nationalities were not, and were merely living quarters with a few guards stationed to keep order. The Russians were the most hated and feared and subsequently the most cruelly treated. Aircrew were considered the most valuable prisoners. If they escaped, they could again return to the skies over Germany. They were therefore not permitted to join work parties and suffered the closest confines.

A new number, a POW one
(Stobart).

The first couple of days Bert struggled with the truth. 'I thought this is a bloody dream … I'm not a prisoner.' There was so much to take in and how could he accept that only he and Jock had survived. Those amazing men he had flown with, killed. He wondered if Noel and his family had been told he too was dead. When would they hear he was alive, how could they cope with the news that he was a POW with an uncertain future and no release date?

The POW airmen in his hut had taken the same emotional journey and there was nothing they could say or do to lessen the weight of it. Bert needed to become a valued member of a new band of brothers, whose preoccupation was simply survival. He needed to adapt to this alien environment and quickly.

His most influential visitor was WO John Dempsey Hunter (400800), who was the appointed man in charge of Australians. Hunter was a long way from his duties as a hardware assistant in the border town of Albury, NSW. He had enlisted on 8 November 1940 and served with RAF 14 Squadron. Hunter's operational experience was as exotic as the nationalities in Stalag IVB. On 24 July 1943 he was shot down in a 'widow maker', more formally known as a Marauder B26. The Marauder was an American aircraft which had commenced operational service with the United States Army. The nickname was adopted because of the high accident rate amongst early models during take-offs and landings. The 150 miles per hour (241 km/h) needed on the final approach to prevent the aircraft from stalling was intimidating for pilots used to the regular slow approach speeds.

Hunter had perfected that skill. On a shipping reconnaissance patrol, his Marauder came under repeated attacks from enemy aircraft off the Italian coast. 'Attacked three times. Third time engines failed.'[44] The aircraft fell into the Mediterranean Sea. Hunter sustained head injuries and was fortunate that an enemy seaplane crew dragged him out of the water and flew him to Marseilles, France for hospitalisation. His Australian navigator P/O Richards Egan (407525), WOP/AGs WO Maxwell Frederick Stephens (406664) and WO Lawrence Murphy (401627), as well as the English second pilot, front and tail gunners,

Stalag IVB (AWM).

survived with minor injuries. Hunter believed their survival was due to the actions of Murphy, who dived into the sinking aircraft to find and release the dinghy, when crew found their life jackets unserviceable. After the usual fortnight interrogation, he had been transported to Stalag IVB in August 1943 with his crew, except for Egan, which made incarceration more tolerable, so he appreciated Bert's dilemma of not having the same comradeship.

Responsibility weighed heavily on camp leaders like Hunter, the welfare of the POWs but also the necessity to maintain constant but diplomatic communications with German authorities. So much depended on fair treatment from the commandant and German guards and he needed to convince his POW charges to be compliant while not compromising their morale and fortitude.

His biweekly meetings with the German commandant had to be handled with the same firmness and diplomacy, as he explained the complaints and suggestions. The Germans were unsure of how to handle the aircrew. Hunter observed that his captors 'seemed rather scared of our potentialities'.[45] As numbers increased, they were herded into their own compound. 'Conditions at the camp were very poor', but by 'various means, mostly by bribery and foraging parties we managed to improve some of our conditions'.[46] The four 25-watt bulbs to each hut were gradually replaced with stronger bulbs only to have them confiscated during searches. Hunter turned a blind eye to raids on the coal storage until 'one of our party was shot'. But the cold pushed men to continue the raids and with some success.

Hunter was sympathetic to new arrivals like Bert Stobart. He oversaw the supply of essentials and clothing for aircrew who arrived with nothing but what they stood up in. He could check on their physical wellbeing but could do little to assuage their mental torment. Each new POW needed to make peace with his situation. Bert walked the perimeter and watched the German guard changing. It was still so hard to believe; he had fought an air war and never seen German soldiers up close, now, he was in the land of the enemy.

CHAPTER EIGHT

'You'd move the maggots aside because they used to go with your soups.'

F/S Bert Stobart (RAAF)

Bert Stobart was trying to adapt to life as a prisoner; it would take time and patience. His mind was full of the panicked exit from the burning Lancaster and images of his dead crew. He was concerned that Noel and his parents knew he was alive. They would have been quickly advised that he was missing and perhaps information had filtered through already about five being killed … even Jock believed he was killed. At the first opportunity he filled out the one-page card allowed, addressing it to his RAAF elder brother Cliff, believing that was the fastest route. Cliff needed to notify everyone concerned as fast as possible. He also asked Cliff, 'Would you arrange comforts from Australia, Kodak House, for me – cold winter.' Unfortunately, it was not fast enough.

Bert was unaware that letters received in England had been returned stamped 'Deceased'. It was a cruel shock for Noel and the Stobart family. Belatedly, the RAAF realised the error, issued an apology and assurance that Bert was safe and incarcerated in Stalag IVB. It was assured letters could be sent frequently and next of kin parcels sent from Australia quarterly, all addressed:

Kriegsgefangenenpost
Name, Rank, Number
Englischer
Name of Cam,
Germany
Deutschland

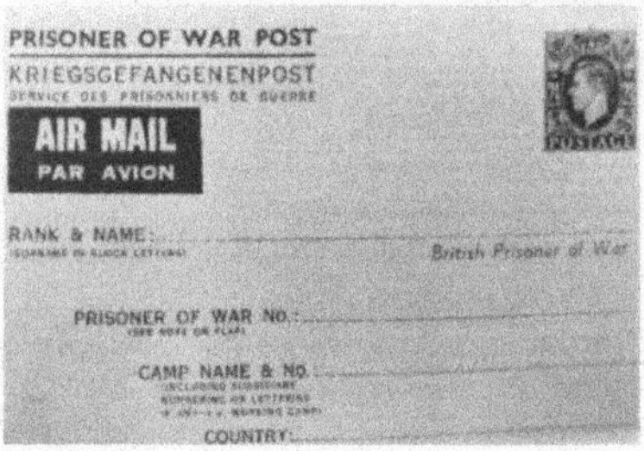

On 17 November 1943 Noel began typing a letter.

> *Allie Sweetheart,*
>
> *Hello Darling how are you? I am just the happiest girl in the world to know that you are safe – all my prayers have been answered sweetheart. It is funny Allie but all the time I just had a feeling that you were alright – I even dreamed of it. I am so much in love with you darling that I knew you would just have to come home to me sometime … and why not when I have the best fiancé in the whole world.*

Having returned home from work, Noel continued writing in ink, and offered family news, and how she was returning to the beach they so enjoyed, closing with, 'I'm crazy about you.'

From his mother: 'My Own Precious Darling Albert', expressing gratitude that he was safe, or as safe as he could be in a German POW camp. One minute the RAAF had him dead, the next they announced he had been promoted to Warrant Officer (WO). It was a strange war.

The German POW rations were appalling.

> *They were giving us potatoes and soup and a bit of horsemeat or something like that. And you'd have the horsemeat with the bones in it and sometimes you'd have maggots in it, and you'd move the maggots aside because they used to go with your soups … mainly potatoes.*

His hut with 200-odd individuals 'felt crowded, almost overpowering'. His bunk offered a thin mattress and palliasses 'full of straw' and a small wool covering,

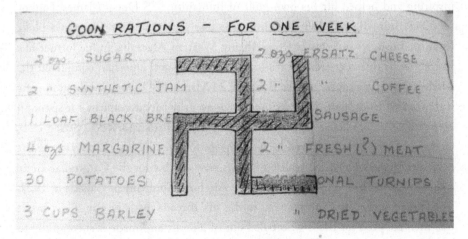

German captors were referred to as 'Goons' (McCleery).[272]

offering scant respite from the numbing cold at the commencement of what was to be a very bad winter. He had been given as much of the surplus clothing store as could be afforded a new arrival, and it wasn't enough. Then, Bert received his first parcel, manna from heaven; or at least the London committee of the Australian Red Cross Society. They would never know just what a relief that parcel with his name on it was. Christmas had come early. He certainly opened the parcel with as much anticipation as a child on Christmas Day, and, rummaged through the contents with delight. The parcel just kept on giving.

One vest, one pair of pants, one pair of pyjamas, one pullover, one pair of gloves, a toothbrush, a shaving brush, a towel, two pencils, one balaclava, two tablets of soap, a comb, a face cloth, ten razor blades, one muffler, two pair of socks, one tooth tablet, one shaving stick, one tin insect powder, one tin boot polish, and two glorious pounds of chocolate.

He realised he had a silly grin on his face and the smile broadened when he thought to himself how just weeks before the sight of a comb, or a pencil, or a razor blade had not caused the slightest excitement, or appreciation. His morale rose exponentially and he almost felt human again. The next opportunity to shower could not come soon enough – he could shave and use real soap. Now he had a pullover, a balaclava, socks, a muffler and gloves and a second pair of pants to survive the snow and ice. The chocolate was a luxury and would be shared, particularly on Christmas Day.

Gradually other aircrew introduced themselves. Their stories were the stuff of the boys' own adventures and the comics Bert had enjoyed as a boy. He figured his own was likely one of those too now, but he found what others had survived inspiring and helped lift his own guilt of humanity. F/S Donald James Tunney (406048) from RAAF 458 Squadron was one such character. He was a bloke from the bush, a wool-classer from Albany, Western Australia, in his former life. Just about as different from Bert's life as one could get. Don had completed the wireless operator's course, unlike Bert. On 24 March 1943 Don's Wellington crew had taken off from Malta but was shot down over the Mediterranean. He spent 15 hours afloat before being captured by the enemy and transported to Stalag IVB, Germany. Don Tunney figured he was eligible for the Goldfish Club. Bert didn't envy him that, although he realised he was now eligible for the Caterpillar Club, a club founded by Leslie Irvin of the Irvin Airchute Company of Canada in 1922. The name Caterpillar Club referred to the silk threads made by the silkworm. It was then adopted for those who baled out of aircraft and made it successfully to land due to their silk parachutes.

F/S Don Tunney, pre-POW and as a POW (AWM).

On his arrival at Stalag IVB Don Tunney's hair was clipped to scalp level, his clothes were fumigated and he was made to walk through a long shower to be deloused. It reminded him of the sheep-dipping operation on Aussie farms. His first two nights were spent sleeping on the concrete floor until space was found in a three-decked bunk. 'Life in IVB was no picnic. We were always hungry and uncomfortable, and, in winter, bitterly cold.'[47] There was no argument from Bert Stobart on that statement. Just as they had supported each other in the air they needed to support each other now.

Bert was provided with the weekly British Red Cross food parcel. These were combined with those of his group of four and rationed accordingly, for when parcels may not be received. He was, however, entitled to barter, and included in the weekly parcel were 50 cigarettes. The advantage of being a non-smoker was immense. Cigarettes in a POW camp were very lucrative currency and those who needed the regular nicotine hit were liable to trade anything they had – cigarettes for a tin of condensed milk, or tin of meat – which in turn enabled Bert's group of four to eat better. Bert quickly caught on to the fact that the French were well provisioned.

The French got on very well with the Germans and we used to say if you wanted to know the time ask a Frenchman because they would want to buy your watch and things like that. And you certainly wouldn't get the right price for them ... and so they weren't very popular, people ... the French lived very well in the prison camp.

Red Cross rations kept POWs alive.

Bert bartered for a full-length coat – luxury! German guards in the early stages of his captivity were quite congenial. The alternative to guarding POWs was being sent to the Russian front. They too craved English cigarettes but to barter with them for personal comfort was discouraged by hut commanders, as more important items needed to be acquired by illicit trade with guards. His wealth increased more as he traded for the different contents of Canadian and United States Red Cross parcels. A Canadian book enabled him to commence a diary, which he jokingly titled 'My Trip Abroad'. By pestering different POWs, he discovered an abundance of artists, cartoonists and storytellers, which enriched the long months ahead and bequeathed a lasting legacy of life in Stalag IVB. How much he wanted to write a long loving letter to Noel, but POWs were restricted to a single card, on occasion, and these were heavily censored.

Being able to participate in work parties outside the camp, even under guard, offered the opportunity to pilfer or surreptitiously, grasp the odd vegetable from a field. This was denied airmen.

An overcoat and the RAAF WO POW (Stobart).

So many nationalities now prisoners (Stobart).

Collecting wood was particularly important to fuel the hut stoves for warmth but aircrew again needed to depend on the benevolence of their army brethren, which diminished along with the available wood supply and an intense winter.

Now more adequately attired for the climate, Bert began to wander the perimeter of the air force compound, and through the wire observed the different nationalities in other compounds. The language barriers prevented meaningful conversation, but it seemed Russians, Yugoslavs, Afghans, Turks, 'just about every European you could mention' were incarcerated in Stalag IVB.

He had been unimpressed with the favourable treatment endowed on the French but was appalled at the treatment of Russian POWs. Allied POWs were unsure whether this was due to the Russians not being covered by the Geneva Convention, or due to the long-established hatred between the two nations. As Russian soldiers advanced in WWII they were greatly feared. Russian troops were unsalaried. Their superiors, therefore, turned a blind eye to the treatment of civilians, as soldiers fulfilled any physical need and desire.

It was better understood after the war, when it was realised that Nazi Germany had engaged in a policy of deliberate maltreatment of Soviet POWs in keeping with their racial purity theory, which declared ethnic Slavs as sub-human. An estimated 3.3 to 3.5 million Russians died due to starvation, ill-treatment and over work.

Heinrich Himmler, enforcer of the Nazi racial policy reviewing a Russian POW
enclosure.

At Stalag IVB Russians were starved, maltreated and denied medical care. Bert
could but watch. They risked coming into Allied compounds in search of food, any
scraps, digging into waste areas and discarded Red Cross tins.

> *They were a pitiful sight and then when the Germans would see the Russians*
> *there, they'd probably come up and they had this thing like a baseball bat and give*
> *them a whack over the head and that sort of thing, belt them around, because the*
> *Germans hated the Russians, and the Russians hated the Germans.*

The Allied POWs attempted to share
what they could, but they had little, and
even less as the war progressed. It left
a lasting impression on Bert Stobart,
watching Russian soldiers, many with
limbs missing, suffer. 'You saw everything

SKILLY · UP!

The daily German skilly (soup) was of very poor quality (Stobart).

that was going on … blokes hobbling around on their stumps.' The Russians were
expected to live on potatoes. When one died the other Russian POWs held the
body up during the morning parade so as,to receive their ration. There were boy
soldiers, not yet in their teens, made to wear brown jackets with SU (Soviet Union)
marked on the back. They quickly picked up English and even the Australian sense
of humour.

> We looked after the kids as much as we could, give them a bit of something to eat,
> when we had it. They were very, great kids.

The cutting of the bread issue (Stobart).

But there was little else Bert, or the other Allied POWs could do to ease their lives.

In the air force compound, as the winter closed in, POWs endured their own battle to survive. The huts were long, with no insulation, and broken windows boarded up with cardboard. The temperature outside dropped to minus 16 and inside it hovered around minus six. Men used every piece of clothing they had to stay warm, 'it got terribly cold'. The colder it got, the hungrier the POWs felt, and ignoring hunger pains required great discipline. 'If you didn't eat too much or take too much you could survive.' The days became, all about food, and Bert's book began to fill with visions of the same.

They had taken for granted being fed well, growing up, and in the RAAF. The

Cookhouse staff.[273]

Stalag IVB stage production (AWM).

one advantage of being in Bomber Command was the bacon and eggs prior to operation and on return. A simple egg now would be heavenly, a roast dinner, decent vegetables, basically anything fresh that didn't come out of a can. The coffee issued by the Germans was made from acorns, 'ersatz'. Bert thought it horrible but when you desperately needed a hot beverage, it had to do. The loaf of bread issued needed to be cut carefully to ensure equal portions for the group of four or five. The execution of this was scrutinised carefully.

Aircrew who had entrusted their lives to others began to lose trust in the same aircrew who shared their food. A cartoon relayed that perhaps even those lucky enough to work in a camp kitchen fared better than those not as fortunate. Hunger changed men.

It took time before Bert was permitted into the most inner sanctum of Stalag IVB. Although he was known by several airmen, camp leadership needed to be hyper-vigilant in case hunger or threats had influenced the loyalty of an Allied POW.

The mind needed to be kept busy. Bert was impressed with the classes and lectures available. The wealth of education and pre-war work experience within the ranks of aircrew, made for many interesting lectures, discussions and debate. The Red Cross sent books when possible, and these were well and truly thumbed and shared.

Bert Stobart never had much of a musical ear so was very impressed with the entertainment other POWs produced. 'The army had come into camp with many of their musical instruments, so the standard was high.' Seemingly out of nothing, costumes and stage props were manufactured, scripts written, and quite passable actors found.

Stalag IVB musical complete with 'ladies' (AWM).

Particularly popular were the female impersonators. Under normal circumstances these 'ladies' would not be given a second glance, but these were not normal circumstances.

Bert had always fancied himself a bit of a handyman but the cleverness of some was remarkable. He was taught how to make an 'immersion heater'. The bottom and top were removed from a tin. It was modified with wood and, a wire was attached, enabling water to be added and brought to the boil. A type of coffee percolator was also made.

Inventiveness – a coffee percolator (AWM).

Further ingenuity was demonstrated in the manufacture of the all-important, particularly coveted 'blower', for use inside the huts and at night-time. There were several models, but they were often manufactured from a Canadian milk powder tin, a fish can and canvas. It was mounted on a board and weighed about 2 kilograms. Compact, quick, portable, smokeless and burning only a bit of charcoal, this home-made turbine arrangement could boil a billy for tea or coffee in about three minutes. Another model was constructed from Red

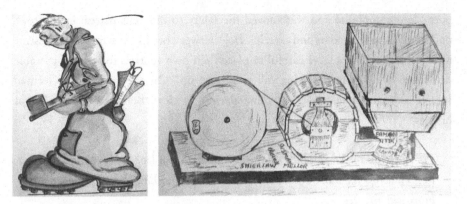

The 'blower' was highly prized (Stobart).

Cross tins, a couple of nails, and a sacrificed belt, which drove a metal blade fan. With a few sticks of wood or charcoal food could be warmed.

Then there were those who had specialised skill.

> We had a bloke in our camp, an RAF navigator, and before the war he worked for His Masters Voice. He was in our group and apart from being a funny bloke he was a genius. One day he said, 'I think I'll make a wireless'. We didn't believe him, but he made one.

To assist they became scroungers. By trade, resourcefulness, and a degree of theft from camp surrounds, they accumulated the list he requested. Wire was easy as was the small tin that had contained rolled oats. Guards provided what they believed to be innocuous items in exchange for cigarettes. A pair of earphones was secured.

Bert and his group sheltered their craftsman while he was industrious and only when he had finished did they reveal their secret to the hut commander. It was very dangerous to have a wireless and if discovered the consequences for hut inhabitants was dire. The fervent desire for news overcame that fear. Carefully, after lights were

An example of a POW secret wireless (AWM).

extinguished, the wireless was tuned to the British Broadcasting Corporation (BBC). Bert and his companions wrote up the important details and between hands and huts the information was distributed. News raised morale significantly and great care was made to protect the purveyor of precious knowledge.

The wireless had been built into a

portable gramophone and was moved for safety to different places: in the roof, under bunks, in the toilets and even in a hole between bricks. As with all clandestine undertakings, POWs were careful to place their own sentries to warn of possible detection. The normal warning call was 'Jerry up!'. On one occasion a German soldier nicknamed 'Pickaxe Pete' came alarmingly close. Bert had the wireless at his feet.

I'm sitting on the bunk, and I saw him. I stood up and looked at him and spoke to him, across the bunk and in the meantime, I'm pushing the radio under the bunk with my feet.

A noisy diversion was created by other POWs and the guard left. 'He never knew how close he was to finding it.' Suspicions though had been raised and the POWs in IVB received a visit from members of the feared German Schutzstaffel (SS). They were none to gentle with the POWs or their belongings but did not discover the wireless. 'Fortunate because they would have shot us.' The wireless inventor within Bert's group of four was henceforth known as 'Genius'.

We thought he was bloody mad when he said, 'I'll think I'll make a wireless.' We should have asked for a tank, or an aeroplane!

Camp Christmas menu (Stobart).

It had been difficult for Bert to adjust, he doubted he could ever fully, but there was comradeship and a degree of security within this new band of brothers, Allied airmen crammed together in small, badly ventilated spaces with three-tier bunks. His new best friend was his 'mucker', the man with whom he shared Red Cross parcels and rations.

On occasion a hut-wide sharing took place. Christmas was one event worth celebrating. Hut members spent time and effort decorating and allowed themselves to indulge in stockpiled treats, to create a

Christmas festivities (Stobart).

feast – by POW standards. But it did little to appease the knowledge of Christmas at home. For the Australians, snow outside reminded them of the cards distributed to celebrate 25 December. Australians, oddly, preferred cards that depicted pine forests and trees glistening in an English winter, rather than images Christmas 1943 in Stalag IVB (Stobart).

Bert had had his fill of snow. He yearned for the Melbourne heat and cooling off in the bluer than blue ocean off Brighton Beach. Like those around him in the

Stalag IVB (Stobart).

crowded hut, he could but think of his family. They would be commemorating the day and enjoying Christmas lunch very differently. A walk outside in the brisk air did little to lighten his mood. Oh to be free of the wire fence and guard houses! It was fortunate that WO Albert 'Bert' Adrian Stobart was unaware that 1943 was not to be his last Christmas in Stalag IVB, and was the best.

He too was soon introducing downed airmen to their caged existence; too many airmen. Stalag IVB was destined to hold nearly 30,000 POWs. Overcrowding became dire, food at times non-existent. The Allied invasion exacerbated life for prisoners of war, and led to the death of many.

Stalag IVB in the snow (Stobart).

For aircrew, 1944, was the worst year of WWII (McCleery).

CHAPTER NINE

'Für Sie der Krieg ist fertig!' ('For you, the war is finished').

They fell from the skies with increasing regularity. As the air war progressed further into Germany on longer operations, bomber crews became more vulnerable to the dangers below and in the air. From November 1943 to March 1944, losses averaged 5.1 per cent. Fewer than 25 out of each 100 crews survived their first tour of 30 operations. On a single night Bomber Command lost more aircrew than Fighter Command did in the Battle of Britain. The highest loss, 11.8 per cent, was incurred on the Nuremberg raid on 30 March 1944.

The crew skippered by F/O James McCleery (415585) had continued to defy the odds, but the war was not yet won. The Australians in the crew were a tight-knit group, having known each other since basic training in 1941. McCleery (415585) had departed Australian shores on 15 January 1943 as a pilot, not yet 20. On the same ship was another West Australian, 22-year-old WOP Victor Widdup

GERMANY HERE I COME!

MAY 11ᵗ 1944

Drawing by F/O James McCleery (AWM).

(415596); Victorian 20-year-old navigator Wesley Betts (410209); and South Australian bomb aimer, 22-year-old, Henry Jeffries Long (417091). In England they teamed up with 20-year-old Western Australian air gunner Donald Jeffrey Dyson (427309). The young crew were determined to remain together and were pleased to be posted to RAAF 460. Englishman, Sergeant A. F. Hamilton joined as rear gunner. Securing a flight engineer came with difficulty. The engineer they were assigned was Polish and much older than the crew.

The Australians in the 460 Squadron crew skippered by F/O James McCleery. Left to right, back row: Don Dyson, Wes Betts, Vic Widdup. Front row: Henry Long and Jim McCleery (McCleery).

We lost a motor one night ... when I was coming in, to land and he ran up the back and disappeared and I had to feather it and do the whole lot myself.[48]

McCleery asked for another engineer and the next also proved unsatisfactory. Finally, Englishman, Sergeant W. A. Law completed the crew.

Too many operations, too many targets, too many killed, so McCleery was made Acting 'C' Flight Commander when Squadron Leader Eric George Delaney 'Ricky' Jarman RAAF (404507) and his crew disappeared over Friedrichshafen on the night of 27–28 April 1944. Three 460 Lancasters were shot down during that attack. Jarman wore a DFC, as did his Australian navigator F/O Marmion Wilfred Carroll, (408034) and bomb aimer, F/O Francis Gordon Jackson, (404503). Australian WOP Hector Ronald Harrison (404467), Australian rear gunner Thomas Joseph Lynch (414807), and mid-upper gunner Ronald Leslie Neal (411227) were extremely experienced flying officers. Only the English engineer Douglas George Champkin, wore sergeant stripes. It seemed rank, and experience meant little and Lancaster LM523 was shot down by night fighter piloted by Hptm Heinz-Martin Hadeball Stabi at Lahr, east of Strasbourg at 01.40.

It was particularly poignant that the only woman official war artist, Stella Bowen, had just that day drawn rough pencil sketches and taken photographs at Binbrook for a painting to represent Australians in Bomber Command. That night they went missing. Bowen completed the painting in a London studio but said: 'It was horrible having to finish the picture after the men were lost. Like painting ghosts.'[49] Bowen's grief was visible in the completed artwork, in the menacing nature of the Lancaster, the solemn expressions of the crew and the dull red ribbon linking the names like a wreath.[50] What Bowen and 460 authorities did not know was that Lynch, in that most precarious of positions, rear gunner, had survived with a significant injury and after months of hospitalisation became a POW.

For 460 Squadron and the McCleery crew, left to fill the lead position in 'C' flight, it was an ill-omen. The disillusionment and fatigue had set in and McCleery considered that Bomber Command's Air Marshal Arthur Harris, commonly known as 'Bomber' Harris by the press, and by his aircrew as 'Butcher' Harris, in his single-minded pursuit of saturation bombing, was disregarding the human cost. Those assigned desk positions had no understanding of what aircrew faced every night. McCleery agreed to take a desk-bound English intelligence army major on an operation. Over the target

Lancaster LM523 aircrew, painted by official war artist Stella Bowen (AWM).

area and being subjected to heavy flak, McCleery called to the guest, 'Come and have a look at this.' The guest rapidly disappeared back into the belly of the aircraft and upon landing, 'he said "never again, I'm never going again"'.[51]

On the night of 11 May 1944, the attack was on the railway yards at Hasselt, Belgium. Lancaster ND674 became a kill for the MG 81 Z machine guns of Unteroffizier Woitanowski. With a flaming starboard engine and wing and a full bomb load, McCleery was left with no option but to issue the bale-out order. He watched helplessly as Betts got tangled up with his helmet and parachute and the navigator's jaw was broken. Then as he descended under his parachute canopy, 'I can remember seeing the aircraft go into the ground and, whoosh, up she went.'[52] The Australians in the McCleery crew had stayed together for years but no longer. Don Dyson somehow escaped and reached Allied lines. Long found himself shunted into Stalag Luft 7. Widdup was sent to Stalag 357. Officers, McCleery and Betts, were sent to Luft III. Jim McCleery drew his journey into captivity in his POW journal.

His 21st birthday was memorable not only because it was spent in a German POW camp but because, despite the severe shortage of food, 'the boys put on a party for me'. Rations had been quietly saved so a birthday cake could be made. It was traditional for a door key to be given on a 21st birthday; that would have been a fantastic gift, but the camp gates remained tightly shut and guarded.

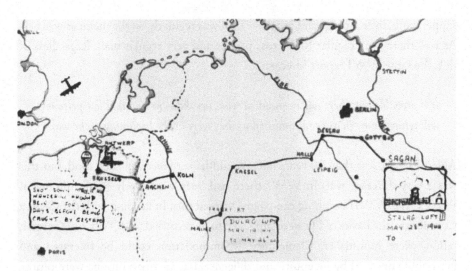

Map drawn by Jim McCleery (AWM).

British officers, investigating the welfare of Allied POWs of the German army in 1916, reported that the Germans supplied, 'Meat balls, noodles with prunes' for dinner and for supper the same day, 'roast veal, sausage, cocoa'. The next day the menu changed. For dinner it was, 'Pork, beef, white beans, rice' for dinner and for

Illustration by Jim McCleery (AWM).

supper, 'pork, liver sausage and groats'.[53] Beef was regularly on the menu as was fish. As well there were regular Red Cross parcels and very regular mail. Regardless of this, the same WWI report forecast:

> *It is probable that there will be many nervous breakdowns and that few prisoners will return home in as good condition as they were at the beginning of the war.*[54]

Allied POWs, less than 30 years later, would have rejoiced in such food, but this was a very different war. In WWI there had been a relatively small number of POWs. The WWII bombing campaign changed this. In keeping with the Geneva Convention, the basics of life were supposed to be accorded to POWs, but German rations were minimalist. Elementary accommodation could be tolerated and invariably improved by ingenuity and diligence, but German rations were pitiful, and food became the overriding concern for all POWs. F/L Alfred Playfair wrote, 'I have an appreciation for well-cooked good food. My appetite is excellent I think I know what hunger is *now*.'[55] Lunch was four slices of bread, dinner was 2 oz of bully beef, 2 potatoes and 4 spoons of barley.[56] There was commonly no breakfast. A Red Cross parcel was meant to be distributed to each POW, each week, but these were withheld either at the whim of the commandant, or, as the war progressed, due to supply interruption.

Jim McCleery and his companions could but watch as the Germans regularly emptied or punctured Red Cross tins so that POWs could not stockpile food for

The Germans punctured Allied Red Cross food tins, purportedly, to stop escape attempts (AWM).

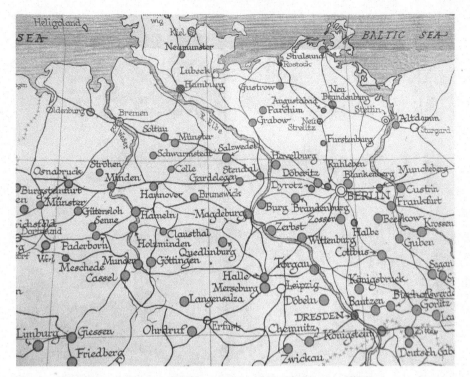

The proliferation of German POW camps in 1944 (McCleery, AWM).

an escape attempt. Subsequently, much was spoiled. There were 12 in McCleery's Luft III room: four Australians, four Canadians, two New Zealanders and a member of the Fleet Air Arm. They were fortunate to receive three Red Cross parcels a week between them. Each man took it in turn to cook for the others for a week, attempting to produce a satisfying meal out of very little.

With an increasing number of Allied aircraft being shot down, and the capture of Allied ground forces, the Germans needed to expand their network of POW camps rapidly, with separate ones for officers and non-commissioned ranks and tighter security for air force than others.

The conditions within the camps depended on a number of factors, not least of all if the camp was run by the Gestapo, German army or Luftwaffe. The foremost were the cruellest while the Luftwaffe demonstrated magnanimity, particularly to other airmen. But with the Allied POW population expanding rapidly at a time when German resources were diminishing, conditions within camps became progressively grim during 1944 and barely survivable in 1945.

POW welfare also depended on good leadership within their own ranks, on conscientious individuals striving to raise morale through the painstaking organisation of activities to reactivate the bodies and minds of once busy and

Cricket was taken very seriously. Stalag 383 Australian team (AWM).

vibrant men. Invariably this occurred through sporting activities that encouraged not only physical activity but an outlet for competitiveness for spectators and contestants trapped in their very unnatural environment. No time was lost in upholding national loyalties.

In Bert Stobart's Stalag IVB a clay wicket was made in the transit compound. Bert had played cricket for Melbourne Grammar, so he was anxious to be selected. Seventeen teams were formed and named after various regions within the Allied territories. An organiser was WO Edward Joseph Colclough (402314). His loyalties became confused by his enthusiasm to play cricket. Born in Sydney, with an Irish heritage, he had belonged to RAAF 458 Squadron, which itself had a confused war. Established in Australia, 458 was moved to RAF Bomber Command and an airfield in Yorkshire. In 1942, 458 was relocated to the Middle East, firstly to Egypt, then Dardinia, then Italy and Gibraltar. Colclough's Wellington was shot down over Sicily in July 1943. In 1944 he was a member of the 'Somerset Cricket Club', named after a very English county. The cricket-mad 24-year-old topped the bowling with 73 wickets for a 7.05 run average and this included vanquishing teams from Victoria and Western Australia.[57]

An entire book compiled by Australians Jim Davies and Jim Welch imprisoned

POW national games. The Australian athletic team (AWM).

in Stalag 383, at Hofenfels, Germany, was devoted to the cricket matches between old enemies England and Australia, and slightly friendlier adversary, New Zealand. Bounty from Red Cross parcels and dye enabled a semblance of national uniforms. The results were mixed with the test matches being drawn between England and Australia and the smaller New Zealand contingent no match for the larger ones.[58]

National rivalries took prominence with the organisation of a POW Games. Again, uniforms were manufactured from imaginative workmanship, though the athletics team struggled with appropriate footwear. Team selection was taken seriously as was the pride felt representing your country. A strange array of prizes were on offer; the most highly regarded was not a medal or cup, but an extra tin of food or several cigarettes.

The gathered crowd was unlike any other sporting audience, but they enjoyed the day and it felt good to cheer on your national contingent and boo the opposition, even if at the end of the day you could not go home.

At the beginning of winter, soccer, rugby, rugby league and something that only slightly resembled Australian Rules, took prominence. Then the heavy snow and ice put an end to the games Australians enjoyed. Only the Canadians were happy, after they built an ice rink, skated, and played ice hockey.

Jim McCleery was pleased to discover that at Luft III education was highly efficient and a substantial reference library had been amassed. Psychology, philosophy, law and languages right through to mathematics, structural and motor engineering and commercial subjects were available. Students wishing to study for their Australian matriculation found books for all subjects. Periodical examinations

Canadian ice hockey, Canadian-POW style (AWM).

were conducted on a wide variety of subjects using examination papers sent through the YMCA and International Red Cross. Lecture and examination rooms were situated in each barracks, with instructors coming from the ranks of educated aircrew.

Sport, education, comradeship, F/O Jim McCleery from Melbourne wondered if his POW log did not give the wrong impression and make Luft III sound like a holiday camp. Holiday camp it most certainly was not, and although he realised he was not much of an artist, he picked up the coloured pencils and drew the life, and those things he most missed. Except one page did not allow him to include everything – how did you draw freedom?

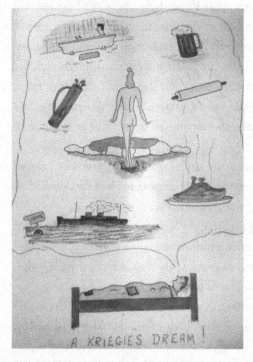

Jim McCleery's drawing of the life at home he yearned for (AWM).

Life for F/S Jack William Fenton Liley (409157) had already been traumatic before this war enveloped the world.

My contemporaries and I had all been deeply, affected by the 1914–1918 war and the terrible casualties that had been suffered. I had been personally affected by the loss of my father from war injuries when I was 11 and he was 38. This effect was mainly through my mother who lost a husband whom she deeply loved, but also left her with little support in a large and strange city, in which she had to battle to support us in a depressed economic climate at the tail end of the depression.[59]

POWs on the move (AWM).

Milton Liley served as a gunner with the 4th Australian Field Artillery from September 1915. He was wounded twice in three months on the Western Front in 1916, the second time a bad head injury resulted in his repatriation to Australia and discharge in 1917. His son, Jack, finished high school with good grades and wanted to enter university but he and his mother, Norah, had already taken in boarders to make ends meet and Jack needed to find employment. Office work enabled him to study commerce at Melbourne University part time. Without his mother's permission he put his age up from 17 to 18 and joined the Melbourne University Rifles, a militia battalion. When war broke out, not surprisingly, 'my mother refused to give permission for me to enlist in the army'. Although Liley had suffered the consequences of WWI, the 19-year-old was still drawn into WWII by the same sense of adventure and loyalty that had enticed his father. With new manpower legislation liable to conscript her son, Norah decided to give her permission for her son to enlist in the RAAF, believing it was a safer option. 'As things turned out I had joined the service that suffered the heaviest casualties.'[60]

RAAF training was 'very tough', but he scored high in the three months Observer's course and its complex lessons in navigation, compass, and instruments, meteorology, maps and charts, reconnaissance, aerial photography, signals and aircraft and ship recognition. Jack Liley's arrival in England introduced him to a country damaged by war. 'The beach looked good but was covered in barbed wire and buried mines.' Given the choice of coastal command or bomber command he chose the latter because it involved some pilot training, and was posted to No. 1 Advanced Flying Unit in Wigton, south-west Scotland. Liley found Wigton a 'terrible place, the weather was awful with almost continuous rain and mist, which made for very bad flying conditions'.[61] Within the normal flying circuit stood Cairnsmore Mountain, which aircraft flew into due to reduced visibility – 22 deaths during the three weeks he was there. He was detailed to, 'help carry the mangled corpses on stretchers'.[62]

> *I have never forgotten helping to carry a stretcher with a blanket covering what appeared to be a heap of bones and watching the blood drip out of it thinking 'this could be me'.*[63]

Having barely survived British weather, he opted for a Middle East squadron, RAF

Stalag Luft I (AWM).

The only clothes issued by the Germans were wooden clogs (AWM).

40. Over the ensuing months, all of his classmates were killed in the skies over Europe. On 20 April 1943 he too was shot out of the sky. Capture by Italian forces meant a tortuous train, truck and march to a German POW camp. Liley then endured not one but three different camps, Stalag Luft I in Barth Germany, Stalag Luft VI in Heydekrug, Lithuania, and Stalag Luft V in Tychowo, Poland.

Stalag Luft I was built on a barren strip of land jutting into the Baltic Sea about 105 miles (169 km) north-west of Berlin. A large pine forest bordered the west side of the camp and, to the east and north, the waters of Barth Harbour. Many thoughts ranged through his mind as under armed escort, he and others were marched through the town of Barth.

The external perimeter of the camp was menacing. Two rows of barbed wire 4 feet (1.2 m) apart attached to 10-foot (3 m) posts. Every hundred yards (91 m), a guard tower mounted with a machine gun and a pair of spotlights provided constant vigilance and permitted an unobstructed view of all within the confines of the enclosure. Sixteen feet (5 m) inside the tall double fences was a single-strand barbed wire fence with warning signs that any POW touching or stepping over the wire, would be shot without warning.

As Jack Liley entered this camp, men dressed in assorted air force uniform and wooden clog footwear greeted him. They were hungry for news and the advent of new POWs provided this. The old 'kriegies' (*Kriegsgefangenen* – prisoners of war) were as generous as they could be.

POWs were locked in their huts at 10 pm, or 9 pm in winter. An atmosphere heavy with cigarette smoke and sweat was difficult to bear. Liley was grateful for the recreational facilities POWs had created and involved himself behind the scenes in the theatre productions. Just as he was becoming slightly comfortable in the alien surroundings he was shunted to another camp. With the capture of United States ground forces, Luft I was turned into an American camp. Another difficult train trip to Stalag Luft VI.

Stalag Luft VI, Heydekrug in Wehrkreis I Königsberg, in the Memel area of East Prussia (now Silute, Lithuania), was a short distance from the delta of the Nomunas River, on an 8-acre flat and sandy site. Stalag Luft VI was the most northerly and easterly of all the German POW camps. Accommodation comprised of four brick barrack blocks, each divided into nine whitewashed rooms, as well as a dozen or so wooden huts, two cook houses and two latrines. Two new compounds were under construction. For the 100 Allied POWs already ensconced, the arrival of hundreds more meant their relative comfort disappeared. Huts were now crammed with prisoners sleeping in three tiered bunks, with just enough space between the man above them or the ceiling.

Arriving at Stalag Luft VI, Heydekrug, the exhausted prisoners were yet again photographed, fingerprinted and examined by the camp's medical personnel to ensure that they were vermin free. The camp continued to grow rapidly. The completion of new compounds did not result in more personal space, just more POWs. Luft VI held around 2000 British and Commonwealth prisoners in one compound, 2000 Americans in another and 1000 Russians in the third. Ten brick barracks were home to 552 men, and 12 wooden huts housed 54 POWs. Although heating was generally satisfactory, ventilation was bad because the shutters were ordered closed because of guard-dog patrols. And still more POWs arrived. The barracks capacity was estimated as 6168; Stalag VI soon held 10,400 POWs. German rations diminished quickly. The potato allowance was reduced from 400 to 300 grams, the quality of turnips deteriorated, and there were no fresh vegetables. Liley considered himself fortunate if he received one Red Cross parcel a week.

Jack Liley had struggled with the cold Scottish weather. In this northern part of Europe, it was night two-thirds of the time, very cold, with metres of snow in winter. With only five wooden slats to lie on he spent much of the nights listening to the howling wind. Twice a day, regardless of the weather, prisoners assembled

Stalag Luft VI (AWM).

outside for roll call. Even the summers seemed bleak in this part of Europe and the ever-present guards and guns were a constant reminder of the freedom he once enjoyed.

The order to move again brought relief and disorientation. By July the advance of the Red Army meant Stalag Luft VI POWs needed to be evacuated to the Stalag Luft IV at Gross Tychow (now Tychowo, Poland), near the Baltic Sea. Hurriedly gathering their few possessions, there was hope that the next camp would be less crowded and provide better provisions and accommodation; there was always hope before another arduous journey.

The first POWs entered Stalag Luft IV in May 1944. By July, Jack Liley and his group of 2400 Americans and 800 British personnel arrived. They found a camp divided into five compounds separated by barbed-wire fences. Three compounds were for Americans and one for British and the remaining Americans. Each of the 40 huts housed 200 men. Rooms were supposed to hold 16 men in two-tiered bunks, but some contained 24 POWs. A third tier of bunks were installed, but still men needed to sleep on floors with no mattresses. None of the huts could be properly heated, with just five iron stoves in the whole camp. Each compound had two open-air latrines and huts had a night latrine with two seats. There were no washing facilities. A Red Cross inspection reported 'fleas and lice are in abundance; no cleansing has been done'. The hope Liley and his fellow POWs harboured totally

There was always hope that a new POW camp would offer better conditions (AWM).

evaporated when they found that even their rations were worse than previously and there were no means of cooking collective food outside the kitchens. The camp commandant refused to grant any improvements. He also ensured that only German authorities oversaw the distribution of Red Cross parcels and medical supplies. Five wagons of American food parcels were seen to arrive but were not distributed. After his capture, Jack Liley had been taunted by German soldiers with the statement '*Für Sie der Krieg ist fertig!*'; 'For you, the war is finished'. He just so wished it was.

CHAPTER TEN

'I often wished it were possible to hitch a ride with them.'

WO Jack Douglas Garland (RAAF)

The gunnery officer was a gaunt, humourless man with a scar extending from his left eye to his chin. Below his brevet was the DFM ribbon. The scar and DFM said all that needed to be said, which was just as well, as he was a man of very few words. The newest aircrew could not have avoided the intimidating hush. This they had first witnessed at lunch when aircrew, returned from the previous night's raid, appeared in the mess. There were no welcome greetings. Their faces were expressionless. They sat together eating their meal with barely a word.

It was April 1944, yet the day was raw with a cold, biting wind blowing in from the North Sea. The just-joined gunners assembled in a classroom, their colourful uniforms in sharp contrast with the WO who stood before them. His uniform was worn and even the DFM ribbon looked faded. He cast an eye over the men before him, listened to the jocular banter which betrayed youthful bravado and nervousness, and raised his hand for quiet. 'You realise gunners are seen as the wild troublemakers?' His face remained stern. There was a light-hearted murmur. 'Most of you will be hosed out of your turrets before you're much older.'[64] The room went very silent.

The battle-weary gunnery-officer speech had been repeated countless times to thousands of gunners in the hope that this blunt statement would alert them to the dangers, and need to remain vigilant at all times. But it was also delivered with the knowledge that these young gunners had little control over their lives in the air. The statistics were sobering. In this 460 Squadron alone between 22 September 1943 and 22 April 1944, 65 aircraft had not returned with only a small proportion of their crews surviving to become POWs. Only 18 of these were rear gunners.[65] Bomber Command losses were staggering.

F/O Thomas Joseph Lynch (414807) could remember that strongly worded speech heard as a new arrival. He had enlisted in Brisbane in November 1941. By RAAF standards he was 'old' at 29 so his aircrew mustering was limited to gunnery. Thirty-four operations on Wellingtons had been completed by July 1943, attacking the Italian cities of Sardinia, Naples, Rome, Messina and Naples. Lynch found himself training aircrew; now he was one of those gaunt, war-weary instructors wearing faded blue Australian battle dress, delivering 'that' speech, and who kept his head down in the mess not wanting to speak directly to the youngsters who arrived to replace the dead.

Adrenaline was addictive; training others was tedious. He besieged posting authorities and finally was posted to RAAF 460 and Lancasters. It was now 1944 and operations over Germany were accelerating: 22 March it was Frankfurt, 24 March it was Berlin and 26 March it was Essen. In just those three operations over five days 115 Bomber Command aircraft and crews did not return. By the end of the fortnight his own crew, had also bombed Nuremberg and undertaken 26.55 hours of night-time bombing. On the Nuremberg operation on 30 March 1944, no fewer than 96 aircraft and crews were shot down. The city names began to blur: this night it was Cologne, the next Düsseldorf, then Karlsruhe and Essen.

On the night of 27–28 April 1944, Lynch and his crew, skippered by Squadron Leader Eric 'Ricky' Jarman, were to bomb Friedrichshafen. They had spent the day smiling for the benefit of art, and his nation's public relations. The crew was to symbolise Australians in Bomber Command in a painting undertaken by war artist Stella Bowen.

Lynch felt more at ease hours later, flying at 20,000 feet (6096 m). This was his 48th operation. Sitting in the rear turret was like having an armchair ride. Those at the front of the plane had the hard work. There was nothing to do as the searchlights and flak intensified and the light show enveloped him. Lynch had full

The Jarman crew, Lynch third from left (AWM).

view of the destruction below, fires burning everywhere. Suddenly a line of dark red flashes. The Lancaster buffeted wildly when the flashes mushroomed. The ensuing minutes were chaotic as the bomber disintegrated, another successful British kill for night-fighter pilot Hptm Heinz-Martin Hadeball Stabi. Three 460 Lancasters were shot down the night of 27–28 April. Of the 21 460 Squadron aircrew, Lynch was the only airman to survive and for some time he was uncertain he would.

Lynch remained unconscious until 5 May. He awoke to find himself in a Luftwaffe hospital in Baden Baden. There was no immediate recollection of how he fell from a Lancaster and arrived in a German hospital bed. Lynch slowly checked his body, what was there and what was missing? It was a shock to find his right leg was no longer attached to his body. The news that the rest of his crew had been killed sent him further into depression. Hospital staff assured him the war was over, at least for him. They were kind and attentive. He was asked if he would like to write to his relatives in Australia, only to be interrupted by a uniformed individual, who declared this was not allowed until Lynch had been processed through Dulag Luft, the interrogation centre for aircrew. Medical staff ignored the instruction and posted his letter. It took six months to reach Australia but was still the first his family heard that he was alive. The officious RAAF had clinically stated: 'Missing over Germany, believed killed'.

German patients entered his hospital ward and angrily berated him. One placed his hands around Lynch's throat and threatened to kill him for bombing Germany. A guard was placed at the door of his room. Lynch was moved under guard by rail further into enemy territory. Once in Frankfurt he saw how much of the city lay in ruins; he decided not to mention that he and his crew had bombed Frankfurt. Another hospital, more blurred months as staff attempted to clear up the infection in his wound, which swept through the rest of his body. American wounded were placed in his ward but refused to speak to him, suspecting that Lynch was a German spy. 'German spy with one leg and a bad infection?'[66] The situation was absurd. His condition deteriorated. A German officer informed him that the 'Allies had staged an invasion but were repelled by German forces back into the sea and most had died.'[67]

It was 1945, and the infection still controlled his body. Further operations removed more of the leg. It did little to ease the pain and when sleep did come, the dreams were vivid and unwelcome. Lynch awoke one morning to find his bedding and nearby wall covered in blood. 'I had never thought so much blood could come from one person.'[68] That was until a few weeks later, 'when I saw blood spouting from a young American's mouth.'[69] Lynch weathered six months without company, then one American and then an Australian, then another three months alone. Tom

F/O Thomas Lynch (AWM).

Lynch may have been the only RAAF airman who welcomed being transported to a POW camp and the close company of others. It was however nonsensical that a one-legged, weak Australian air gunner be incarcerated, and the senior Allied officer lobbied that Lynch be part of a convalescent exchange. While he waited, his reduced duties consisted of, 'cutting a loaf of bread into 24 slices'.[70] He realised how badly the war was going for Germany when he observed army guards scraping out the empty Red Cross tins.

Thomas Lynch was loaded onto a 'train trip to freedom', though this too, 'was agonising thanks to the Allied fighters which strafed rail stations'. He felt particularly 'hopeless' when caught 'unprotected' on the ground, with one leg. Lynch was consoled by thoughts of all Allied crews he had known who, did not have the opportunity, to return 'even on one leg'. There was relief when his contingent crossed the German border and he arrived in Marseilles, France, to board a ship as part of prisoner exchange. The sight of the English coastline brought tears to the eyes.

> There were a few of us who did come back, but many will not return, ever. They went so suddenly that it is best to think of them as being away on long sorties and some day they will call up and say 'This is J for Johnny' coming home.[71]

WO Jack Garland (403186) was captivated by the sky, or at least the vapour trails. Beautiful blue skies and the vapour trails of hundreds of American heavy bombers flying to their targets, he just, 'wished it were possible to hitch a ride with them'.[72] He thought back to when he was a member of a heavy bomber crew winging their way on an attack. There had been purpose, deadly intent, even exhilaration at taking the war to the enemy. Now, he was reduced to standing watching the vapour trails of others. He had been free up there, he was not free down here, and that was getting very old. How many years? Two and a half. How many days was that, how many hours? Up there in the sky he recalled a tinge of guilt when Bomber Command was ordered to bomb cities. That guilt dissipated as mates died. Years as a POW, forever hungry, forever filthy, witnessing malicious treatment, had ensured there was no guilt left.

How ignorant he had been as a teenager anxious to join the fight. Talk of war was, 'unconcerning, my mates and I thought the whole thing a bit of a swizzle'. He had watched newsreels with Britain's Prime Minister Neville Chamberlain 'waving his piece of paper', saying there would be no war. 'Like the words and utterances of all politicians it should have been taken with a grain of salt'.[73] He was sitting with friends in a Sydney milk bar on that Sunday when war was announced. They had no real understanding what that meant but quickly enlisted in the militia for a 'bit more fun', and then the glamorous RAAF at 20.

Garland was one of 72 WOP/AGs who sailed on the RMS *Aorangi* for additional training in Canada in January 1941. Seventy-two, full-of-potential young Aussies, of whom, as far as he knew, 37 had already been killed on active service and five had become POWs. He watched the vapour trails and could remember the cold fear he felt when the notice board listed his RAF 97 Squadron crew was to fly that night. Fear that was 'suppressed to the best to your ability'. The words 'maximum effort will be launched tonight with over 1000 aircraft participating' ensured the fear remained in the pit of the stomach, until you were in the air, busy, supporting your crew and with your heart only returning to a 'more normal beat when you heard "Bombs Away"'. His crew, his brothers, gone in an instant, that

Garland and Sgt Fletcher McKendrick (403201) who was killed over North Africa and has no known grave. (AWM).

night when they were coned by searchlight and flak tore metal, and bodies.

In a strange way the night on 27–28 August 1942 had played out in slow motion. The port fin and stabiliser disappeared, and the rear turret was swaying drunkenly on its lower mounting. It hung there for a second and then fell away taking with it a young Canadian gunner on his first operation. The Lancaster was spinning towards earth, but Garland couldn't stand to reach the rear door. He dragged himself upwards using the aircraft ribs. He hit the release just as there was a tremendous explosion and he tumbled into thin air. Rapid thoughts, 'Need to open the parachute'; 'Something wrong with my leg, something warm and sticky running down my neck'. He saw the aircraft hit the deck and explode, 'Who still in it?'. Trees flashed up and branches tore at his face before a sudden jerk as the parachute canopy caught and he hung there dangling 25 feet (7.2 m) above the ground. Germans below indicated he should.

I had just jumped 14,000 feet [4267 m] from the aircraft and wasn't in the least interested in the last 25 feet [7.2 m] without a parachute, particularly with something not quite right with my leg.[74]

He swung there watching those below him bustle about; it was almost comical. They returned and stood in a circle with a stretched tarp between them. Garland released his harness. The next he remembered was being wheeled into an operating room in a Duisberg, Germany, hospital. He had been concussed, had a broken leg, shrapnel lodged in his neck and two black eyes. While in hospital the RAF bombed the city. All the patients except him were wheeled down into the cellars – the German staff believed he should be left to witness the horror.

His English flight engineer, Fred Ambrose, turned up in hospital but with a sobering story. The rest of their crew were dead. They had been found huddled together in the nose of the Lancaster. Centrifugal force as the bomber spun to earth had prevented them from opening and baling out through the front escape hatch.

En route to Stalag IXC he managed to escape but limping on a bad leg meant recapture was inevitable. His German captors were unimpressed, and he was sentenced to three months road labour. He and the rest of the road gang of 50 spent time in handcuffs and their night accommodation was terrible, locked up in an air raid shelter.

Mice, cockroaches were running all over the floor, the place smelt of stale urine and there were a few wooden bunks that no doubt held a variety of small animals ready to devour any person that had to spend time in the place.[75]

RAAF 466, crew 87, having breakfast after their first operation. F/S Lyle Doust, sitting middle front facing. Only he and one other would live (AWM).

Garland couldn't believe he was pleased to be led to a railway station and shoved with too many others in a small carriage. Stalag Luft VI was not welcoming, a large camp with many nationalities, but at least the camp commandant, Hauptmann Muller, 'seemed not too indoctrinated with the usual Nazi Party hate', having been educated in England and with an English wife. Garland hoped his injuries were considered bad enough that he too could be part of any repatriation prisoner exchange. This was denied. Having been attached to an RAF squadron with an English crew he was pleased to meet other Australians as they arrived.

One such Aussie was Lyle Doust. He heard Lyle's drawl before he saw him. Doust was a country bloke, his father a stock inspector in rural Yass, New South Wales. Like Garland, he was 20 when he enlisted. His navigator training was long, but his operational tour was short. An Australian newspaper photographed his crew (crew 87) having breakfast, looking relieved, and speaking with other crew, after their first operation – an attack against the city of Frankfurt on the night of 20–21 December 1943. Only he and one other of the aircrew in the photograph survived the war. The next two operations were 'gardening', dropping mines off the Dutch islands of Terschelling and Schiermonikoog. The crew's fourth operation was the night of 21–22 January 1944, against Magdeburg, a heavy manufacturing

centre south-west of Berlin. It was just after midnight when Oblt Hans-Heinz
Augenstein, in his MeBf110 G-4, fired cannon at the rear of the Halifax.[76]

Direct hits shattered the port engine and wing. The order to bale was issued,
and as Doust sat directly above the front escape hatch, he lifted his folding seat,
clipped on his parachute and bent down to open the hatch. The slipstream ripped
the hatch upwards slicing a large gash to the forehead of Doust. Like Garland,
Doust was ejected from the aircraft. He was unconscious but his parachute ripcord
had been pulled by New Zealand bomb aimer, F/S Johnny Dobson, who followed
him out. The pilot F/S Conrad Johnston, a dairy farmer from Wingham near Port
Macquarie; rear gunner, F/S Jack Thompson from Sydney; English WOAG Sgt
Len Wykes, MUG Sgt John Morgan and flight engineer Sgt Syd Hennan, did not
survive.

Like Jack Garland, Lyle Doust landed in a tree. He 'was bleeding badly and
swinging on his harness in the gale-force winds and driving rain'.[77] Time was spent
in hospital before Doust was sent to Dulag Luft interrogation centre at Frankfurt.
Being a navigator, his treatment was worse and longer than that accorded WOP/
AG Garland or rear gunner, Bert Stobart. The enemy was anxious to understand
British navigation systems to better combat air attacks.

Doust was locked up in a small single room measuring about 8 feet by 6 feet
(2.4 m x 1.8 m), containing a wooden bunk, a palliasse, a blanket and a single-
locked frosted window. There was no opportunity to wash or shave. The radiator
was deliberately turned on to the highest level to ensure the cell was unbearably hot
and stuffy. Solitary confinement was known to extend to three months.

After the initial session of interrogation by a German officer the prisoner might
receive some food and water. An early meal could consist of two slices of black bread,
one spread with margarine or jam. A late meal was a bowl of indescribable soup
and a slice of bread. Dulag Luft was a very unpleasant place. Those on the other
side of the English Channel had blithely told aircrew that they should only provide
their name, rank and serial number. Those on the other side of the channel, 'did not
take into consideration the ways and means which were employed at Dulag Luft
to entice an airman to talk. Often these methods were quite successful.'[78] Physical
punishment could be used, and a less painful method was to offer a starving airman
a huge and delicious meal on condition more details were offered than name, rank
and serial number. It took strong willpower to resist.

When Garland introduced himself to Doust, clearly the navigator has already
been through a difficult period. It took time before the reticent navigator relaxed
and he, Garland, and six other Australians, decided there being strength in
numbers, they were determined to see each other through this captivity. Lyell

Doust recorded that his life as a POW was, in the beginning 'tolerable', then it wasn't, due to 'overcrowding ... insufficient beds', rations 'poor'.[79]

The elected camp leader was WO James 'Dixie' Deans (RAF), who had been a POW for nearly three years. He always appeared impeccably dressed at each roll call. A stickler for good discipline, 'he demanded and got uncompromising loyalty and esprit de corps'.[80] Unbeknown to the POWs he was an MI9 agent, actively collecting intelligence from behind the wire and relaying it in coded letters, via his wife. Deans introduced himself to Lyell Doust as soon as the new POW was led through the front gates. Deans needed to assure Doust of his assistance, but he also needed to ensure this lanky, quiet Australian was not a German spy. Deans was known to ask RAF aircrew questions such as: Where is your hometown? What does your father do for a living? Where in London, is Madame Tussauds? German authorities were anxious to end clandestine activities in camps and escape attempts. In 1944 their success resulted in the murders of 50 POWs.

CHAPTER ELEVEN

'It is every POW's duty to try to escape.'

The statement: 'It is every POW's duty to try to escape' was yet another made by desk-bound English authorities. The very reason Allied aircrew were the most closely guarded was because the enemy realised the value of these men in blue battle dress. The desire to return to England was strong and the efforts to escape were commendable; but the reprisals against those who remained were harsh, the punishment for escape attempts was severe and recapture invariably led to murder.

Within a day or so of the advance party of British aircrew arriving at Stalag VI, Heydekrug, a tunnel was started. By the time the main party arrived, three tunnels were under way though one was quickly discovered by camp guards. Tunnels soon pockmarked the ground beneath and many escape attempts were made. Unfortunately, the Germans were as industrious in their attempts to discover the tunnels and recapture the prisoners.

German guards digging for tunnels.274

When found, the exterior was caved in and the tunnels became open pit toilets. A favourite name for the German guards was 'ferrets'. According to WO Jack Garland, 'Occasionally the floor of a hut would open, and a ferret would emerge having found the new tunnel.'[81] The hut leader was held responsible and taken to the 'cooler', solitary confinement.

At Heydekrug the Germans then dug a deep ditch between the main wire and the warning wire, along the whole length of the compound. It dented the confidence of the tunnellers but made them even more determined. An English airman arrived at Heydekrug with a reputation for tunnelling known by Stalag VI elected leader, RAF WO James 'Dixie' Deans. He was an officer who had swapped identities with a sergeant at Stalag Luft III, Sagan, and come to Heydekrug believing escape was easier. At Sagan, although the soil was similar, the water table was much higher making collapse a constant risk. With many eager volunteers he immediately commenced another tunnel. Within months it was 145 foot (44 m) long and hopes were rising. The Germans brought in a steamroller, which they ran up and down the camp – POWs held their breath. Tunnels collapsed but the 44 m tunnel withstood and work continued.

It took a great deal to dent the willingness to try again and another tunnel was started, this time within an ablution block, its entry hidden below one of the lavatory seats. The tunneller needed to move down through the seat opening, bend double on the brick wall that held back the effluent and carefully inch along until reaching the end wall before squeezing through the entrance to the tunnel, which was hidden beneath an adjacent ablution. This at least allowed the evacuated dirt to be added to the effluent under the toilets, which was then collected by the 'honey wagon' (sewage cart) at regular intervals. Unfortunately, the level of effluent rose to a dangerous level, which in turn started to flood back into the tunnel. Heavy rainfall and a higher than normal water level exacerbated the situation and there was no alternative but to start a new tunnel entrance.

The room used for washing clothes housed three hot-water boilers. A hole was cut into one of the boilers, large enough for a POW to drop down into the tunnel, without restricting the operation of the boiler. This had the added bonus of allowing much needed fresh air to enter the tunnel via air holes, enabling the tunnellers to work both night and day shifts. The downside of this new access point was that the disposal of soil was difficult.

The standard practice of soil disposal was for volunteers, nicknamed 'penguins', to tie the bottom of their trousers and then shovel the dirt into them. They then walked around the camp, gradually releasing the soil. This only worked when the soil was a similar colour. Often, the Germans observed very eager POWs building

'I was only inspecting the drains.'[275]

another 'vegetable garden'. RAF Sergeant William Garrioch had undertaken escape attempts at two different camps without success. At Heydekrug in August 1943, he crawled through a tunnel to freedom. He was recaptured shortly after.

Although tunnels were not favoured by escape committees, it was accepted that tunnels kept the more impatient POWs occupied and diverted German attention away from the more complex and productive escape strategies. Success invariably came from POWs simply passing through the main gate dressed in Luftwaffe uniforms.

Secrecy was paramount and Dixie Deans, needed to ensure only the most trusted men joined the 150-strong escape committee, known as The Tally-Ho Club. Bartering with German guards for vital escape material, such as passes, badges, some uniform items and intelligence was essential and could be undermined by POWs attempting to barter for their personal benefit. Strict control was needed over scarce cigarettes, chocolate, and other goods. Dixie Deans succeeded in dissuading this practice. A swap shop called 'Foodacco' was permitted to allow the exchange of food and clothing for cigarettes, but profits were given to the escape committee.

Australian, Jack Garland was one of the trusted at Stalag VI and was very active, in 'acquiring' essential items, particularly through German guards.

The camp was a beehive of escape activities and Goons enriched themselves through bribes. The lowest ranks were easy to bribe. A photo was taken of them accepting a cigarette and then they were had. They were also struggling to survive.[82]

WO Jack Garland (AWM).

A unanimous decision by the escape committee was needed for an escape plan to proceed. Aircrew with specific abilities were welcomed. Only those directly involved were told the plan. Forging documents, such as passports, travel and leave passes, ration tickets, rail warrants and even currency, became an art form, as did maps, civilian clothing and German uniforms.

Original documents or the copy of an original, procured from the most corrupt guards, allowed for 30 or 35 copies. The workmanship and creativity were masterful. POWs who had been tailors in civilian life were put to work assembling civilian outfits or uniforms out of other garments, and these were enhanced with badges and trim traded for cigarettes. Luftwaffe uniform badges were made from melted silver cigarette linings, while cloth badges were manufactured from the linings of flying boots. Compasses, hacksaws, files, and wire cutters were secreted in from Britain in personal parcels. The Americans began to smuggle passport photographs in packets of Camel cigarettes, but this was discovered, and all Camel cigarettes were confiscated. A necessity for any escape was to have someone outside the barbed wire and at Stalag VI an RAF F/S sacrificed his own freedom to live outside a camp with friendly Germans, to organise the escape of others.

Members of the escape committee nicknamed 'stooges' stood sentry while clandestine activities were underway. One camp group called themselves the 'Cooee Club', using the Australian call of 'Cooee', should a German guard approach too closely. If a surprise search caught POWs unawares, diversionary tactics were employed, even to the point of POWs staging a fight, until escape material was concealed. In one incident, a German guard suspecting something, marched quickly towards a hut only to be intercepted and sent tumbling by a prisoner being chased by another POW. Profuse apologies and frightened expressions followed, but the delay was all that was needed. Another responsibility of the escape committee was to ensure food and cigarettes were secreted to the victims of failed escapes, languishing in appalling conditions in solitary dungeons.

RAAF WO, William Frank Redding (412184), had enlisted in Sydney, NSW, on 22 June 1941 and trained as a WOP/AG. His Wellington XHE475 was shot down during an attack on Mannheim on 16 April 1943. He was the only Australian in the 425 Canadian Squadron crew and on just his 11th operation.[83] By June 1943 he was a captive at Stalag VI and a valued member of the escape committee. Introduced to forged and counterfeit documents he was in awe of the 'really brilliant work' of his fellow captives. POWs had requested Nazi newspapers. German authorities were pleased, believing it a wonderful opportunity to disseminate propaganda. The newspapers contained maps, useful for copying for escape attempts.

Other committee members were no less impressed with Redding. By trade Redding was a cabinet maker and joiner and now found himself tasked with building phony weapons. 'One of the most successful schemes was the two rifles I made.'[84] Finding a suitable piece within the highly prized camp wood supply proved the first obstacle. He then needed to model them on the real thing without of course ever being given access to a German rifle. Day after day he walked as closely to guards as he dared, 'trying to notice and retain every dimension ... one needed a retentive memory'.[85] The butt of each rifle he stained brown. Redding then honed metal pieces which he attached, painted black, and worked to a high polish. Both rifles enabled successful escapes.

WO Redding was also kept busy building dummy parcels and false bottoms in boxes. He heard that the Germans intended to move the fence inside the washhouse and that a large wooden barrel used for storing hot water would form part of it. Redding built a false bottom in the barrel into which a POW crawled and successfully escaped. Redding was inspired and began to create dummy panels in ceilings and walls to hide escape paraphernalia. He scrounged timber and three-ply from Red Cross parcels to build small gadgets and holders.

Australians were commonly held in high regard by other POWs.

The morale of the Australian boys was of a high standard, they adapted themselves so easily to strange conditions and were always to be relied upon whenever the occasion arose.[86]

Curbing their enthusiasm sometimes proved taxing. West Australian, WO George Thomas William Farrell (415895) was awarded German close arrest for ten days, for changing identity disks with a non-aircrew POW, in an effort to join a work party and just once, walk the ground outside the wire. He was later punished for attempting to sabotage a German truck, testing the theory that if you peed into a petrol tank of a truck you could 'stuff' the engine.[87]

Such exploits and attempted escapes could have dire consequences for all POWs. Rations, Red Cross parcels and mail were withheld, the two daily parade roll calls annoyingly increased in number and POWs were left standing for extended periods of time, regardless of the weather. When Red Cross parcels were distributed the Germans punctured all the tins and emptied them into one mess of meat, sardines, cheese, margarine – they said it was to prevent the storage of food to enable escape. Solitary confinement was extended to 28 days and guards turned increasingly abusive. Feared most were the visits and searches conducted by the Gestapo. At Stalag VI the Gestapo arrived and were none too gentle with hut leaders. Huts were thrown into totally disarray. Well-hidden valuable escape equipment and documents were discovered.

The Gestapo enjoyed springing hut searches at odd times.

They were an evil crew and ever in their comic opera uniforms of long coats with the collars turned up, their gloves and black hats with the brim turned down they evoked an aura of dread and foreboding. A sudden shout of 'Raus!' they were bundled out of the barracks regardless of weather, didn't mean a thing to the inhuman bastards of the Gestapo.[88]

Ongoing searches and guard behaviour caused anxiety.

At Stalag VI the escape committee decided that despite the loss of valuable material, the breakout was to proceed as soon as possible. Those selected moved to the dispatch point. The escape committee scrambled to cover the disappearance of several POWs by placing dummies in beds ready for the snap inspection. Holes were pushed through walls so that prisoners could pass through quickly and be counted twice. Some 50 POWs crammed into the tunnel with their escape kits.

The night was clear, not ideal, but there could be no further delay and the first men broke through the surface. The gush of fresh air was invigorating, and men pushed up and out to freedom. The opening was regrettably too close to guard posts and as the ninth POW left the exit, gunfire broke out. Guards gathered quickly and commenced firing down the hole. POWs jostled each other to move backwards. Luck prevailed and none were shot, but German reaction was brisk. Soldiers rapidly searched huts and intercepted POWs as they emerged from the now discovered tunnel entrance. The solitary cells, 'cooler', were crammed full of captured escapees for weeks.

Nine had escaped and their comrades behind wire were desperate to keep this from their gaolers. The Germans searched the compound and found the correct number of POWs. Nine dummies had been removed and their hut mates assured that a confusion resulted in nine POWs being counted twice by the guards. The same subterfuge during the morning roll call confirmed this until one of the escapees was captured that day. Another roll call was demanded, but again, men who had once marched flawlessly on RAF and RAAF parade grounds, had difficultly sorting themselves into the most rudimentary lines. The Germans left satisfied they had the numbers correct.

Another escapee was returned, and all POWs were confined to their huts to be counted. The numbers didn't add up, so they were herded onto to the parade ground and instructed to be tallied in single file between two guards. POWs scurried back around to join the queue of uncounted men and the Germans were infuriated that they had many more POWs than they were supposed to have. Another count was attempted, matching each prisoner with their bunk, but again there was a good deal of movement within huts and sick men – dummies – lay tucked in, too ill to be rallied by hut commanders. Again, there were far more POWs in camp than there should have been. The farce continued when identity cards were produced to match prisoners. Unfortunately for the guards, when their backs were turned, cards disappeared. The photographs were to prove useful to the escape committee in the production of false identity cards.

Photographs of the prisoners commenced, to replace the lost cards, but POWs gave false numbers and details and, the exercise was useless. Additional copies of the POW identity cards took weeks to arrive from German headquarters. The last escapee was recaptured ten days into his quest to reach friendly forces. The gaolers of Stalag VI had long given up ensuring they had the correct unit of Allied airmen.

Peter Kingsford-Smith (402241) bore that famous name. He was the nephew of pioneering aviator, Sir Charles 'Smithy' Kingsford Smith. Smithy had enlisted in the 1st AIF in WWI in 1915, and served at Gallipoli before transferring to the Royal Flying Corps, and earning his pilot's wings in 1917. In June 1927, Smithy and co-pilot, Charles Ulm, completed a round-Australia circuit in 10 days, five hours, a notable achievement with minimal navigational aids. The following year they completed the first trans-Pacific flight from California to Brisbane in the Fokker trimotor monoplane, *Southern Cross*. In partnership with Ulm, Kingsford Smith established Australian National Airways in 1929. During an attempt to break the England to Australia speed record in the Lockheed Altair, *Lady Southern Cross*, Kingsford Smith and co-pilot John Thompson 'Tommy' Pethybridge disappeared over the Andaman Sea.

It was no surprise that Peter Kingsford-Smith, along with his brothers Rollo and John, enlisted in the RAAF. Rollo was the commanding officer of RAAF 463

F/L Peter Kingsford-Smith DFC (left), with PO John Ulm, son of Charles Ulm (AWM).

Squadron. Peter arrived in England in May 1941. He soon earned a reputation for 'his cheerfulness and willingness for operational flying in any circumstance'.[89] Peter was a PO on a special duties' operation when this Kingsford-Smith too, disappeared. His RAF 138 Squadron Halifax had taken off at 2006 on 19 February 1943 from RAF Tempsford, in Bedfordshire, England, with eight on board. His co-pilot was another Australian, F/O Robert Charles Hogg (46665). Special duties operations were particularly dangerous because the aircraft needed to fly at low altitude to allow operatives and supplies to drop into occupied territory. The Halifax was at 500 feet (152 m) when both outboard engines and the port wing were struck by flak. Kingsford-Smith wrestled the aircraft to the ground near Tours, France. Those on board scattered. Kingsford-Smith, aided by French farmers, avoided capture for 22 days.[90] By the end of March he had joined other officers attached to RAF Bomber Command, in Luft III.

Established in March 1942 and run by the Luftwaffe, Luft III was huge and as the war endured housed 11,000 Allied air force officers. The camp was situated in the German province of Lower Silesia near the town of Sagan (now Żagań, Poland), 100 miles (161 km) south-east of Berlin. The site was selected because of its thick sandy soil, which it was believed should deter tunnelling escapes.

Luft III model.[276]

Compounds consisted of 15 single-storey huts, each 10 feet x 12 feet (3 m x 3.7 m) containing five triple-deck bunks for 15 POWs.

Aircrew preferred Luftwaffe-controlled camps rather than German army camps as respect was accorded air force to air force. On arrival in the compound new POWs were vetted by their own, with preferably two other aircrew verifying their identity. They were interrogated by POW hierarchy and kept under surveillance. This was necessary to avoid German infiltrators.

Peter Kingsford-Smith joined the escape committee, but he was unable to join the tunnellers due to 'claustrophobia'.[91] He could but watch as tunnellers beat the odds. RAF aircrew, Lt Michael Codner, and F/Ls Eric Williams and Oliver Philpot, built a vaulting horse from plywood from Canadian Red Cross parcels. Each day POWs carried the vaulting horse close to the perimeter fence and conducted noisy gymnastics. Unbeknown to the watching guards, the horse contained men and tools. In two-man shifts the prisoners with metal rods, bowls, and shovels, dug a 100-foot (30 m) tunnel. When the entrance was carefully covered by a board and sand, their fellow POWs carried the horse back to outside a hut. On the night of 19 October 1943, Codner, Williams and Philpot made their escape. Each returned to England.

Peter Kingsford-Smith was a man of the air and found captivity not to his taste.[277]

At Luft III, after a year of patient, hard work, an ambitious but meticulously planned break-out, came to fruition. No fewer than 200 POWs, dressed in civilian clothes with forged papers and some food waited impatiently to escape into the dark night. More than 600 British and Commonwealth air force officers had dug tunnels, assembled clothing and produced in excess of 4000 maps and 500 compasses. Three tunnels named 'Tom', 'Dick' and 'Harry' were commenced.

By September 1943, the Germans had discovered 'Tom'. Beneath the stove in room 23 of Hut 104, the tunnel codenamed 'Harry', proved the most effective.

The chief carpenter was an Australian with a decorated WWII history. Squadron Leader John Edwin Ashley 'Willy' Williams (40652) DFC was a proven air ace while serving in the Middle East and North Africa flying P-40 Kittyhawks. He was commanding 450 Squadron (RAAF) during the second Battle of El Alamein when he was accidentally shot down on 31 October 1942 by a member of his own squadron.[92] 'Delighted' may not have been an appropriate word but Willy was 'delighted' to see his good mate F/L Reginald Victor 'Rusty' Kierath (402364) walk through the Luft III gates. Kierath had been born in the NSW country town of Narromine. He was educated at Sydney's Shore School with John Williams.[93]

The Narromine airfield had been requisitioned by the RAAF in July 1940. No. 5 Elementary Flying Training School (5EFTS) operated there between 1940 and 1944. Kierath, a clerk with the Bank of Australasia, decided his being a pilot was therefore destined and enlisted on 19 August 1940. During training he was re-mustered as an observer. Kierath fought hard to convince the RAAF that they really needed him as a pilot. Unfortunately, the day he sewed on his pilot's wings in April 1941 he heard that his brother, Captain Greg Kierath, serving with an Australian anti-tank company at Tobruk had been killed. By August 1941 he too was serving in the Middle East, flying Hurricanes with RAF 33 Squadron. While

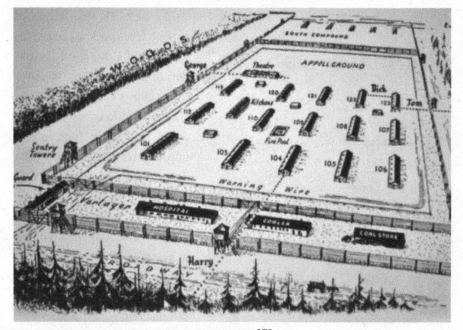

The tunnels 'Tom', 'Dick' and 'Harry', Luft III.[278]

flying Kittyhawks with RAAF 450, Kierath was shot down on 23 April 1943.[94]

Willy Williams arranged for Rusty to be assigned to his Luft III hut and quickly gave him responsibilities within the escape committee as a 'hide specialist', constructing small hide spaces within the compound for forged papers and other escape essentials. It seemed that within their compound few POW bunks did not lose bed boards, to prop tunnel ceiling and walls. 'Harry' was equipped with electric lighting, an ingenious air pump, and an underground railway with trolleys for men and dirt. The tunnel was an extraordinary engineering feat.

POWs were broken into three escape tiers. The first group numbered 30 and included those with foreign language experts or those in the escape committee who had undertaken the largest preparation work. Deemed the most likely to escape, they were dressed in the most presentable suits. The second and third groups were the tunnellers, the 'penguins', carpenters and 'stooges'. Their civilian clothes were not as convincing, and they carried fewer documents.

On the night of 24 March 1944, John 'Willy' Williams and Rusty Kierath were crouched with other Australians in the long tunnel awaiting their turn. Squadron Leader James Catanach (400364) from Melbourne believed he had a better than most chance at travelling through enemy territory because he spoke fluent German. He had been only 18 when he enlisted in the RAAF on 18 August 1940. Having been schooled at both Brighton Grammar School and Geelong Grammar School,

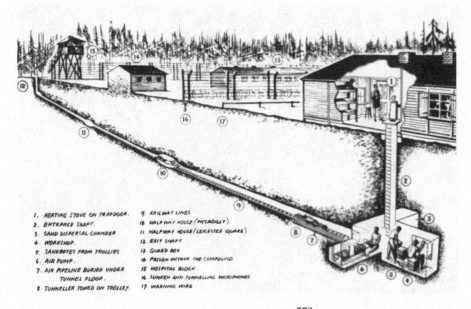

1. HEATING STOVE ON TRAPDOOR.
2. ENTRANCE SHAFT.
3. SAND DISPERSAL CHAMBER.
4. WORKSHOP.
5. SANDBOXES FROM TROLLIES.
6. AIR PUMP.
7. AIR PIPELINE BURIED UNDER TUNNEL FLOOR.
8. TUNNELLER TOWED ON TROLLEY.
9. RAILWAY LINES
10. HALFWAY HOUSE (PICCADILLY)
11. HALFWAY HOUSE (LEICESTER SQUARE)
12. EXIT SHAFT
13. GUARD BOX
14. PRISON WITHIN THE COMPOUND
15. HOSPITAL BLOCK
16. SUNKEN ANTI-TUNNELLING MICROPHONES.
17. WARNING WIRE

The engineering marvel of 'Harry' tunnel at Luft III.[279]

a former rover scout and army cadet, and a salesman in his father's prestigious jewellery business, he was considered, the 'right stuff' by recruiters to be a gentleman pilot. His trajectory was rapid as Catanach proved a natural aviator. After many operations he was piloting an RAAF 455 Squadron torpedo bomber, when awarded a DFC. 'On three occasions, in spite of, severe damage to his aircraft', Catanach had flown his Hampden bombers back to base without further injury to his crew. On 5 September 1942 he and his crew were not as fortunate.[95]

Another two were, WO Albert Horace Hake (403218) and Sydney-born F/L Thomas Barker Leigh (RAF 46462). Hake desperately wanted to qualify as a pilot. The married 24-year-old from Sydney had trained as a draughtsman and was working for an airline company when he enlisted on 4 Jan 1941. He was piloting Spitfires with RAF 72 Squadron when his wife Noela was advised her husband was missing on 4 April 1942. He had been with the squadron just 42 days.[96]

Leigh had left Australia to become a merchant seaman in England. He then became fascinated by aircraft and entered an RAF apprenticeship in 1935. With the war came the opportunity to train as aircrew and he became an RAF 76 Squadron Halifax rear gunner. It could be well understood why Leigh was so anxious for freedom: he had been shot down on the night of 5 August 1941 and nearly three years as a POW meant crowding into a stuffy tunnel caused little discomfort.

At 2130 on 24 March 1944 the outer end of the tunnel was breached. All the planning and hard labour had not prevented miscalculations. Freezing temperatures

A German guard enters the exit point of 'Harry'.[280]

had hardened the ground meaning the final dig took over an hour, an unexpected delay causing those crammed in the tunnel discomfort and concern. Then, as they burst through it was found 'Harry' was around 20 feet (6 m) short of the woods, meaning prisoners had the added risk of crawling across exposed ground. The escape had to proceed. Men hurried across the snowy ground to the shelter of the woods, each having to pause long enough to avoid the strobing searchlights and movements of sentries.

Progress was brisk until bombers such as they had once crewed released bomb loads in an attack on the region. Immediately all camp lights were extinguished and the number of guards doubled. The raid continued for an hour before the escape could proceed. Precious time had been lost and just before dawn it was decided the 87th man in the tunnel must be the last. In a terrible twist of fate, a sentry patrolling the perimeter decided to move to the edge of the woods to relieve himself. He noticed steam rising from the ground and then three POWs emerged with their hands raised. The guard fired into the air and his armed compatriots ran in support. There was no alternative but for the remaining men in the tunnel to withdraw and to hastily throw months of precious escape material into furnaces. Peter Kingsford-Smith observed, 'the huts were surrounded by guards ... heavily armed with machine pistols, grenades and appeared panic stricken.'[97]

The camp commandant, Freidrich-Wilhelm von Lindeiner Wildau arrived, his face livid. Searchlights flooded the compound and German soldiers ran into huts screaming 'Raus! Raus!' (Out! Out!) With much pushing and shoving, POWs were removed and ordered to strip. 'If we weren't quick enough shirts and vests were torn off us.'[98] Aircrew stood naked in the snow and icy wind with the guards in no hurry to process each POW. Once allowed to dress in basic coverings they were ordered into two lines. One by one, the prisoners moved forward, to be identified by way of their POW cards. Delays and confusion were attempted through false names, but the mood of their gaolers was dangerous. Inspections and searches increased and more guards were posted. A fortnight later Luft III POWs were paraded and the commandant sternly delivered terrible news.

On 29 March 1944, the 22-year-old squadron leader, James Catanach, was sitting in a Nazi prison with three fellow airmen escapees. They had almost made it to the Danish border, almost. After two years as a POW, for Catanach, freedom, while fraught with danger, had tasted wonderful. He and 21-year-old New Zealander, F/L Arnold Christensen (RNZAF), had caught an express train from Sagan to Berlin. After hiding overnight, they continued their quest to reach neutral Sweden and succeeded in avoiding detection to board a train for the northern German port city of Flensburg. It was in this city on the Baltic coast that they were noticed and taken into custody. Keeping company with them in the jail were fellow Luft III escapees, Lieutenants Nils Fuglesang and Hallada Espelid, Norwegians, who had served with the RAF. The men attempted to remain cheerful; they had managed to escape this far, and now at least they would be reunited with mates at Luft III, after weeks in solitary. Photographs were taken on their capture before members of the Gestapo arrived.

SS Major Johannes Post, accompanied by Oskar Schmidt, interrogated each airman. Post was an ardent Nazi who enjoyed intimidating others. The POWs were handcuffed and pushed into waiting cars, Catanach, in the custody of Post.

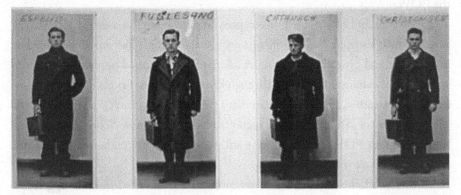

Photographs of the recaptured Luft III escapees
(www.bbc.co.uk/archive/stalag-luft-III--the-great-escape-1944/zmjsmfr).

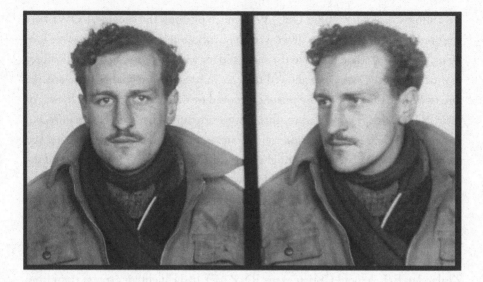

Left: Sqn Ldr John 'Willy' Williams. Right: F/L Reginald 'Rusty' Kierath.[281]

They were driven into the countryside before Post instructed his driver to stop by the side of the road. Catanach was ordered to get out and cross the road towards a meadow gate. Post pulled a Luger 7.65 mm pistol from his holster and shot the Australian, killing him instantly.

Adolph Hitler had been enraged by such a blatant mass escape of Allied aircrew. He summoned Luftwaffe Reichsmarschall, Herman Goring and Reichsführer SS, Heinrich Himmler, and ordered them to execute all 76 escapees on recapture. Goring, whose responsibility Luft III was, cautioned that Allied reprisals could result to such murder and violation of the Geneva Convention. Himmler suggested that 50 be executed. This was agreed, and extensive manpower directed to recapture the POWs.

By 29 March 1944, dozens of escapees languished in Nazi gaols, all unaware of that which awaited. Willy Williams and Rusty Kierath had stuck together but the weather had proved unrelenting. A blizzard had dropped heavy snow and the aviators were exhausted trudging through knee-high snow. Locals did not venture out in such weather, so the two Australians were observed and taken into custody. They were consoled by the fact that mates from Sydney's Shore School had escaped from a German POW camp and were still together. Photographs were taken and they awaited their return to Luft III.

In Stalag VI the many escape attempts had also resulted in more aggressive treatment from the guards, and soldier reinforcements. Two prisoners attempted to escape under the cover of darkness. As they neared the wire fence, they were spotted by the watchtower machine gunner. The POWs stood with hands raised. A guard approached, shot one and ordered the other back to his hut. The POW died of his wounds. Another POW was shot for being found outside his hut during curfew. The deaths stunned, as did the callous funerals. The Germans used a reusable coffin. The body was loaded into a large wooden casket which extended over the grave. Bolts were removed and the body fell into the hole, after which the coffin was removed for the next victim.[99]

It was April 1944, and the Stalag VI POWs were told to fall in on parade. Heavily armed soldiers arrived and formed a circle around them. WO Dixie Deans marched out from behind the German adjutant, Major Heinrich, to take his place stiffly at the head of the parade. His demeanour was as solemn as they had witnessed. Heinrich read slowly from a document with an interpreter offering the English translation. There had been a large escape from Luft III, and many had been shot as a deterrent to all POWs wishing to attempt escape. Movement and angry muttering within the ranks was immediate, the wrath palpable. The Germans raised their guns menacingly. Deans shouted an order for his men to maintain order and the Germans slowly retreated.

At Luft III only six had been returned and thrown into solitary confinement and camp morale was high, buoyed by the belief so many had made it to safety. Two weeks later the remaining POWs at Stalag Luft III received news that 50 of the recaptured escapees had been shot for 'resisting arrest or making further escape attempts after arrest'. Among the list of the murdered were the names of five Australians: Williams, Kierath, Catanach, Hake, and Leigh.[100] Their RAAF records were simply marked 'Died while POW', and families received no details.

CHAPTER TWELVE

'At the back of the mind of any sane POW is fear.'

WO Ronald Charles MacKenzie (RAAF)

The murders reverberated throughout German POW camps, on both sides of the wire.

Australian 460 Squadron Leader Lorraine Joseph Simpson (401542) was stunned; it could have been his name included in the gruesome list of names now circulating through his Luft III camp. Simpson's crew had been shot down while on an attack on Berlin on 27 January 1944. Being a builder's assistant in civilian life, his knowledge had assisted in the tunnel construction, but having arrived late in the creation of 'Harry', others involved longer were deemed more deserved. 'Being more deserved' had a hollow ring, yet another quirk of fate with regards timing and chance. The names, the aircrew, were acquaintances. 'The whole camp went into mourning,' he wrote.[101] Fourteen escapees were returned to Luft III. From solitary confinement they shouted of seeing POWs in handcuffs being led away by members of the Gestapo and not being seen again.

The Commandant of Luft III was Luftwaffe. He and his deputy had rigidly followed the Geneva Convention to the best of their abilities and consequently were well respected. They were immediately replaced. The new Luftwaffe commandant was nonetheless appalled by the Gestapo executions. He permitted the POWs to build a memorial to their murdered companions. The principal designer of the memorial was the Australian-qualified architect who had entered the RAF and flown with RAF 169 Squadron as a navigator, F/L W. Wylton Todd. Simpson was one of the first to volunteer and there was no shortage of others. 'It took about four to five months' to turn the memorial into reality. Eventually 'the vault was a beautifully neat design and had stone scrolls on which each deceased officer's name was inscribed'.[102] Above the large air force eagle engraved on the front were the words, 'In memory of the Officers who gave their lives'.[103] The ashes of those executed were placed into urns within the memorial.

More stories circulated throughout camps concerning POWs murdered by German authorities and how these same authorities were disregarding Allied

The memorial to the executed prisoners of Luft III (www.StalagLuft3.com).[282]

airmen being beaten and murdered by German civilians; of aircrew summarily 'lynched' as they parachuted to the ground.[104] It felt more important than ever to demonstrate defiance and solidarity. Defiance was difficult but if there had been any casual relationships and conversation between gaoler and prisoner these ceased. As tired, hungry and deprived as they were, it was necessary to maintain their pride. For Australians and New Zealanders, Anzac Day commemorations were never more important than in 1944.

An auction of scant possessions, particularly those left by the murdered, was conducted. Driven by emotion the bidding rose to ridiculous amounts, uniform pieces going for far in excess of what they cost brand new in England. Officers

At Luft III they gathered to commemorate a national day.

Stalag IVB parade (AWM).

subscribed sums from bank accounts in England. The proceeds were donated to the families of the murdered and particulars sent through the Red Cross to Britain.

At Stalag IVB Bert Stobart joined others to dust off their best uniform remnants and march. There was an unusual solemnity but determination within the ranks.

At Stalag 383, Hohenfels, Australian and New Zealand POWs staged a concert titled 'Anzacs on Parade', which included members of a Maori battalion. Photographic prints were traded among the prisoners for four or five cigarettes each, which in turn raised funds for camp recreational activities.

Allied camp leaders were, however, deeply concerned with the general atmosphere amongst those they attempted to represent. The simmering anger and

Stalag 383 (AWM).

unrest could easily erupt, and the Germans had now shown a willingness to execute. Concerted efforts were put into re-emphasising participation in camp activities, more lectures, more sport. Art and craft exhibitions were organised with the prizes being very coveted cigarettes or a tin of jam. Camp newspapers attempted greater flair. And then, 6 June 1944 heightened emotions.

WO Roy William Mirfin (425186) was asked to take over the handling of the Stalag Luft VI secret wireless organisation. When he was 18, Mirfin, like Bert Stobart, had chosen gunnery because it was the quickest way to war. He was posted to RAF 61 Squadron in August 1943 and was shot down the following month.[105] Having worked as a sound engineer with Brisbane's Western Electric company pre-war, he was the obvious choice, and quickly proved himself an adept scrounger. Mirfin immediately built a crystal set. He obtained some carborundum for the crystal from the cookhouse (which in turn got it from a corrupt guard), and an ordinary sewing needle and wire from the electrically heated flying suits.

'For earphones we had small American coffee tins full of soap as an insulator and wound the coil around it and magnetic razor blades. For the diaphragm we used the sealed top of cigarette tins. The reception was not too good and had a limited range, but they could pick up a few German stations.'[106]

After about a week they received radiograms through the YMCA through which were smuggled four spare valves. Minute radio receivers then came in through American Games sets.

The secret radio in Stalag VI was the lifeline to the outside world. The radio, which, remarkably, the Gestapo had not discovered, was hidden inside a gramophone. On one occasion, camp leader WO Dixie Deans had been listening to the BBC news when a surprise search was conducted. He hurriedly moved the radio back inside the gramophone as his hut door was thrust open. The German soldier even lifted the record off the turnstile and examined it, but the radio remained hidden. On another occasion Deans and another managed to start a record playing as a German officer entered. To distract from their wild efforts of hiding the radio the POWs danced with each other.

On the morning of 6 June 1944, the radio was connected to the clothesline that doubled as a makeshift aerial and the 'two knobs fashioned from toothbrushes' were again tuned to the BBC, when, through the static came the most amazing news.[107] British, American, and Canadian forces had landed on beaches along the coast of Normandy, France – 'D-day' had finally arrived. For all his excitement Deans was concerned; he realised he had a serious problem. The news could create a groundswell of optimism and excitement and possibly even an uprising within the ranks of the thousands of British POWs. The French coastline was a long way

"He's been doing it all day!" (Walley)283

from Stalag VI, German forces were strong and likely to fiercely contest every piece of occupied territory; how could he contain the most exuberant?

It was a common concern amongst Allied camp officials as the most welcome news filtered through. POWs had been humiliated, starved, and treated appallingly. How could they now curb the resentment that would undoubtedly ensue with the invasion of Europe by Allied forces? Hut leaders cautioned that outward signs of joy could signal to the guards that there were indeed secret radios. POWs could not appear boastful or defiant to guards who had long arrogantly bragged that the armies of the Third Reich were undefeatable, that, the mighty Atlantic Wall defences ensured German coastal defences were impregnable. The reactions of German camp guards were unpredictable but news of D-day was likely to make them even more anxious and trigger-happy. What would the consequences be for those behind barbed wire?

POWs had long been assailed by German camp loudspeakers broadcasting their own version of the news followed by strident propaganda and music. One camp cartoonist suggested this had been well countered by encouraging members of the Scottish fraternity to play their bagpipes.

On 6 June 1944, as the news of the Allied invasion circulated in whispers, loudspeaker systems turned to the highest volume, announced:

*This morning the Allied armies landed in force on the coast of France, and this is the day the German Army will show its superiority and push the Allied Armies back into the sea.*108

The cheer that rose 'could be heard on the beaches of Normandy' a POW wrote.109 What began as a whisper, quickly became a murmur and then a roar, 'as wildly excited prisoners tore around the various barracks spreading the welcome news',

INVASION

JUNE 1944

The OKW announces that last night after a tremendous aerial and novel bombardment the Allies began their long prepared and by us long awaited offensive against Western Europe — — —

Drawing by RAF rear gunner Roy Child.[284]

Squadron Leader Simpson observed.[110] A tremendous wave of optimism swept through the camp. The diaries of aircrew were regaled with bolder handwriting and uplifting thoughts. RAF WO Playfair wondered if it was possible for non-POW, 'to visualise our delight'.[111] Camp artists allowed their imaginations to flow.

The euphoria gathered momentum at thoughts of the terrific possibilities this news meant. The optimists believed it could be as early as six weeks, as late as three months, before they were free men again. The pessimists muttered it could take another three years.

At least there was an exuberance that the Allies were advancing after years of retreating. Finally, the first whiff of victory could be enjoyed, regardless of what the German broadcast screamed. Groups of men gathered to scan carefully guarded maps, plotting the possible Allied advance with ink and pins, planning for their release route home.

They reflected that it had been the same European maps with coloured thread, in Bomber Command briefings, that had landed them in POW camps, but this was different – the word 'freedom' could be entertained. In the excitement none realised that although the Allied advance opened a new chapter of WWII, their excitement was premature and the most dangerous chapter of their lives as POWs had begun.

McCleary (AWM).

At Stalag VI, illicit liquor that had been stored under floorboards to celebrate an invasion was discovered by German guards. After sampling the concoction, they confiscated the entire stockpile for their own enjoyment, much to the angst of the British POWs. Added to their disappointment was that they then needed to watch and listen to 4 July 1944 American POW celebrations. Despite the worst infestation of fleas, the Americans celebrated their national day. From US Red Cross parcels, they had secreted away prunes, sugar and raisins which had been brewed into alcohol, called 'Kickapoo joy juice'.

Less than a week after the D-day landings the Stalag VI theatre was ablaze and burnt to the ground. Some said it was the best show ever witnessed in the theatre. The POWs proved very ineffective in putting out the flames, with ill-aimed buckets of water 'inadvertently' hitting German guards. Faulty electrics were blamed but the fire had been deliberate. The theatre needed to be sacrificed to conceal from the Germans the removal of parts of an amplifier donated by the Swedish YMCA. These could then be cannibalised to turn the secret radio into a transmitter.

News of the massacre of POW escapees had been learnt in Allied headquarters and a message was transmitted that POW escape attempts should cease, because with the end of the war in sight in was endangering lives unnecessarily. For some

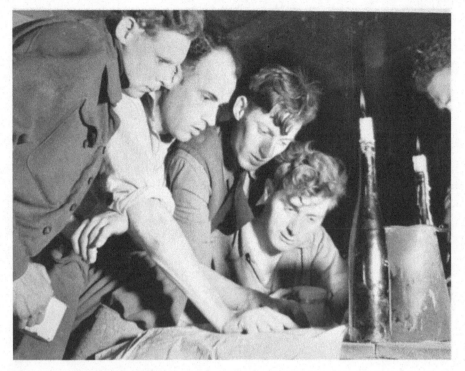

Planning a way home (AWM).

this was a relief, for others it meant frustration. WOP/AG, WO Ronald Charles MacKenzie RAAF (402465) was one of the relieved. He certainly was not one of the optimists and wondered if this was because he felt so much older than his 28 years, or, more likely, because he had been a POW for too long. Hard to believe he had been shot down three years ago, almost to the day – three years he had been in this hell of 'hunger and cold', three years his life had been on hold from whatever was normal. He learned quickly operating with Bomber Command that 'the mathematical knowledge made one realise how slim the chance of survival was'.[112] As a POW the odds were not much better, 'at the back of the mind of any sane POW is fear'.[113] His eight weeks in solitary had severely diminished his physical and emotional strength. MacKenzie had watched too many escape attempts fail to support any more. 'No-one escaped for long, we were in the middle of Germany'.[114]

Months before he had seen four burrow under the fence and disappear. The usual attempts to conceal their absence had failed and the Germans had ordered all British aircrew out into the winter snow. They were forbidden from re-entering huts for several days. The escapees were then found frozen to death in a ditch where they had sheltered together in an attempt to stay warm. The bodies were returned. Yet again MacKenzie attended another funeral, another 'nightmare',

Another Australian aviator buried a long way from home (AWM).

someone buried in frozen ground in the land of the enemy. He struggled with his emotions when the bagpipes played 'the lament, an appropriate ending which can tear at one's heart'.[115]

POWs had been concentrating on the Allied attack from the west. They had not considered the attack from the east. The distant rumble of heavy artillery from the Red Army's summer offensive made this a reality. German guards became increasingly agitated. Their contempt for Russians had become fear. Stalag VI at Heydekrug was close to the Polish border and the Russians were sweeping through Poland with remarkable speed, better attuned to harsh winter weather. Allied prisoners did not care who freed them, but they were rapidly becoming part of the battleground itself, at the mercy of everyone. What actions would the German army take toward those who had become even more of an impediment? There were now around 10,400 POWs in Stalag VI. The exuberance felt the month before evaporated when it was learnt Heydekrug civilians had been evacuated.

POW camp sentries were placed on watch to observe any unusual activities within the ranks of those who guarded. Hut commanders enacted the 'W' plan. Instigated to create reserves of food in case of serious shortages, the second phase was in the event of the military situation resulting in German guards abandoning their posts and the reserve needed to last until friendly forces arrived. POWs were encouraged to fashion rucksacks from any material found, should they need to evacuate. Efforts were made to quash negative rumours concerning POW welfare, but discussion continued: Would the Germans decide that POWs were too serious a drain on resources and manpower? And if so, what was to be their fate? Could they be massacred to prevent them from taking up arms again? Regardless of the ugly questions that hung in the air, normal activities were encouraged and in mid-July at Stalag VI that extended to the fiercely contested cricket test between Australia and England.

Each side believed they were winning when German soldiers abruptly entered the compound and with raised guns and angry voices ordered the POWs out. The artillery gunfire had intensified and the Russians were believed to be hours away. The test was disbanded as POWs ran to their huts to gather their belongings. Camp stores were emptied. The American compound was cleared first. Excess food and possessions rained down into the British compound as the Americans moved past under guard. Shortly after, the same columns returned. German authorities were clearly confused and fearful. Hours later the Americans were marched out again. It was very early morning, and in the British huts men quickly assessed what they could carry, made more difficult by no indication of where they were going, and how long it would take to get there. Spare food and cigarettes were consumed, upsetting stomachs and elevating anxiety through the rapid intake of nicotine.

Hut by hut, section by section, the camp emptied. It was unnerving to be leaving, for this place, as uncomfortable as it had been, had still been home and offered its own form of security. They were broken into smaller groups to be dispatched to various other camps to the west. British and Commonwealth aircrew were separated from the rest, 900 in total, with several American flyers added to their number. Yet again their future was precarious, and this was quickly accentuated as the remaining German civilians emerged to hurl insults and stones while they passed through villages. The guards with their snarling dogs did nothing to discourage the abuse.

It was a stifling summer day and on arrival at the railway station POWs were ordered into the confines of cattle trucks – 60 men into each, 60 men unable to sit, in unbearable heat, with no ventilation. They defecated and urinated were they stood, the stench within the carriages overwhelming as the train lurched along the track on the nightmare 36-hour journey north.

The first part of the awful journey finished close to Memel/Klaipeda docks on the Baltic. A dilapidated freighter awaited, and the aviators were herded 'like so many sheep', described WO Thomas Roberts RAAF (416905), into the holds of the merchant ship *Insterburg* to undertake the voyage to Swinemunde. Conditions were 'atrocious'.[116] When Roberts, an accountant, enthusiastically enlisted in the RAAF from Adelaide in October 1941 this experience was inconceivable. For three nights and two days the only possibility to sleep was to have their legs across the next POW. There was only the food they carried with them, no water was distributed, and only the most 'primitive of latrines'. A bucket lowered on a rope offered the only toilet. There was one single bulb to light the darkness. No rations were offered and the food they had left camp with needed to be rationed. Sea water was used to brew tea. Once, they were allowed up on deck. This was abruptly curtailed when a POW dived overboard. He was shot in the water. It was a relief when the rusty transport docked; fresh air never smelt so good.

The relief was short lived. POWs were stripped of their footwear and belts and handcuffed. The cruelty never stopped. POW aircrew hobbled over rocky surfaces to the railway station and again were shoved into cattle trucks. They guessed they were somewhere near the German–Polish border – which seemed strange since they had come from the German–Polish border and ended up at the same – but none of this was logical. The talk quietened with the unmistakable sound of aircraft overhead. Shore gunfire broke out. The term 'sitting ducks' was not one the POWs cared to entertain.

They were left in the cattle trucks for a night and part of a day. Above them the Allied bombing raid rocked the carriages and they pleaded with whatever God they believed in that the bombs missed. An all clear was sounded and the train lurched off. Mercifully, the trip was short, and they were unloaded at Stargard, 35 miles (56 km) inside Poland. New German guards awaited with bayonets fixed. The POWs were handcuffed in pairs and ordered to double march, 'encouraged by liberal use of bayonets, rifle butts and dangerously waving revolvers'.[117] Heavy back packs made the run difficult, and they attempted to discard items on the way. This proved problematic and chaotic as items caught on their handcuffs and dragged along the ground.

More soldiers lined the roadside and an officer in a vehicle drove alongside shouting, 'These men are murderers of women and children, now is your chance for vengeance'.[118] Soldiers began slashing pack straps with bayoneted rifles, which resulted in an obstacle race for the prisoners, as well as injuries. If a prisoner stumbled and fell, he was either jabbed in the legs with a bayonet, hit over the shoulders and head with rifle butts or the guard dogs were set on him. 'I saw dozens of men with bayonet wounds and a number who had been savaged by dogs.'[119] The screams grew louder, and smashed rifle butts were testimony to the fury unleashed on those unable to take shelter or fight back. For Garland, 'the memory will live with me forever … the snarling of slobbering Alsatian guard dogs'; the screams from 'fanatically zealous members of the master race' accompanied by rifle butts.[120] They were pushed into an interrogation hut, stripped of clothes, and then 'every orifice of the body probed accompanied by a boot up the backside'.[121]

F/L Eric Livingstone Maher RAAF (33231) had been a POW since 1942 and he still did not appreciate the German temperament he was exposed to.

There is no race quite like the Germans for displaying bad temper. They rant and rave, gesticulate, stamp their feet and work up in colour from natural through a fiery flush to a ghostly white. Just when one thinks they would burst a blood vessel with anger and effort, the whole colour scheme changes to white, a deadly white.[122]

For 9 kilometres the contingent of Allied airmen ran, the stronger piggybacking the weaker. They arrived, many without their possessions and with 'plenty of cuts, scratches, and bayonet wounds'.[123] They arrived at their new camp at Gross Tychow Stalag Luft IV, exhausted and traumatised and minus the few possessions they had cherished.

WO George Thomas William Farrell RAAF (415895) was from Three Springs, Western Australian. The name conjured up hills, greenery and babbling creeks, but his hometown was flat wheat-belt country. It was so named by the surveyor C. C. Hunt, a man more famous for the wells he dug than his town naming. He found three places suitable for wells, springs. From the wheat belt to England to being shot down over Germany in October 1943, Farrell wasn't impressed with what he now saw. The barbed wire was familiar as were guard towers, the bleak grounds and the basic huts. It seemed inconceivable that Stalag Luft IV could offer worse living conditions than Stalag Luft VI, but it did. The standard daily menu at Stalag VI had been breakfast a cup of tea or ersatz German coffee, plus one slice of black bread and jam. Lunch consisted of a bowl of potato or turnip soup, if indeed it could be called soup, or the rare tin of stew, if indeed it could be called stew. At night it was whatever your group could share from a Red Cross parcel plus a potato or turnip. At Stalag Luft IV Gross Tychow, rations diminished further. WO Farrell wrote in his diary that his eight months in the camp were 'thoroughly unpleasant and tense'.[124] Later he wrote, 'arrival unpleasant, departure was much worse, not over in a few hours but stretched over three horrible months'.[125]

CHAPTER THIRTEEN

'I did not expect to be here.'

WO Bert Stobart (RAAF)

Another year, 1944, had started very cold in Stalag IVB. WO Bert Stobart wrote in his diary that a lack of fuel had led to POW raids on the German coal store, which in turn had led to 'shootings'. The night raids on the coal store were judiciously planned because of the danger. A chain gang of volunteers crept towards the store through the snow. The first group broke in, the next group loaded the briquettes into containers, which were then laboriously passed from hand to hand. The coal then needed to be hidden in well-concealed places such as beneath floors. Guards were ordered to shoot on sight, and they did.

There was a steady stream of British aircrew brought into camp, all with the same bewildered expression Bert wore when entering beneath the huge intimidating Stalag IVB facade the previous year. By February 1944 they numbered 1500. Bert

Stalag IVB (Stobart).

Cramped huts, but some still needed to share bunks and others slept on the floor (AWM).

struggled to welcome the new arrivals. There was not a lot he could say but speak with the most cheerful voice he could muster and offer rudimentary information. He was certain he failed to sound in any way optimistic, and knew all too well it was best to give them time and space.

Stalag IVB was grim. Each iron roofed barrack was constructed of unpainted, dilapidated weatherboards. Some had weatherboard ceilings but in others the boards had already been removed to fuel stoves. In the middle of the compound was the primitive concrete and brick ablutions block. There was only cold water and exceptionally low water pressure. The water came out of small nipples and dribbled into a horse-trough. In winter, the water pipes froze.

The huts were a mass of rickety three-tier wooden bunks pushed together in banks of 24. Many of the bed boards had been removed for fuel or escape tunnels. The remaining ones were strategically placed to support the shoulders and head, the hips, and the lower legs. The individual on the top bunk had just enough head room to sit without knocking their head, assuming they were not tall. Bedding issue consisted of a thin hessian palliasse and two small WWI paper-thin blankets with an objectionable smell and which disintegrated in any attempt to launder them. Straw was offered but this was found heavily infested with bugs and lice. There were no wall linings and most the windows were missing their glass panels. The huts therefore were referred to as being 'naturally ventilated', but this meant misery in cold months. Externally the windows were covered in barbed wire.

Just as Bert and his crew had avoided befriending new aircrew back in England because their lives were commonly very short, as his own sense of hopelessness intensified, more POWs simply meant more crowding and discomfort, and even less food.

Rations deteriorated. With time the half an ounce of margarine, four slices of bread with a spoonful of sugar and a potato, which was our daily ration, diminished.

The water ration and washing facilities did not increase as more arrived, it meant greater competition for the already rapid fortnightly cold shower. Sanitary conditions deteriorated as toilets overflowed, and illness became rampant. An outbreak of typhoid and diphtheria meant Bert spent his April birthday quarantined – not that it was worth celebrating anyway.

And still they came, so many from his own RAAF 460 Squadron, but he recognised none of these airmen who looked barely old enough to shave – had he ever looked as young as these men? When would it end? Britain's Prime Minister Winston Churchill had declared that bomber aircrew would win the war, but he didn't need to fly one and these traumatised youngsters arrived with the same stories, of being ripped from bombers and falling from hell, into another form of hell, of brother crews not surviving burning wreckage, of seeing airmen murdered as their feet touched the earth and they believed they had survived.

The stories they brought with them were horrifying. It seemed that Allied authorities continued to underestimate the power of the enemy. A new name to his ears, but a familiar story, was a place called Mailly-le-Camp, where yet another attack went very wrong. It was the night of 3 May 1944, and the target was a German Wehrmacht military barracks and elements of the 21st Panzer Division near the French village of Mailly-Le-Camp east of Paris. Bomber crews were briefed that this was an important strategic location. To destroy German tanks and personnel may prevent resistance and delay when the Allies invaded. They were ordered to fly at a low altitude to ensure success. Because this was deemed not a lengthy or particularly dangerous raid, they could only record a 'third' of an operation in their logbooks. The bomber stream consisted of 346 Lancasters and 16 Pathfinder Mosquitoes. A malfunction in radio communication meant the Morse code signal to commence the bombing run was unreadable and the Lancasters were kept orbiting the assembly marker on a cloudless night with a bright moon.

They made easy targets for the scrambled night fighters. A total of 42 or 11.6

'Shoot up' by a Ju.88 — Stalag IVB.

Ju 88 too low over Stalag IVB (Stobart).

per cent of the Lancasters were shot down killing 258 aircrew. Of the 18 Lancasters from Bert's 460 Squadron, six were destroyed, all shot down while they awaited the necessary bombing instruction. Only three crews survived. A week later, on 10 May 1944, during a raid on Lille, France, a problem with target indicators caused yet another delay resulting in 13 per cent loss rate. Bert's belief in the competency of those who ran the war had waned long again, perhaps as long ago as when he found himself one of two survivors of his crew of six mates, and the stories coming into camp during 1944 did nothing to improve this reckoning.

There was a Luftwaffe training unit not far from Stalag IVB. Hauled out of their huts before six for the morning parade, aircrew POWs wistfully looked in the direction of the German airfield as aircraft took off. Young aviators regardless of nationality were fearless and out to impress. 'They would come over in the morning and give us a bit of a fly past and show off.' More experienced aircrew knew the dangers and Bert and his companions made it a habit to bend over while pushing their hands up, to entice the Germans to fly their aircraft lower. 'We'd try and catch them in the wires that were around the camp.'

On 30 April 1944, a Ju 88 pilot was too daring. The aircraft first hit a guard tower causing the German soldier to exit rapidly. Those on the ground weren't sure if they were hoping for a disaster or recovery, but tragically, as the Ju 88 pilot struggled to regain control, his plane hit two POWs before climbing rapidly, taking some of the eastern fence barbed wire with it. The mirth on the faces of watching Allied aircrew quickly turned to dismay. Two Royal Canadian Air Force airmen had been innocently walking the boundary. Sergeant Herbert Mallory was hit by a propeller and killed instantly. His companion, Sergeant Wally Massey, suffered a fractured ankle. The irony of these two Canadians having survived being shot out of the sky only to suffer this fate was not lost on the shocked onlookers, and the prank was never attempted again.

Tunnelling was not going well at IVB. After sacrificing their valuable bed boards, internees had hoped for something better than having the tunnel collapse under the weight of the heavily laden sewage cart being wheeled away from the ablutions block. Fortunately, there were no tunnellers digging at the time and the Germans dissuaded further work by emptying the contents of the latrine cart into the tunnel.

After that discovery, the commandant ordered all Red Cross food tins to be punctured so as to discourage the storing of food for escape attempts. For several weeks jam, powdered milk, beef stew, and any other tinned product was emptied into dishes in an unpalatable mess. After strong objections from the elected 'Man of Confidence', Canadian, WO Jack 'Snowshoes' Meyers, the commandant relented and ordered that the tins be simply punctured.

Some guards ensured Allied aircrew suffered. One particularly disliked guard was nicknamed 'Blondie', Prussian by birth and manner. There was elation when he was posted out of the camp. The pleasure was short-lived when his replacement proved as nasty. Nicknamed 'Pickaxe Pete', the guard was described by WO Assheton Taylor as having 'a shocking temper, with a very short fuse, plus a vitriolic tongue'.[126] No-one knew his real name, and no-one cared. His personal joy came from increasing POW misery. He moved through the huts carrying a pickaxe in search of unpunctured food tins. He gleefully shouted 'Ho, ho' with every discovery and as he brought down the pickaxe.

In August, the first D-Day Allied prisoners arrived in camp. 'They had been very badly treated, two months in transit.' The soldiers, 1000 of them, were starving. Food somehow needed to be found. As in other POW camps D-Day had lifted the spirits of IVB POWs. POWs had not considered the direct effect the Allied advance would have on their welfare. Stalag IVB already had 20,000 POWs in a camp intended for a maximum of half that. Soon the 20,000 grew to 30,000, and then 40,000 and 'our already overcrowded conditions were to become much, much worse.'

By August 1944, the waves of American Super Fortress bombers passing over the camp became common viewing during the day and raised the fading morale of those who watched from below. The nightly Lancaster raids incurred different images and emotions. They could lie in their bunks and remember how good it had felt closeted away in their position 20,000 feet (6 km) above the earth, surrounded by like-minded resolute crew, winging their way to attack Germany. It was good for the soul. But the noise of the Merlin engines above also brought less welcome visions, of the destruction of aircraft and mates and the nightmarish ordeal of survival.

Now they needed to wait and be patient and any news of an Allied advance was of the utmost importance. The secret radio was vital, and every piece of the BBC evening news was forensically examined and relayed throughout the camp. 'Immersion heaters' became every more crucial. Built from a Red Cross tin, 'you'd take the bottom and the top out of the tin, and you'd jam some wood in the thing'. A wire was then attached so that it could be attached to electricity. The heaters were used to boil water, but they were also used to disguise the electricity required to run the radio. 'We made them to put the Germans off the scent.'

As if to remind POWs that the German Reich was still in charge of their destiny, on 25 August 1944 several large trucks of heavily armed SS troops, escorted by motorcyclists, roared into the camp. Accompanied by shrill German screams, POWs were bustled out of their huts. The search resulted in their few treasured personal possessions being trashed, but importantly, the secret radio was not found. It was an unnerving experience and was followed by further restrictions for air force personnel only. They were confined to their immediate area, all sporting activities were terminated, and exercise severely reduced. Any rations needed to pass through added security and greater time-consuming procedures. As pitiable as the daily watery soup was, now the delivery was further delayed so that when it finally arrived at the aircrew compound it was cold. Aircrew rightly wondered why their POW experience should be worse.

Red Cross parcels were intended to be issued every week to every POW, with each parcel divided between a group of three or four. Bert knew that 'If you didn't eat too much or take too much the group could survive a shortage of parcels.' By September, the Red Cross parcel per POW was reduced to half a parcel per man per week. Absolutely nothing was wasted. Toilet paper was considered another unnecessary luxury by their German captors, so anything paper was rationed for use – Red Cross tins labels, chocolate wrappers, and particularly popular were pieces of any German newspaper.

In October more POWs arrived from yet another badly orchestrated battle. Operation Market Garden saw British paratroopers dropped near Arnhem in northern Holland. After securing bridges and roads, reinforcements in the form of the United States 2nd army were to arrive. Allied command had again underestimated German resistance and not taken into account the likelihood of heavy autumn rain. The paratroopers faced extreme counter-offensives and the 2nd army, bogged down in the conditions, were unable to reach their target to assist. Of the estimated 10,000 paratroopers who landed at Arnhem only 2400 were able to rejoin Allied lines. A column of exhausted, hungry, wet, and muddy soldiers, supporting their wounded, stumbled through the Stalag IVB gates. Bert Stobart and his hut companions made room and did what they could, which was far too little. 'We helped them as much as we could, but we were short of everything.'

In November, IVB occupants rose to see 960 Polish women arrive and placed in a separate compound. With the Russians closing in on Warsaw the Polish people fought the Germans for 63 days. Around 15,000 Poles and 10,000 Germans died before Polish authorities surrendered. The sight of women was novel, but they remained but two days before being transported to their death in concentration camps. The information just added to the gloom in camp.

The bread ration was further reduced, and it took surgical precision to ensure everyone received equal portions. By late 1944, with the Allies targeting German supply lines and infrastructure, POWs suffered. If any Red Cross parcels did arrive the Germans never shared. 'Germany wasn't getting any food … food trucks weren't getting through.' Bert had thought the German ration of potatoes and horsemeat had been terrible, now he wished he had some. There was no alternative but to share with new POWs. The quotas dropped to minuscule quantities and then nothing at all. Bert thought it just as well his stomach had 'shrunk'.

He could just recall what now seemed a splendid 1943 Christmas lunch, the decorations, colourful menu and certainly the food. On Christmas Day 1944 there was no effort made to decorate, the menu was barely pencilled on a piece of cardboard and without descriptive

Rationing the bread (AWM).

XMAS '44
STALAG IVB
GERMANY
menu
SOUP
PEA SOUP
DINNER
PORK TURKEY SPAM
VEG
MIXED VEG POTATOES
DESSERT
PUDDING STODGE MILK
BISCUITS CHEESE
COFFEE
MIXED CANDY

There was little Christmas cheer by 1944 (Stobart).

embellishment. Even with stored rations, it was a miserable lunch.

It was a very bad winter, the coldest for 40 years. At Stalag IVB temperatures dropped to minus 16 outside. The lack of fuel meant the temperature inside huts rarely exceeded minus six. The fire did little to warm long huts without insulation. Men huddled around barely burning stoves, wearing every piece of clothing they possessed and the lice situation worsened. Fellow Aussie, WO Keith Skidmore, was a mid-upper 460 Squadron gunner until he plummeted to earth on the last day of July 1943. He had been one of the first to say 'Getya' when Bert arrived in camp. Skidmore now struggled to say 'Getya' to anyone, spending much of his day in bed.

Elected leaders attempted to promote activities but hunger and cold extinguished enthusiasm. The only sport that could be undertaken was boxing, but emaciated men had little strength for physical contest.

Men had once carved chess pieces out of wood, but with every piece of wood needed for heating there were no pieces for craft. More bed boards were sacrificed, every second batten from the bunks, table legs, even roof rafters in the desperate attempt to stay slightly warm. Card games and checkers made from left-over cardboard proved the only entertainment.

Noel's letters were not getting through and Bert was starving and fed-up. In his diary he wrote in strong handwriting 'I did not expect to be here'. Now, on days he merely wrote the date and the word 'Nothing'. His world was monochrome, a dreary grey. He so longed for the strong colours he had been born into, but monochrome and monotony were the two 'm' words that governed his existence. Hunger did not start with 'm', but malnutrition did. The Germans never tired of causing discomfort. They never tired of routine and monotony. Shouts of '*Raus, raus! Schnell, schnell!*' (Out! Fast!) every morning at 6 am regardless of the cold. If the counter was inept, or the senior guard not happy, POWs could be left standing for hours. An airman broke ranks and, waving his arms, ran to the boundary and

Board games provided the only diversion from the monotony (AWM).

stepped over the warning wire. He was shot dead. On New Year's Day another airman was found to have hanged himself in the ablution block. Two days later another airman broke the curfew only to be shot by a guard, the body left slung over a barbed wire fence until morning.

Bert realised how important it was to keep his mind busy. He turned greater attention to his book, titled 'My Trip Overseas', approaching POWs of any nationality to draw, paint, produce a poem or story, or letter in this cherished book. It not only sparked interest within the huts, but the entries were inspiring and more.

The camp held talented men. Bert described to one in detail the house he wished to build in Melbourne for him and Noel when they married. A great deal of time was spent looking at that drawing, imagining how the black and white was going to be transformed into bright colours, how they could spend many hours filling the garden with greenery and more colour, how, one day, the bedrooms might be full of children.

From 16 December 1944 to 25 January 1945, the previously serene forests of the Ardennes were transformed into a violent battle ground. The target of the Allied attack was the Belgian city of Antwerp. In frigid conditions 30 German divisions launched a counteroffensive. The surprise German attack was timed perfectly to take advantage of the weather and the deep snow drifts, record cold

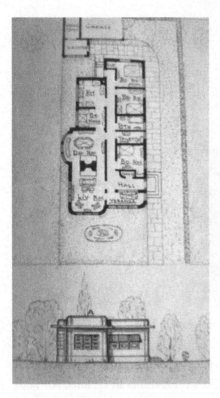

The house that Bert dreamed of
building (Stobart).

temperatures, freezing rain and thick fog brutalised opposing forces. The Battle of the Bulge as Allied forces would know it, proved the costliest fought by the United States army in the war, with an estimated 105,102 casualties, including 26,612 missing or taken prisoner.[127]

The POWs of Stalag IVB watched as closely guarded long lines of battle-weary American soldiers staggered into the camp. Bert Stobart wrote, 'Americans very badly off'. Bunks now needed to be shared. To make room aircrew moved in with each other, 'blokes needed to bunk up together'. If boards were available a board was set down the middle of each bunk, otherwise palliasses were filled with straw and rolled down the middle in an attempt to offer a modicum of propriety, 'that gave the Yanks some room'. For the even less fortunate, straw on the cold brick floors needed to suffice.

During all of March 1945 they received just half a Red Cross parcel each.

By mid-March at least the days were lengthening and mercifully there were breaks of sunlight through the heavy cloud cover. It was so good to walk outside without freezing. But with the burst of fresh air came an outbreak of flu which spread rapidly through the overcrowded camp. With the arrival of spring came an increased infestation of lice and bedbugs. German fumigations were rare and hot showers even rarer, so the blood-sucking bugs thrived. Men suffered bites and rashes. For the hardy, bathing in the still freezing water helped, but for everyone there was the threat of the disease this plague could cause. Acute diarrhoea broke out and spread rapidly. It was easy to comply with the order to starve oneself until the bug had worked itself out of the body.

They eagerly listened to every news bulletin they dared; freedom seemed close, but so were the battlelines. A German ammunition train appeared outside the camp under cover of the woods. POWs emerged to watch an American P-51 fighter appear and begin his attack run. 'There was a lot of cheering and waving', as the pilot successfully destroyed the ammunition supply. Recognising that gathered

Digging trenches to save them from their own bombers (AWM).

below were POWs the pilot flew over again and 'waggled his wings.' 'We had a great view of that … it was a great booster.' For a brief time, smiles lit up huts. Air raids were 'thicker, closer and heavier' and they dug trenches. The sound of artillery and machine-gun fire was becoming a constant. The POWs of Stalag IVB prayed the unarmed behind wire would be spared.

'The Jerries have cut rations further', Bert Stobart wrote, 'not too keen on the food – we haven't any and getting thinner'. His last cigarettes were traded for paper,

charcoal, boot polish and paint, when he decided the best artist could transform the small black-and white photo of his fiancée into a large painting. It was comforting to have Noel smiling down on him in technicolour. Now he just had to get home to her, but that was becoming more and more challenging.

Noel (Stobart).

CHAPTER FOURTEEN

'We saw the bomber keel over and crash … all on board were killed except the tail gunner.'

F/S *Thomas Lonergan (RAAF)*

The fourth child of Jeremiah and Gladys Lonergan was born on Remembrance Day 1924. It was only fitting that their son be named Thomas Patrick Lonergan after his uncle who was killed in the previous world war at Bullecourt, France, on 3 May 1917. By 16 November 1942, having just turned 18, the younger Thomas Lonergan enlisted in the RAAF as number 432828, to follow his namesake to a war in Europe.

He thought himself fortunate to become an aircrew trainee given the large number of youth vying for the same. Recruiters could afford to be very selective. Those accepted needed to be educated above the average Australian male and preferably with further tertiary qualifications as well as white-collar work experience. An interest in the technical was a bonus. A proven physical sports background was preferred.

Thomas Lonergan was the type of candidate sought and he was posted to Initial Training School and then Elementary Flying Training School. His wonderful trajectory faltered when it was deemed that he was not a natural born pilot; 'tense' in the air was added to his record. He was sent to Bombing and Air Gunnery School at Evans Head and, like Bert Stobart, was awarded his Aircrew (G) badge and sergeant's stripes.

Just a week after his 19th birthday Thomas Lonergan embarked on a troop ship bound for England. The journey via the United States was the wildest dream for any teenager and he spent his first Christmas away from home in the mind-blowing city of New York. His 20th birthday and next Christmas would be spent in a German POW camp.

Cy Borsht (Borsht family).

Lonergan's progress in Bomber Command was identical to that of Australian gunners before him. The crew selection did not, however, go exactly as planned. The pilot commonly approached those wearing different insignias. Lonergan watched quietly 'as the "gun" pilots teamed up with the "gun" engineers and the "gun" navigators who all knew each other'.[128] An air gunner from Queensland, Sgt Ronald 'Glynn' Cooper (434622), though himself not yet 20, approached Brisbane pilot F/S Cyril 'Cy' Borsht (426416). 'Aren't you a friend of my brother?'[129]

Cyril Borsht a junior draughtsman before he enlisted, was days away from turning 21. The confident Cooper then approached 20-year-old F/S Brian (Snow) O'Connell (428820) from Sydney, a former clerk with the Department of Agriculture who had been studying Economics at Sydney University to be the navigator. F/S Maxwell Ray Staunton-Smith (428029), a natural sportsman, and still a student when he enlisted from Hobart in 1942 at 19, was asked to be wireless operator/air gunner (WOP).

The reserved Borsht recalled that as the Australians moved to their quarters, he overheard Staunton-Smith being asked who his pilot was. The WOP answered: 'Some little bandy Jewish bloke. I hope to Christ he can fly.'[130] It was already known that people of the Jewish faith were being persecuted. Later, the true extent of Nazi crimes against humanity were revealed, but Borsht felt he needed to ask his new crew did they have any objection to their captain being Jewish. There were surprised looks and shakes of the head. The very, young Australians bonded so quickly they combined their savings to purchase a Vauxhall car even though only Cy and Max knew how to drive.[131]

As conversion to Lancasters occurred, RAF F/S Sergeant Tom Laing (1561720) took on the bomb aimer duties and RAF F/S Eric Leigh (2204264) became their flight engineer. They transferred to Silverstone RAF base in Northamptonshire on 30 March 1944. That night Bomber Command suffered terrible casualties in a raid on Nuremberg. Of the 795 aircraft, 95 bombers were shot down. Their initiation was typical for 1944 when an Allied advance also meant increased fatalities in

W/Cdr Rollo Kingsford-Smith (AWM Geoffrey Mainwaring).

the air war. They watched a battle-damaged Lancaster limp back from operations with three engines. It was unknown if the pilot was injured but his control of the aircraft was minimal. In an attempt to land, a wing clipped a roof. 'We saw the bomber keel over and crash ... all on board were killed except the tail gunner.'[132] And it was not just the death of aircrew. A member of the Women's Air Force Auxiliary was towing a load of bombs to an aircraft when a faulty fuse caused one to ignite. 'The poor girl was blown to pieces, and, spread all over the remains of the tractor,' just one incident Tom Lonergan would remember forever. 'Life goes on' as the airfield apron was quickly cleared, and aircraft readied for an operation.[133]

On 25 November 1943, a new unit was formed in Waddington, Lincoln, England from RAAF 467 Squadron. The squadron RAAF 463 adopted the motto, 'Press on Regardless' and the first commanding officer was Wing Commander Rollo Kingsford-Smith, nephew of adventurer aviator Sir Charles Kingsford Smith and a brother of Peter, who by 19 February 1943, languished in the German POW camp Luft III.

On the first page of the squadron logbook Rollo Kingsford-Smith proudly stated:

> *This day, November 25th 1943, will indeed be a memorable one, for the Officers and Airmen who formed the Advance Force of yet another Royal Australian Air Force Squadron in England the RAAF. Its official designation – No. 463 (RAAF) Squadron. The birth of the new Australian Squadron was celebrated in a manner both typical and prophetic.[134]*

The squadron's first operation was to bomb Berlin, but the commanding officer wrote:

Photomontage of the seven crew members from 463 Lancaster bomber 'D for Dog', killed during a raid on Berlin, 3 January 1944. Left to right (top row): F/O John Watson Gage from Peterborough, England; Sgt Albert E. Cowell, from London. Second row: F/S Colin Hemingway, 417839, from South Australia; Victorians PO Jack Weatherill, 410621; and PO Peter Louis Symonds, 408054. Bottom row: Queenslander F/S William Donald Toohey 426401; and F/S Francis Noel Looney, 423290 from New South Wales.

> *The misguided and deluded people of that once glorious city, but to the great distress and disappointment of the members of No. 463 Squadron, aircrew and ground crew alike, owing to adverse weather conditions, the operation was cancelled ... tomorrow we will be 'bang on' for wherever the target for the night will be.*[135]

By the time the Borsht crew joined 463 Squadron on 18 July 1944, the pride remained, but the bravado had dimmed. The word 'prophetic' had indeed been a 'forewarning', as Kingsford-Smith added to most log pages 'aircraft missing'. Over the ensuing three years RAAF 463 and RAAF 467 based at the same airfield, although rarely with more than a combined aircrew strength of 350, saw 1100 airmen vanish. Squadron losses of 28 per cent in one raid or 35 per cent in one month were common. Within 463 Squadron, by war's end, 74 crews had completed a tour of 30 operations, but the chance of this was only 2.6 per cent.

The empty beds and photos not quickly removed were unsettling – so many young Aussies obliterated.

There was a marked reluctance to befriend newly arrived 'sprog' crew because more than likely they would not be around long, but what did you do with photographs of you and a mate who had 'bought it'? PO Lindsay Samuel Fairclough (415412) from 463 loved the candid photo of him and fellow West Australian F/S James 'Jim' Mudie (29886), but Jim was killed in the operation over Germany on 2 January 1944. Did he leave the photograph on display to remind himself of the good times or did it only remind him of the mortality rate of service with RAF Bomber Command? Lindsay Fairclough was himself killed when shot down on a 463 attack on Germany four weeks later, the night of 30 January 1944, and staff were left to pack away the photograph of the grinning Australians.

On 6 June 1944, D-day, 463 Squadron crews were not told that their flight over enemy territory was a decoy flight to assist the largest seaborne invasion in history.

For the Borsht 'sprog' crew their first operation did not occur until 12 August 1944 when Allied armies were advancing quickly across Europe. F/S Lonergan was restless the night before because as far as he was concerned, 'this is the first day of the war for me'. The wait had been long and arduous, but 'God help me' because he was still only 19.

Jim Mudie, left, and Lindsay Fairclough (AWM).

Take-off was 1900 but the ground crew had started their day around 0800. A team of about six ground crew were assigned to each Lancaster and they took the care of their bomber very seriously. F/S Max Staunton-Smith was impressed with how ground crew treated both the aircraft and the Borsht crew – perhaps the aircraft even better than the crew.

If you blew an exhaust stub, it cost you a pint of beer each. We came back one night, and we'd blown 15 exhaust stubs, so we took them down to the pub at Waddo – The Horse and Jockey – and bought them beer at 11 pence a pint. But they'd wait up all hours of the morning for you to return from your mission – they were colossal.[136]

The maintenance of bombers was laborious and time-consuming and the pressure to get them back into the air the following night, relentless.

Aircrew had to accept whichever Lancaster they were allocated for a raid and over ensuing months the Borsht crew flew seven different Lancasters. They were not supposed to have a favourite, but they did: 'G for George'.[137] It could have simply been the 'feel' of the aircraft, as a later poem penned by a 463 Squadron POW explained.

Ground crew (Stobart).

Here is a tale of Georgie Lanc.,
Fast as the wind, sure as the bank,
Quadruple power, Octuple gun,
Beautiful bomber to battle the Hun.[138]

It may also have had something to do with the art that adorned the nose of 'G for George'. The fuselage was painted with the cartoon character 'Snifter', a loping bloodhound which featured in *Man* magazine, an Australian publication better known for its risqué 'girlie' photographs and cartoons than its worthy journalism. After every operation in 'G for George', 'a post and a piddle' was added to the artwork.

On their first flight the Borsht crew flew 'J for Jig'. Tom Lonergan had no clear memory of what nose art adorned this Lancaster. He was too anxious to see anything but directly in front of him, as he pushed leaden legs up the short ladder into a fuselage smelling of metal, paint, oil and something more sinister. Outwardly, crew all appeared calm and confident but Lonergan had no doubt that inwardly they felt like he did, stressed and with 'stomach tightening'.[139] He squeezed up

RAAF 463 'G for George', being loaded with bombs (AWM).

into the mid-upper turret by pulling down a moveable step and the drop seat he secured beneath his body. There was no room for his parachute, so it lay stowed inside the belly of the plane. Lonergan believed he 'had the best all round view', but likely his pilot Cy Borsht and Glynn Cooper tucked away in the rear turret may have disagreed with him.

The target was the Opel manufacturing plant south of Frankfurt, Germany, where intelligence believed the destructive V1 flying bombs were being assembled. Trying to remain vigilant for night fighters the 19-year-old Australian became, 'transfixed by the extraordinary spectacle of the burning city of Russelsheim below' and, the 'pyrotechnic display all around us as searchlights, incendiary flares and fiery shell bursts' lit up the sky.[140] His commanding officer, Wing Commander Rollo Kingsford-Smith was to describe such a sight as:

> It was a cauldron of hell, magnificent, awesome, and we had to fly into it and through it. It scared all the self-confidence out of me. I remembered how to pray.[141]

Lonergan thought there would be relief once the bombload was expelled, but he was wrong; throughout the return flight they were 'a sitting duck'. Those three hours through the unnerving darkness seemed to take forever. The sight of the

Lancaster mid-upper gunner in turret (AWM).

Lincoln Cathedral as they approached Waddington was fantastic.

Another welcome sight from his mid-turret as Borsht straightened the Lancaster, was their ground crew standing and waving from the airfield apron. 'No-one was more excited or more relieved than me to have experienced and survived my first mission.'[142]

There was little time to 'savour the exhilaration of my first bombing raid on Germany, because just two days later we were off on our next'.[143] The operation was against Gilze-Rijen, Holland. The Borsht crew had thought night-time bombing was nerve-racking, this attack was in daylight. 'Visibility was perfect' but the enemy seemed a lot closer, particularly as the target was a Luftwaffe airfield.

Three days later the Borsht crew bombed a German bomb supply depot at L'Isle Adam, France. Lonergan spent time in hospital with an ear infection, but the crew had kept flying with a substitute gunner. While he had only three operations beside his name, his crew had flown 11 so were given nine days leave. He felt a bit of a fraud but could but take advantage of the opportunity to act like a tourist in war-torn England. August had not been a good month for 463 Squadron with 21 airmen killed.

When the Borsht crew returned to operations, they were allowed to drive

It was customary for ground crew and non-flying aircrew to wave as aircraft took off (AWM).

their 1937 Vauxhall car to dispersal rather than wait of the trucks to collect them. Getting seven blokes into the Vauxhall with all their flying kit was a tight squeeze. It made the Lancaster felt downright spacious.

Their next operation was a daylight attack against a German garrison based

Releasing bombs over the Luftwaffe airfield at Gilze-Rijen, Holland (AWM).

at Brest, France, on 5 September 1944, the next two on 10 and 11 September against German forces in the France regions of Le Havre in support of British army divisions. Aircrew were aware how much danger their operations were for civilian populations in occupied territories as they reinforced the Allied advance, but there was little they could do except ensure their bombs fell on target.

They had only just finished the daylight attack against Le Havre when called to participate in a night attack against targeting factories in Darmstadt. Bomber Command hierarchy declared the operation an 'outstanding' success. An extensive firestorm not only destroyed the manufacturing capacity but killed an estimated 120,000 citizens. For crews they could only justify their actions as 'kill or be killed'.[144]

The 463 Lancaster captained by Flying Officer James William Taylor (418585) was shot down by a night fighter. The Borsht crew feared their friends in the crew, which was similarly made up of

Flying over the Netherlands (AWM).

Destroyed rear turret (AWM).

Australians and an English flight engineer, had been killed. Little were they aware that their own destiny would reflect that of the Taylor crew, and they would meet as POWs, except both engineers. It was another reminder of the very real dangers. A 463 Lancaster arrived back minus its rear turret. Hit from above by another bomber the turret and the rear gunner within were ripped away.

Crews needed to stifle the thoughts and horrors witnessed to continue as yet again, operations accelerated with the Allied advance. Some operations left enduring fear. For Tom Lonergan this was his 8th operation, flown on 12 September, against Stuttgart. A force of 204 Lancasters was sent to destroy chemical factories. 'The northern and western parts of the city of Stuttgart were erased.'[145] Many decades later a repatriation psychiatrist reviewed Tom Lonergan's anxiety and wrote, 'I suspect he denies the intensity of his fear; although he recalls that on a raid over Stuttgart, he was terrified.'[146]

They were barely out of their teens and too much was being asked of them. For the Borsht crew as with so many others, the routine had become a blur. Daily briefings, maps revealing new targets, but in so many ways the same, they began to merge over the broad map of Germany: Bremerhaven; Rheydt/München-Gladbach; Dortmund Ems Canal, Karlsruhe; Kaiserlautern; Bremen; Nuremberg.

463 Squadron captains briefing. A target like Flushing was a change from night
operations (AWM).

Mates didn't return and like those before them, the Borsht crew were reluctant to
befriend the newly arrived.

For F/S Tom Lonergan his 18th operation came on 23 October 1944. After so
many long night flights over German cities, a small 112 Lancaster raid against gun
batteries based around Flushing, The Netherlands, was almost a relief. Flushing
(now known as Vlissingen), was situated on a North Sea island of Walcheren. It
had been joined to the mainland by a causeway, but a previous raid had breached
the sea wall. Control of the adjacent Belgian port city of Antwerp and Scheldt
River and estuary were crucial for Allied shipping to land troops and supplies.

Rain and wind delayed the departure time until 1600 but the Borsht crew were
assigned their favourite Lancaster, 'G for George'. It was a little worrying when the
four Spitfire fighters escorting the bomber stream turned back due to the weather
and poor visibility, but it was a short flight and as far as the gunners, Tom Lonergan
and Glynn Cooper were concerned, poor visibility and bad weather deterred
German fighters also.

Over the intercom came the navigator's voice, Brian O'Connell, telling his
skipper to descend to 4000 feet, 'ten minutes to target'. The Lancaster was skimming
along below the grey cloud cover now. From the rear turret Cooper's voice had
some urgency, 'Skip, there's light flak coming very close.'147 The bomb bay doors

were open, and the engineer PO Eric Leigh lurched backwards as he was hit by anti-aircraft fire. His stomach wound bled profusely. Borsht shouted to O'Connell to come to assist.

The WOP Max Staunton-Smith watched as an 88 mm shell ripped through his radio set. He jumped up to move into the astrodome and another shell tore through where he had been sitting. The port inner and starboard engines were hit, and fire spread quickly from the bomb bay into the interior of the fuselage, making it impossible to jettison the bomb load. The 22-year-old pilot lost no time in giving the order to abandon the Lancaster. Staunton-Smith hesitated and asked Borsht, 'Do you need me anymore?'. 'For Christ sake get out!' came the reply and the WOP jumped through the aircraft rear door just before both gunners.[148]

Leigh urged Borsht to leave him behind but that wasn't an option, as far as his skipper was concerned. Borsht set the controls as well as he could, attached the parachute to the bleeding engineer and dragged Leigh down the steps to the front hatch.

I left my seat and helped the engineer to the forward hatch and pushed him out. The aircraft was blazing and close to stall. I baled out at 1000 ft.[149]

Leigh became stuck in the front hatch so Borsht could but push him out with his boot and follow. 'Sadly, I could only hope there was sufficient life left in Eric for him to activate his own chute'. Unfortunately, that was not the case and Leigh died. The aircraft crashed into the sea. Borsht landed on the narrow strip of land a mere couple of hundred metres from the very gun emplacements he was attempting to bomb. He quickly released his chute and took off running. The urgent screams from German soldiers caused him to halt and raise his hands.

Tom Lonergan tumbled out of the rear hatch. For the mid-upper gunner, 'it was the sweetest moment in my life' when his parachute 'finally opened and I realised I wasn't going to die'.[150] As he dangled from the silk canopy he was blown towards the German emplacements with 'shells buzzing all around me, and the sound of bombs … exploding underneath me'.[151] He landed heavily on a Dutch dyke. German rifle shells whistled too close. Max Staunton-Smith was not as fortunate and a shell tore into his arm.

German soldiers rapidly captured Lonergan, Cooper, Staunton-Smith, Laing, and Borsht – F/S Brian 'Snow' O'Connell was nowhere to be found. He had been very, fortunate. Landing clear of the gun emplacement, he approached a Dutch family, and was quickly handed to members of the underground who ensured his return to England. Tom Lonergan wondered if it was not a case of 'the luck of the Irish', but then Lonergan was a fairly Irish name also.

Within weeks the 20-year-old F/Sgt Tom Lonergan was pushed through the Stalag Luft VI POW camp gates. His welcome was restrained; he was a 'Johnny come lately', another mouth to feed, another body to jam into the already overcrowded hut. The condition of some aircrew was startling: their bodies were clearly emaciated, their expressions were glum, they were mere shadows of the men they once were.

CHAPTER FIFTEEN

'Another lousy day ... couldn't be bothered getting out of bed ... bags of rumours – all baloney in my opinion.'

F/S Robert Shannon (RAAF)

The stories being brought into camps by the newest arrivals were disturbing and added to the pent-up emotions within POW huts. RAF 57 Squadron Rear Gunner Sgt John Forward (RAFVR) reached Luft 7,[152] Bankau, near Silesia, Germany (now Bakow, Opole Volvodeship, Poland) during the last days of December 1944. He was the sole survivor of his crew of five RAF and two RAAF, sent to attack the railway yards of Giessen, Germany, on the night of 6–7 December 1944. Three parachuted safely from the shattered Lancaster: Forward, the Australian bomb aimer, F/S Neil Francis Dallaway McGladrigan (426895) and the RAF Engineer Sgt John Scott. Forward was processed and sent to Dulag Luft for solitary, interrogation and then transported to Stalag Luft 7. Sergeant Scott was taken prisoner in the town of Gladenbach and shot. McGladrigan was placed in a town

F/S Neil McGladrigan (RAAF) (AWM).

jail. He was beaten severely during an interrogation. A day later, two days after his 22nd birthday, the airman from Brisbane was taken into woods and shot. Both airmen were buried in shallow graves.

The POWs had thought 1944 was bad; 1945 was worse. The optimism bolstered by news of the Allied advance diminished under increasing hunger and feelings of hopelessness – the war needed to be over, it was taking too long for British forces to free them. F/L James Edward Holliday (404432) had been away too long from his home in Brisbane, way too long as a POW.

Most of his war had been spent behind barbed wire and he was well over it. His RAAF record could never tell his story. It simply recorded that his first flight with RAAF 458 Squadron was 19 February 1942, and his 18th, and last flight, was 7 August 1942. All very clinical. The uninformed would think he had a brief, unspectacular war. Under certain circumstances he might agree but the word 'war' needed to be redefined. His Wellington bomber crashed during an attack on Tobruk. Holliday trudged through the Middle East heat and sand attempting to skirt the El Alamein battle lines for 16 days. His luck ran out when he was captured by Italian soldiers and then transported to Stalag VIII (later known as Stalag 344) Lamsdorf, Upper Silesia, Germany.[153] It was 11 September 1942 and the next years were grim. It wasn't just the deprivation of all things required to sustain a healthy individual, the overcrowding, the three-tier rickety bunks, the miserable rations, but the humiliation was compounded when the Germans decided to chain him and other POWs.[154]

Early on 8 October 1942, POWs in Stalag VIII were ordered onto the parade ground, lined up and counted. New German officers and soldiers 'armed with rifles and tommy-guns surrounded us'.[155] Other unarmed soldiers carried bundles of Red Cross parcel string. A raucous speech was delivered condemning the 'barbaric behaviour of British troops on the Island of Sark who had tied and then shot five German troops'.[156] The Fuhrer had demanded an apology from Winston Churchill. Soldiers moved in and tied the hands of POWs. They were returned to their barracks, hands all tied in front, but quickly realised that it was possible to nibble through the string and free others. Aircrew wondered what the hell this all had to do with them: if the 'barbaric behaviour' had occurred, they were in the air force, not the army, and they had many stories concerning barbaric behaviour against their own upon parachuting into occupied territories.

The following day they were again tied and those who freed themselves a second time were removed to the guard house, hands tied so tightly 'circulation stopped' and made to stand for hours.[157] After three weeks the string was replaced with dog chains, the end being padlocked around each wrist, then it was police-type handcuffs, separated by 18 inches (46 cm) of chain. POWs then found that a bully beef can opener was ideal for unlocking handcuffs. German guards wearied of this and began to ignore the indiscretions. Unfortunately, a senior officer arrived and demanded that all POWs be kept chained. The chaining was extended to Stalags 7, 383 and IXC.

In Jim Holliday's Stalag 344 Lamsdorf camp, RAAF 460 Squadron WO Raphael Sherman (404804) found himself with the daunting responsibility as senior Australian when suddenly all commissioned officers were taken from the

Stalag 344 Lamsdorf (AWM).

camp. Sherman could just remember how quiet and mundane his life had been as a chief clerk with the Brisbane office of Colonial Mutual Life Insurance. Life insurance, almost worthy of a chuckle. He had no assurance of life past the present day. How anxious he had been in 1940 for the excitement that the RAAF and war promised. Now he yearned for a return to that quiet and mundane life in Brisbane, with family, friends, a comfortable home, and food, lots of food.

Stalag 344 Lamsdorf offered none of those things Raphael Sherman so yearned for. The compound was a mere 50 by 90 yards (46 x 82 m). Crammed in were huts with a small toilet and washroom which housed 195 aircrew, 60 of whom were forced to sleep on tables, forms and on the doors off lockers laid on the floor. The huts had been built on a slope so the top ends were decidedly above the lower ends, which collected the moisture and mould. There was one tap in each hut and the water turned on for only three hours per day. The toilets were intended to accommodate 40 and there were 1000 POWs. The cisterns, more often than not, did not flush so the toilets quickly became 'decidedly unsanitary'. Each hut had a large central heating stove, but the week's fuel supply only lasted one day. The German cookhouse provided swede soup, cooked potatoes and occasionally hot water, but the rations were irregular and meagre. Aircrew envied the freedom of army personnel who were allowed outside the camp under guard, either for work parties or recreation, thus also offering the opportunity to barter cigarettes or chocolate for food. Army POWs believed aircrew had it easy because they were not required to work; air force personnel observed the work party opportunities they were denied. Having to depend on the charity of army POWs, which was not always forthcoming, did little to assuage emotions which were already close to the surface. When new aircrew arrived, Sherman visited and distributed what surplus clothing, soap and cigarettes he had. Once a month he forwarded requests, complaints, and suggestions to the German commandant, but it resulted in little improvement In September 1942, with the chaining of POWs, the relationship with the commandant deteriorated dramatically.

The first reason concerning German captives on the island of Sark was changed and he was told it was a reprisal for the alleged ill treatment of other German POWs, particularly those taken prisoner during Operation Jubilee, the Allied raid at Dieppe. The amphibious attack on the German-occupied northern French port was, however, a German victory. Allied losses were massive with 3623 of the 6086 Allied soldiers killed, 106 RAF aircraft lost, and 33 landing craft and a destroyer sunk. It was yet another harsh lesson for Allied high command: the lack of the necessities for a successful ambitious attack, such as the adaptation of mobile equipment for beach landings and, importantly, the requirement for artificial wharves had yet again, resulted in a huge human cost. Sherman reasoned it more likely Hitler was exaggerating the situation for propaganda purposes, but it was those with the least control over their destiny who suffered. He and other camp representatives made unsuccessful complaints.

> When the German Commandant expressed their intentions to us, we protested that it was contrary to the Geneva Convention, but they refused to take this into account. We were told plainly that resistance would only mean shooting.[158]

Sherman held grave fears for his charges but could do little. One of his POWs was 20-year-old F/S Murray Arthur May (404916). He had sat down with May on his arrival in camp, in an attempt, to assure the 20-year-old that he was now safe, safer than he had been. May's operational war had been short. He had been posted to RAF 53 Coastal Command Squadron. On 8 April 1942 he was the WOP/AG on a Lockheed Hudson tasked for a reconnaissance operation over the North Sea at low altitude. Off the Dutch Frisian Islands, a convoy of ships was sighted and, the English pilot decided to attack. Their aircraft was immediately hit by anti-aircraft fire from the ack-ack ships protecting the convoy. The Hudson was further damaged when German shore batteries opened fire. For the young Australian it was horrifying.

A massive rackety onslaught which was earsplitting because of their close, proximity. Why we were not blown out of the sky I will never know.[159]

The worst was not yet over. The aircraft crashed into the sea and began to sink. May clambered up into the astro hatch at the top of the fuselage only to see two German fighters levelling out to attack. 'I didn't see my whole life appear before my eyes – there wasn't time.'[160]

Fortunately, the fighters broke off, but the water was freezing. Aviators could survive 15 to 20 minutes in the North Sea. Only the Canadian navigator, F/S Dave Moran, was able to follow May out of the astro hatch. They inflated their Mae West life jackets and May shouted to the Canadian that they needed to get to shore quickly. The Canadian replied he could not swim. May pulled away as the Hudson disappeared. He turned to see the navigator had not moved. He had not been joking, he really could not swim. 'I was already feeling the effect of my freezing environment and was faced with self-preservation.'[161] The Australian swam back to Moran. The navigator clung to the back of the WOP and May struck out again for the shore. 'My swim strokes shortened as my arm muscles felt the drag effect of propelling two bodies.'[162] As he fell onto the shore with Moran still attached May was 'almost frozen stiff'. German soldiers with rifles raised stood inches away and

Australians chained at Stalag 383 (AWM).

May wondered if even this wasn't, 'more comforting than the deathly cold water'. Now May, and other Australian aircrew were roughly handcuffed by their captors.

The Germans had ensured that work parties were not handcuffed but as aircrew were not allowed to participate in work parties they suffered most from the cruel policy, 'we were perfect targets'.[163] They were tied with crossed wrists each day for the next two months and then placed in handcuffs each day for a further six weeks. The punishment was demeaning and stressful and undertaking the smallest of tasks was difficult and painful.

The chaining of Australian POWs was discussed in the Australian parliament. A formal objection was issued and accompanied by information concerning the good treatment of German POWs in Australia, but it wasn't until early 1943 that the German stipulation was countermanded at least for the Australians. WO Sherman conferred with other Australian aircrew and the decision was unanimous.

> We immediately refused to be unchained, stating that we were still British and that we would take our share of the discomfort and hardship in the same manner as was being meted out to others of British nationality.[164]

The Germans were perplexed but the Australians were determined. POWs had little left but their self-respect, beliefs, and resolve. Not only did the chaining contradict their interpretation of fairness, but their belief that solidarity with British aircrew was paramount. It became clear 'that the Germans were continually trying to drive a wedge between the Dominion and UK personnel'.[165] The impasse was resolved by moving the Australians to a separate and more secure barrack.

Jim Holliday had endured the chaining and 552 days in Stalag 344 before being informed he was to be moved. He had been a sergeant when he became a POW. Since then, he had been promoted to F/S and then PO, F/O and F/L – in his own eyes that was ridiculous. Promotion to officer rank simply disrupted his life further as he was taken to the officers' camp, Luft III at Sagan, where he spent 318 days. It was now years incarcerated and his patience had worn thin. When would he be free of this God damn awful life? Where were his rescuers?

> We have suffered unnecessary indignities. We have suffered for what should have been settled by those controlling our welfare in war. Why should the minions suffer for the stiffed necked to preserve their gold braid and their warm seats?[166]

In every POW camp elected leaders and senior officers struggled to raise morale and to ensure that men, many of whom, like Holliday, had been prisoners of a hard and ruthless enemy for years, were kept under control and not allowed to explode into a premature uprising. They had been behind barbed wire forever, or so it felt, in that debilitating state of being unfree, eternally hungry, deprived of love and comfort, and scarred by the wasted years and the degradation of captivity. Now they had seen a real possibility of Allied defeat turning into victory. Time hung heavily and they turned into armchair critics. Campaigns were expected to finish much more quickly than was practicable; 'delays or stalemates were for us catastrophic', described F/L Peter Kingsford-Smith.[167]

WO Robert Shannon (411231) had had little hesitation in enlisting in the RAAF. He had been born in Greenock, Renfrewshire, Scotland and considered it was his civic duty to enlist from his adopted Australia to defend the land of his birth. The war also offered an opportunity to visit the land of heather and bagpipes as a 21-year-old and become reacquainted with Scottish relatives. Like Bert Stobart, Shannon was another in a hurry who opted to be a rear gunner. He did not mind being attached to RAF 10 Squadron as his loyalties were shared between the British Isles and Australia. In December 1941, the squadron had relocated to RAF Melbourne in Leeming, Yorkshire and he was the gunner in a Handley Page Halifax crew.

The Lancaster bomber received the highest praise but as far as Shannon was concerned, 'these Halifaxes are great kites'.[168] In August 1942 he undertook his first operation, raiding the docks at Le Havre, and any romantic visions of war in the air quickly disappeared. 'It was altogether different than I imagined, flak over area and the searchlights were damn powerful.'[169] His diary began to fill with deaths of Australian mates, aircrew he had tried to crew with, 'now they are gone ... Quite a few of the boys are going now, tough luck'. Another entry, 'Jim Henry went west the other night ... it was their final op, bloody bad show.'[170]

His crew came under heavy fire from a flak ship off the Danish coast, 'barely made it back'. Shot up again over Kiel, 'a mate had several fingers shot off'. His squadron wing commander was shot down over Cologne, more went missing, 'Five kites went, only one came back that makes three out of our ten gone.'[171] On the operation to attack Genoa, Italy, on 26 October 1942, his second pilot was hit in the neck and Shannon was shot in the legs, 'all my crew are screwed'. There were months in hospital, well into 1943. He wasn't sure he would pass his medical to rejoin the squadron, part of him hoped he would not.

There was no such reprieve and by March he was again on operations. On 29 June 1943, Shannon's crew were shot down by an enemy fighter. Shannon was the only one who managed to bail out. Incarcerated in Luft III he struggled with the survivor guilt. As 1943 moved into 1944 and 1944 into 1945, his depression deepened. By April 1945 he had all but given up. 'Another lousy day … Couldn't be bothered getting out of bed. Bags of rumours – all baloney in my opinion.' He sold half of his meagre bread ration for two cigarettes.

> *Well worth it would sooner smoke than eat. Every day gets worse … I dream about home every night. So do the rest of the fellows. Mentally picture the family as it used to be. One thing is certain, all ex-POWs will appreciate the small things in life much more than people who have not been through this sort of thing … God home will seem wonderful.*[172]

He promised that if he ever got home, he would never complain of everyday chores or a boring lifestyle. He would never take any food for granted.

It was nine months, then 10 months since the invasion on the beaches of Normandy. They watched aircraft flying overhead, heard and saw fire and destruction on the near horizon. They prayed the Allies knew where they were. Shannon had heard the optimists say they would be free by Christmas 1944, then January 1945. It was now April, 'everyone is on edge – expecting something to break at any moment'. He had stopped listening to the optimists. He separated himself from his fellow POWs, as much as was possible, because he was criticised for being so pessimistic. He had been a POW too long and too often the dream of being free had been dashed. Shannon was no longer capable of embracing the idea of freedom, lest it be wrenched away again.

The assiduous English author, Percival Christopher Wren, had written adventure fiction dealing with soldiering in Africa. His books were firm favourites with this generation of warriors. A paragraph from one of his books that rang true with POWs was:

> *Only those who have been prisoners have any conception of the horrors of being a prisoner, or the ineffable joy of release, of the terrible rise and fall of the spirit, the fluctuations between the delirium of happiness and madness of despair attendant upon fluctuating hopes and fears as the possibility of release advances and retreats.*[173]

It was a paragraph RAF F/L Alfred Playfair repeated in his own journal and by January 1945 he wrote, 'I think I know what hunger is now. Getting colder, more snow damn roll on the summer or armistice.'[174] During the first weeks of January he returned to bed as soon as the morning parade was over, only to rise for whatever he could find for lunch, a slice of carefully rationed bread. If he could find the strength he walked for an hour in the snow. A good dinner was 2 ounces (56) of bully beef, two potatoes and 4 spoons of barley. If the pipes weren't frozen, it was a cold shower and bed. An avid reader in peacetime, he had lost all interest in reading because the dim light had resulted in vision difficulties, so he lay in his bunk enjoying 'thoughts and hopes for home and loved ones'.[175] Another freezing day and Playfair stayed in bed – and so the monotony continued. 'Very depressed' was all he could scrawl in his diary.

His depression was shared. RAAF WO Ronald Frank Davies (400342) incarcerated in Stalag 357 wrote:

> *For the rest of my life, I will never be able to forget the harsh facts of life as a prisoner of war. We went to bed hungry, we got up hungry, we rose from each mockery of a meal hungry, and we sat, stood, lay, or walked in a state of constant gnawing. … At night we dreamed we were free and at home, and we awoke anew to the dreadful reality. Each new morning, despair clawed at the guts again.*[176]

POWs in Stalag VI had been moved to Stalag 357 at Fallingbostel, in July 1944. It was described by one airman as a 'lousy billet, in the middle of a dirty, dreary camp … with the walls and floor just oozing damp'.[177] Illness increased as rain dripped through holes in the roof, and the humidity of the summer months exacerbated the sweat of too many within. In November large numbers of British troops marched into Stalag 357. Led by their formidable Regimental Sergeant Major (RSM) John Lord, they were members of the British 3rd Battalion Parachute Regiment captured at Arnhem. Consequently, the senior army NCO, RSM Turner assumed command. Aircrew insisted that their elected leader, WO Dixie Deans, continued to be in charge. 'A clash of wills ensued, but Deans proved stronger' and the army RSM relinquished control.[178]

WO Dixie Deans in discussion with German commandants (AWM).

At least WO Ron Davies had something to raise his spirits. The army, to his mind, constantly disregarded the war service of aircrew referring to him and others who wore the blue uniform as 'blue orchids'. The name was derogatory, supposedly, referring to the 'preciousness and scarceness' of air force personnel. How could

Aircrew at Stalag 357 (AWM).

they possibly understand the chilling fear in the middle of the night as one climbed the short steps into a cold and black bomber convinced that they were likely going to their death?

There were now 17,000 POWs crammed into the camp causing severe overcrowding. Each hut with bunks for 150 POWs now needed to accommodate 400. During the winter of 1944, 'the fuel position is grim, and without fires we cannot dry out our rooms'.[179] There were two roads through Stalag 357, made of crushed coke and slag mixed with soil then rolled. The POWs dug up and sifted the small fragments of coke from the slag and soil to help fuel stoves, but it did little to ameliorate conditions. During the early months of 1945 conditions deteriorated further and large tents were erected on the parade ground to house the unfortunate new arrivals. The food situation became desperate, and the POWs realised the end was coming one way or another.

WO Leslie 'Curly' James Terrett (418711) was a very long way from his temperate riverside hometown, Benalla, Victoria. He had enlisted at age 18 as a gunner and with less than 50 operational hours with RAF 158 he was shot down over Leipzig at 20. He had witnessed 'killings' in Stalag Luft 7 and 'reprisals' at 357. His opinion of Stalag 357 was 'large, muddy, and depressing'.[180] He was hungry but the price of a loaf of bread was 40 cigarettes, then it was 70 cigarettes. Terrett did not have 40 cigarettes or 70 cigarettes. It was uplifting that the Allied advance was getting closer but German guards were becoming increasingly dangerous. 'Our tables, stools, palliasses and other articles were confiscated. Reprisals were carried out against us.'[181] An estimated 734 Allied POWs died at Stalag 357 and nearby XIB.

At Luft III, Squadron Leader Lorraine Joseph Simpson (401542) had exhausted his human reserves.

The hours are very long, hours drag. Reading is difficult, writing impossible. Life is one long boredom from dawn to slumber, prison is odious, you feel a sense of constant humiliation in being confined in a small space, fenced in by wire, watched by armed men and webbed by a tangle of regulations.[182]

Camp leaders vainly attempted to settle POWs and asserted how vital it was that captivity acceptance continue. Negativity needed to be avoided but now close companions quarrelled over trifles and found little pleasure from each other's company. 'Petty quarrels are frequent' wrote Simpson, 'our senior officers keep reminding us "unity is strength"', but in his and other camps, 'hunger makes men very irritable, and they develop a quite intolerant and narrow attitude over relatively small matters.'[183]

WO Dixie Deans was busy defusing disagreements and disturbances. Once 'Jerry baiting' – making fun of the German guards, irritating them – had been a common practice, now it was dangerous, as guards became increasingly nervous, volatile, vindictive and more trigger-happy than before. There had been deaths in the camp, a prisoner had been shot while trying to escape; another, gunned down for having left his hut three minutes before the night curfew was over. Australian WO George Farrell had given up carving the days on the timber end of his bunk, it was months now – 10 months, 12, another Christmas with the dawning of a new year not looking any brighter. The guards were becoming 'increasingly arrogant and cruel. I would love to meet them after this.'[184] Wistful thinking – he couldn't convince himself that he, or they, would still be alive in the months ahead. By February 1945 the 900 British aircrew had around 9000 American companions. The camp was bursting at the seams and that could only mean one thing, another move; but where and for how long? Farrell and his camp leader Dixie Deans did not foresee how much worse it was to become.

Another with heavy responsibilities forced upon him was rear gunner WO Alistair McGregor Currie (407822). Prior to the war he had been manager of a sheep station. It had been a lot easier controlling sheep on the open plains of Western Australia than controlling the fate of repressed POWs, now he had assumed the position of camp leader at Stalag 344. 'Quite a deal of verbal struggling with the German Commandant'. Huts which were supposed to hold 112 held 160, huts that should only hold 124 held 175,'I was forever trying to get better sleeping conditions for the men.' Towards the end of 1944 he struggled to maintain discipline.'Morale generally varied with the food situation. When food was short the men became restless, found dissatisfaction with trivial matters.'[185] Joking exchanges turned into raised voices and full-blown arguments.

The questions were unavoidable. What if POW camps became the battlegrounds? With no convivial resolution concerning the men behind barbed wire, would the Germans withdraw? Were POWs to be murdered? The questions were about to be answered. During the first months of 1945, WO Alistair Currie observed, 'the exposure of POWs to danger of gunfire, bombing and other hazards of war', as well as 'beatings, other cruelties and executions'.[186] The marches were given different names: The Death March, The Long March, The Great March West, The Black March, The Bread March, The Lamsdorf Death March, The Shoe Leather Express. Regardless of the name, for the 257,000 British and American POWs, it meant the same: hundreds of kilometres endured over months of, 'beatings, starvation, amputations, frostbite, frozen feet and hands, dirt, lice, filth, degradation, heat, thirst and death, deprivation, misery and death'.[187]

CHAPTER SIXTEEN

'Men were constantly beaten ... men were tied or chained to carts or wagons for punishment.'

WO Alastair Currie (RAAF)

Thomas Patrick Lonergan was named after an uncle killed in WWI by German soldiers. In 1942 having just turned 18, the younger Thomas Lonergan enlisted in the RAAF to follow his namesake to a war in Europe. He became a member of the crew of Australian pilot, PO Cyril 'Cy' Borsht. On the 18th operation, in October 1944, their Lancaster was shot out of the sky by German soldiers. Borsht was sent to Luft III while his surviving crew, Lonergan, Australians F/S Ronald 'Glynn' Cooper, F/S Maxwell Staunton-Smith, an RAF F/S Sergeant Tom Laing, were deposited in Stalag VII.

Stalag VII camp leader WO Peter Angus Thomson (415285) was concerned for young men like Lonergan. The majority of aircrew for whom he was responsible were from comfortable city homes unused to the deprivations they needed to cope with as POWs. Thomson had worked underground in the gold mines of Western Australia and as a jackeroo in Queensland, living out of a swag on a diet of salt beef and damper, 'so this new life perhaps did not hit me as hard as some others'.[188] By late 1944 Thomson carried information he dared not share with those who filled the huts.

Adolph Hitler had argued for the deaths of more POWs as a deterrent to the Allied advance. Another suggestion he and SS Chief Heinrich Himmler favoured was that POWs be interned in the middle of major German cities to prevent further Allied bombing. Thomson was now informed by the German interpreter that Himmler had instructed camp commandants that if there was a chance of POWs falling into the hands of the Russians, they 'were to be shot'.[189] By the beginning of 1945 Hitler was planning his 'last redoubt' by moving around 35,000 Allied POWs into the Bavarian mountains as hostages for his own protection. Thomson never thought he could be grateful to the leader of the Nazi party.

It was a bitterly cold morning on 19 January 1945 when Lonergan and his fellow POWs were abruptly woken by shouting guards and barking dogs. Any slow to respond received a rifle barrel in the ribs. As they stumbled from their bunks they were ordered to pack and be on parade by 5 am. The searchlights reflected off the snow and ice over dishevelled men attempting to assemble their belongings. They were loath to leave any of the precious items so hard to acquire through inventiveness, trade and prudent conservation. Precious equipment such as blowers and camouflaged radios could not be left. It was agony to discard the disguised and forged items painstakingly prepared by the escapee hopefuls, but it was clear that only what could be carried could accompany each man. They layered themselves with all their clothes and blankets and quickly divided any remaining provisions, which they were warned needed to last for a two-and-a-half-day march, or four days, should transport not arrive. Lonergan carefully placed a tin of cocoa, a packet of tea, a tin of sausages and some margarine with the German issued rations consisting of '$1/7$th tin of meat, $2/3$rd loaf of bread, $1/8$th lb of margarine, $1/4$ lb honey, and 2 cheeses' into his improvised backpack.[190]

As 1,565 POWs passed out of the gates that had held them prisoner, they were ordered to stay in orderly columns and warned that for every man who fell by the side of the road, five would be shot. The screaming continued as German soldiers attempted to quicken the pace of emaciated POWs. Gunfire was enticingly close,

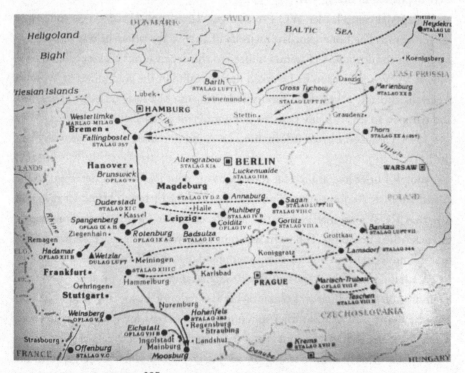

The movement of POWs.[285]

the flashes and sounds of the Allied advance. The Germans were clearly nervous, repeatedly shouting 'Die Russen kommen.' (Russians are coming.) The POWs would have preferred to remain in camp until the Russians arrived, but they were again pawns in a dangerous game.

In December 1944, the movement of POWs had started in earnest. Two days after Christmas 1944, POWs at Stalag VIIIB at Teschen, Poland, began their forced march through Czechoslovakia, towards Stalag XIIID at Nuremberg and finally to Stalag VIIA at Moosburg, Bavaria. In January 1945, Tom Lonergan's group of POWs were force marched from Stalag 7 to their final destination at Stalag IIIA at Luckenwalde, South of Berlin. On 20 January 1945, Stalag XXA POWs at Torun, Poland, were ordered onto roads and two days later Stalag 344 at Lamsdorf, Silesia, Prussia, was evacuated. On 23 January, POWs at Stalag XXB at Marienburg, Danzig, were ripped from their huts. POWs at Luft III, Sagan, were broken into different groups, one headed for Stalag IIIA, another to Marlag und Milag Nord, near Bremen, and the third to Nuremberg's Stalag XIIID, and then Stalag VIIA near Moosburg, Bavaria. On 6 February 1945, prisoners in Stalag IV at Gross Tychow, Pomerania, commenced their 86-day forced march to Stalag XIB and Stalag 357 at Fallingbostel. On 10 February 1945, Stalag VIIIA at Gorlitz, was evacuated. By the first week in April 1945, Nuremberg's Stalag XIIID and Fallingbostel's Stalag XIB and Stalag 357 were deserted.

The months of January and February 1945 were the coldest in the century. Blizzards, heavy snow and temperatures as low as −13° Fahrenheit (−25° Celsius) wreaked havoc within the ranks of poorly dressed prisoners already weakened by malnutrition and captivity. Made to walk up to 40 kilometres a day with little or no rations they scavenged for anything edible, digging in the frozen ground for root vegetables, consuming cattle fodder and eating cats, dogs and rats. When there was not fuel for fire, everything was eaten raw. Men needed to drink from muddy puddles and became ill. Unsanitary conditions combined with exhaustion and the frigid conditions resulted in pneumonia, pellagra, diphtheria, and dysentery. Body lice spread typhus. Trench foot, frostbite and blisters turned gangrenous. POWs unable to keep up were helped by their mates until they could be helped no longer, and bodies were left on the side of the road, German escorts not allowing any to be buried. Stragglers were sometimes escorted by guards into woods and executed. An estimated 8348 British and American POWs died between September 1944 and May 1945.

For Tom Lonergan the grand adventure of being aircrew had soured months earlier. He was one of 134 Australians, one of 1578 POWs in Stalag VII who had listened to the sound of heavy gunfire for days and optimistically contemplated

POW forced marches during January and February killed thousands. Painting by Alan Moore (AWM).

that he may yet celebrate his 21st birthday as a free man. Now he was just trying to stay alive, with the early morning January sky filled with artillery flashes. He was grateful to have secured a greatcoat and new boots and had thrown his bed blanket over his shoulders. 'Bitterly cold – nothing but ice and snow' and they 'passed by columns of retreating German soldiers'.191

By midday, weak men stumbled under their loads and the roadside was littered with books, musical instruments and some bulky objects. How greatly treasured these had been in the camp, items that had civilised an uncivilised existence, but now they were disposable as men battled the elements. Each time they stopped they were cautioned not to fall asleep and to warn mates to wake them should they do so. Tom and his crew mates stayed close. Max Staunton-Smith collapsed and Tom had to drag him to his feet. The following day Max returned the compliment. Through deep snow they were pushed 28 kilometres that first day. As night descended, they sheltered in farm outbuildings and the meal was bread and honey.

Again, they were woken before dawn and on the march by 6.30 am. Lonergan would write, 'Bitterly cold – fingers and ears quickly numbed.' The roads were choked with sad columns of individuals, the POWs stared at by civilian refugees, everyone moving slowly in the same direction, away from advancing Russians. They were pushed on before sheltering in a bombed-out brick building. The number of German guards had fallen to around 80, the aura of defeat obvious. The POWs were 'filthy dirty'. At least this time they were allowed to light fires and the cups of tea and coffee brewed helped ease the chill. The flesh of a dead horse was carved off and cooked.

On the march, trying to find something to eat or burn (AWM).

Each day the ordeal deepened. 'We are in poor shape,' Tom scribbled in his diary. 'Very cold, hungry, tired and despondent … the local population lining the street … abuse us.'[192] They continued to stumble through snow drifts, weakening with every kilometre, and the sick cart filled. Without horses it was left to POWs to pull and push the cart. Guards subjected to the same conditions were becoming increasingly irritable and trigger happy. On 21 January they were pushed on for 42 kilometres. Peter Thomson noted the temperature dropped to −13° Fahrenheit (−25°C) and 'men were picked up from the roadsides in a collapsed and frozen state'.[193] The river Oder was crossed shortly before it was bombed, the river below a solid block of ice. A distance of 34 kilometres, before they were permitted to shelter. Rations consisted of 100 grams of biscuits and half a cup of coffee per man.

The following day they were woken at 3 am and told they must now march at night. In the darkness men were slow to gather their belongings and guards discharged their firearms. Tom Lonergan, Max Staunton-Smith and Glynn Cooper stayed very close, even holding hands as the blizzard made it difficult to see the road. 'Terrible conditions – snow, ice and cold, men falling out on the way.'[194] After 24 kilometres and sheltering in barns outside Jenkwitz, Thomson 'ascertained that 23 men were lost and their whereabouts unknown'. A further 31 sick POWs

Composite illustration (Playfair).[286]

were taken away. Thomson's protests fell on deaf ears and 'nothing further has been heard of them'.[195]

It was 23 January and 20 kilometres. The next day it was 30 kilometres, a day's rest then 19 kilometres, then 21 kilometres then 22 kilometres. 'Men utterly exhausted', Thomson reported, and that the medical officer was having 'a bloody awful time with next to no medical equipment'. Frostbite was dangerous. Thomson observed too many blackened toes. All that could be done was for the toenail to be removed to relieve pressure and antiseptic applied. [196] The main problem was dysentery. No matter how much Thomson 'begged, the boys would eat snow and rotten food'.[197] There was only charcoal to alleviate symptoms.

No transport and no shelter so the POWs were pushed on. They stole milk, anything edible. If they lay for a short time on the mounds of earth where farmers stored winter root vegetables, the ice melted just enough for them to pull out turnips and potatoes. Eating raw root vegetables provided a fleeting feeling of fullness. 'Some of the blokes are catching starlings and sparrows for food', two days later a farmer put out slops for his pigs and 'we beat the pigs to it'.[198]

Again, and again, long before dawn they were ordered out. Any reluctance incurred warning shots. Exhaustion caused POWs to fall asleep during short rest breaks and they froze by the roadside. Max Staunton-Smith collapsed, and Tom Lonergan dragged him to his feet.

> *Cases of frostbite. Rumours that we have lost over 50 people during the two nights of the blizzard, and 10 or so guards frozen to death on the side of the road. Distance marched 2km … food issue half a packet of wafers 1/8 lb margarine … boots frozen.*[199]

On 25 January, from 4 am they covered 30 kilometres to Heidersdorf. During the day they crossed paths with POWs from Stalag VIIIB, who looked in worse condition than themselves. The columns cheered each other before being forced on their separate ways. This seemed insane: did the Germans know what they were actually doing? The routine was vicious, with each miserable day and night blending into another, the sick multiplying faster than the kilometres walked. Australian navigator WO Sam Birtles (418049) wondered if they 'wanted to live or die. It really was the worst feeling I've ever had in my life.'[200] Boots froze solid. German guards were hungry, cold and exhausted too and their sense of duty was almost admirable. Lonergan figured Aussies would have said 'Bugger this and left'. Some days 20 kilometres, others 30 kilometres, some days half a cup of soup, other days a piece of bread, 'very cold, hungry, tired and despondent … weather worsening; this march is becoming a nightmare'. On the last day of January cause for celebration: POWs received two cups of porridge and raw onions.

There was no alternative but to keep going because to stop was fatal, if the cold didn't kill you the Germans would. On 5 February they straggled into the Goldberg railway station. It was a relief to see a train awaiting. Again, they were shoved into cattle trucks, 54 POWs to each, cramped and unhygienic, but at least the marching was over – all 240 kilometres of it. Water was passed into the carriages but all they had to eat was the raw oats, flour and porridge they had left. Conditions rapidly 'become unbearable as men urinate, vomit and excrete in odd corners'.[201] Three days after they joined the train, they arrived at Luckenwalde, and marched into Stalag Luft IIIA, a camp already crammed with 20,000 POWs.

WO Peter Thomson recorded:

> *The morale of the men is extremely low. They are suffering from an extreme degree of malnutrition and an outbreak of dysentery. There are numerous cases of frostbite … They are quite unfit for any further moving.*[202]

In barracks intended to house 200 POWs, 400 now attempted to find any space to call their own. Beneath the floorboards stagnant water pooled, the floors were filthy and slimy. There were no bunks, palliasses, blankets or eating utensils. The first hot shower in three weeks and hot soup, were glorious. Exhaustion took over and men collapsed on a thin bundle of straw which did little to ward off the cold, but they were alive. Strength was slow to return, blisters slow to heal and mental wellbeing the slowest of all to overcome.

More aircrew arrived, in a terrible state after a long forced march. Lonergan caught sight of his skipper, PO Cy Borsht, before he disappeared into officer barracks. With so little to offer, no beds and cramped conditions, the resident POWs felt helpless to assist. The airmen were full of lice, exhausted, some clearly showing signs of frostbite and many with dysentery. They lay down on wood shavings on the floor and didn't move. All there was to offer was hot watery soup. 'Filth everywhere,' wrote Lonergan. It was distressing when one approached Lonergan to offer his watch for bread. 'He was an Aussie … Gave him half loaf. Told him to keep watch – very grateful.' Proud men reduced to begging. It was February and there were still no signs of Red Cross parcels. The German guards were increasingly prone to taking any cigarettes and provisions from the POWs at gunpoint. On 28 February three RAF and one Canadian raided the French storeroom of Red Cross parcels. They were shot.

Lonergan was a scrounger who changed identity discs with other POWs to join work parties outside the wire. He 'acquired' whatever he could by stealth or barter and was anxious to help his skipper Cy Borsht. Officer and NCO barracks were separated by a 20-foot-high (61 m) barbed wire perimeter fence with a road running down the middle. Set back 30 foot (91 m) from each perimeter fence were high warning wires. Germans stationed in the watchtowers shot anyone who stepped over a warning wire.

Borsht had indicated that they desired cigarette paper. Tom Lonergan stuffed some into a shoe polish tin and threw it over the wire fence. Unfortunately, the tin landed on the roof of a hut and then slid into the gutter. Borsht shimmied up the downpipe to collect it. From behind he heard a guard shout and the distinctive noise of a rifle being cocked. Borsht froze. He turned ever so slowly to notice Lonergan had stepped over the warning wire as a diversion and was offering the guard a packet of cigarettes. The guard uncocked his gun, took the cigarettes and walked away.

On 1 March nine wagons of Red Cross parcels arrived for the French. POWs stood by the wire salivating as they watched the parcels unloaded. The French refused to share, 'typical of the French' wrote Lonergan. American and British camp leaders approached the German commandant who agreed that these would indeed be shared. Two days later morale rose when each group of four were handed a parcel. A week later it was manna from heaven when 25 wagons containing 80,000 Red Cross parcels were delivered to the Americans, who shared equally. For Lonergan it was the largest meal for months. 'Two tins of "Kam" between four, and a milk pudding. I am as full as a sack of oats.'[203] Three days later another 18 wagons arrived. Clearly the Allies were ensuring these were allowed through. The POWs were overjoyed; surely now they could survive until being freed. With fuller stomachs and radio news that the forces of both General Patton and Field Marshal Montgomery had crossed the Rhine, almost a party atmosphere was enjoyed, rugby and soccer games were played, and gambling left some with more cigarettes and others fewer.

Yet again the celebrations proved premature, and despondency descended, 'Where the bloody hell were the Allies?' The bounty of Red Cross parcels had been consumed; now a box of raw potatoes could be exchanged for 100 cigarettes. Three hundred officers, including Cy Bosht were removed from camp, it was believed for a place named Moosburg. Two aircrew attempted escape and were shot dead, 'one had four bullet wounds … bad blow to my morale'.[204]

Similar tragedies were taking place as columns of emaciated POWs were pushed beyond the limits of human endurance, across an area of 500 square miles (1300 km). WO Alistair Currie could have been amused had the circumstances not been so grim. He had been a sheep station manager in the vast hot plains of New South Wales. For ten years he had overlooked the day-to-day running of 'Wirryilka Station' near Menindee. Now he was the herder of aircrew in a freezing European winter, and he felt powerless to assist them. For more than three long years he had been a POW. He could only just recall being home for his daughter Jane's eighth birthday. She was now 12 and her sister Janet going on 10. He had thought of them and his wife Isabel throughout the endless days of captivity, and had escaped once to work his way home to them, but was recaptured.

Currie was elected camp leader and compound commander at Stalag 344 Lamsdorf. The responsibilities were many and taxing, not only dealing with German authorities, but relations within the camp required great diplomacy and patience, even tension between army and air force personnel. Increasingly 'the men became restless' and 'dissatisfied'.[205] RAAF POWs, 84 of them, had preferred their own company. It wasn't that they didn't wish to mix with the others, but they did not need to explain the colloquialisms, or to justify their own war experience.

From 22 January 1945 Currie was the leader of the POW column forced from Stalag 344 on the horrific 270-kilometre Lamsdorf Death March, attempting to keep these men moving and alive. As the POWs became weaker and the guards

A long march (AWM).

even more impatient the situation deteriorated. He was powerless as a guard killed a POW and a Canadian airman was wounded by another guard. 'Men were constantly beaten … men were tied or chained to carts or wagons for punishment.'[206] He protested to the Germans about their 'disregard' of the Geneva Convention but the 'beating and flogging of the sick by sadistic idiots' did not stop. Currie reminded himself that, most of his crew did not have the opportunity to return home. Aussie pilot Sgt Einar Due (404876) and second pilot P/O R. E. Greenwell (403170) nor the Englishmen, Flt/Sgts Sheahan and Ives. He had spoken of herding sheep with Due, who had been a grazier outside Roma, Queensland. The bodies of his crew had been washed ashore near St Nazaire, France. He could clearly remember their laughter. He just had to keep going for them, for Isabel, Jill and Janet, but the body and spirit were waning as his own loss of weight, strength and mental exhaustion caused him to doubt.

RAF WO Dixie Deans had been a most worthy camp leader at Luft IV Gross Tychow and Stalag 357. From 6 February 1945 he found himself in charge of 2000 POWs on a month-long march across Poland and Germany to Stalag XIB at Fallingbostel. Unfortunately, his group expanded with more POWs, and they were forced back on the roads in the direction of Lubeck. WO Jack Garland (RAAF)

POWs on the march from Lamsdorf (AWM).

had been one of Deans's trusted and industrious committee men, now Garland felt fear for the unknowing and fear of the knowing that the Germans could act ruthlessly. American Red Cross–issued blankets were used to make a pack of sorts to hold precious belongings,'as the Goons told us to evacuate'.[207]

They marched, straggled on, feeling fortunate to find a barn for shelter. The only meal invariably was steamed potatoes coated in 'the good soil of Germany also protected and flavoured with an ample coverage of cow manure'.[208] No longer was it possible to find splendour in the sight of fresh deep snow glistening under a winter sun, there was only the urgency in keeping up with the column and scrounging for food. Kohlrabi was a vegetable that could be cooked for hours and still remain hard and flavourless. Turnips were no more flavoursome. One day 25 kilometres, another 38 kilometres, herded into open fields covered by snow and told this was where they would sleep. POWs dug small holes, to crawl into. Being dressed in all the clothes they owned did little to ease the discomfort, men huddled together for body warmth but there was little of that. Those with intact boots had the dilemma of whether to remove them at night. To leave them on meant trench foot; if they removed them, it was difficult to get swollen feet back into boots and that meant frostbite. Fourteen days and 237 kilometres through snow, sleet and rain in 'a Godforsaken country'.[209] They were told that groups of two and three had

Passing a German flak tower such as that which had shot so many out of the sky. Painting by Alan Moore (AWM).

better chances of surviving and they scratched the earth for frozen potatoes, ate them raw and suffered dysentery. 'Dysentery again rearing its ugly head ... for those who needed to squat urgently by the side of the road, a rifle butt.'[210]

Then there was nothing to eat and nothing to scrounge. Garland and his small band decided to improvise.

> It occurred to us that horses survive by chewing chaff and we attempted to make
> a soup from it, chaff does not get any softer the longer it is stewed so it was a case
> of drinking the resultant clear soup and acknowledging that you would need the
> constitution of a horse to digest chaff.[211]

Garland's father had been to Gallipoli and had spoken of the horror of lice infection, which spread typhus, now he too was so cursed. Weeks of deprivation and cruelty saw only the strongest survive. Older guards were falling with exhaustion also. Water was in very short supply and 'we purchased it from the guards at five cigarettes per cup.'[212] Those without cigarettes went thirsty.

Finally, a train, but the trip was gruesome, POWs crowded into a rail truck with 80 others, most suffering from dysentery, 'tempers were frayed, and they were awash in faeces and urine– one man died'.[213] The trip took only an hour but they were left in the cattle truck for 23 hours. They knew not where they were, unaware they had just crossed the German border. Their thoughts were on survival, sheltering from the penetrating cold, attempting to ward off frostbite and dysentery. Another river to cross, the Elbe, unaware that they were close to yet another POW camp, IVB, which contained another throng of POWs. It was the end of March when they reached Stalag 357 situated in Fallingbostel, north of Hanover, 52 days and 518 kilometres, later. It was a massive camp with 20,000 French, 30,000 Russians and 1500 Commonwealth POWs. Conditions in the Commonwealth compound were appalling and even the guards would not enter for fear of typhus. On 6 April 1945 they were ordered out again, joining thousands of other POWs to march again. Night merged into day, days into weeks Commonwealth and American men who had once been warriors were now consumed with staying alive.

The marches had different names, some covered 500 miles (800 km) others nearly 930 miles (1500 km). On 17 December 1944, at what became known as the Malmedy Massacre the SS had murdered 71 American POWs. Between September 1944 and May 1945, the official estimate of Commonwealth and American POW deaths was 3500, but this did not account for the unaccounted for. A later estimate was 8348.[214]

CHAPTER SEVENTEEN

'We were waiting and waiting for the Yanks or the Russians to get us out of the place, but they weren't in a hurry.'

WO Albert Stobart (RAAF)

WO Albert 'Bert' Stobart did not realise how fortunate he was. 'Fortunate' is not a word he was using during his captivity in the first months of 1945, but Stalag IVB was one of the few camps not evacuated, its POWs spared the horrors of the marches.

Bert wondered if he could survive the terrible winter of 1945, if he could survive the overcrowding, 'more prisoners arriving', if he could survive on the near negligible rations. For the entire month of March, he received half a Red Cross parcel and the 'skilly' (soup) each day had become merely brown water. If he was 'fortunate', he found something resembling a piece of turnip or potato, sometimes it was just grass. 'No food, no nothing.' He hated the cold but at least the cold limited the spread of illness. By March with the weather warming up, 'Typhoid and diphtheria epidemic causing quarantine ... disease prevalent'.

It was purely the news of the Allied advance that sustained life now. His 23rd birthday on 11 April 1945 was 'uneventful', in the normal sense. Machine-gun fire and booms from larger guns surrounded the camp. A small tank battle was observed. Fighters tore across the sky, 'air raids are getting thicker and closer and heavier. The Russians are coming, so are the Americans.'

Fellow Australian IVB POW, WO Gordon Stooke, could not resist the call of nature any longer and walked briskly towards the latrine. He felt the 'rat-a-tat-tat' of machine gun fire an instant before he heard it and 'hit the dirt'.[215] A United States P51 Mustang roared over his head. Stooke froze and then slowly took account of his various body parts. All seemed intact. A bullet clip was embedded in the ground just above his head. He reached out and picked it up – a souvenir which stayed with him the rest of his life.

German guards were downcast and muttered to anyone who would listen, 'Deutschland kaput' (Germany finished). There was little sympathy but as a precaution they stayed indoors and at night remained dressed. Between the noise of battle and great anticipation, there was little sleep. The morning of 23 April, Bert and others emerged to silence, 'the German guards had gone'. The threatening watchtowers were empty. A cheer echoed throughout Stalag IVB. They expected to see Russian soldiers with automatic weapons at the ready reinforced by tanks, and armoured cars arrive. Instead, a single Russian appeared and opened the camp gates. Three Cossacks on horseback rode up to the Russian compound and rode out again. It was an anticlimax; however, the gates were open, no-one, friend or foe, was around, 'we were liberated'. Or were they? A conference was quickly held, and it was decided that the gates should be closed again, but at least this time from the inside. 'We realised we had to be careful not to be caught up in the crossfire between the remaining Germans and Russians.' 'Free' a word which came more readily to the lips than 'fortunate'.

The Russians offered no food so small parties were sent to forage. Hunger was acute and Bert joined groups sent to take chickens and rabbits from German farms, anything edible. It felt so very strange walking on the outside. Locals were accorded no sympathy by hordes of starving POWs. They waited and waited, 'we were waiting and waiting for the Yanks or the Russians to get us out of the place, but they weren't in a hurry.' They had needed to be patient for months, years, there was no more patience. 'We thought the Americans would send trucks to collect us. We thought they might put on some aircraft but no they didn't.'

More Russian soldiers arrived. The German commandant had remained, and

(Stobart)

a Russian walked up to him, drew his revolver and shot the commandant dead.

WO John Hunter (RAAF) was the elected camp leader of Australians in IVB, and his frustration increased daily. Liberation meant so little for his POWs. They listened to the BBC and heard the 8 May celebrations to mark 'Victory Day Europe', but in his camp the German guards had been replaced by Russian ones. By 15 May, 'God, it gets almost unbearable to think we have

(iwm.org.uk)

been free in name for over three weeks but that we are no nearer home and loved ones.'[216]

More days and the BBC's jubilant broadcasts caused resentment and disillusionment. When the Americans were so near and had transport for them, why could they not be allowed to go. 'We would not mind any discomfort if we were amongst our own troops and hearing our own language.'[217] Did anyone really care about them? Had authorities and families forgotten? The thoughts were irrational, but these were not rational times.

Germany was in turmoil and POWs were again mere pawns in yet another battle for conquest, power and prestige. Splintered British and American forces were hamstrung in their attempts to free POWs. United States and Russian forces linked up at the River Elbe, but it was all about the race to Berlin. On 30 April, the Russians won the race and Hitler committed suicide.

On 16 April 1945 those incarcerated in the infamous Colditz Castle were liberated by British soldiers. Stalags 357 and XIB (at nearby Fallingbostel), when liberated by units of the 2nd British Army, were found to contain mostly Australians and New Zealanders. Members of the US 14th Armoured Division were horrified at the condition of the American and Commonwealth POWs they liberated at

They were forced to continuing marching from advancing forces (AWM).

Stalag VIIA, Moosburg, on 29 April. Built to hold 14,000, Stalag VIIA now held 130,000 from evacuated stalags with 500 living in barracks built for 200. Some lived in tents while others slept in air-raid slit trenches. At Stalag 344 the Russians arrived, locked the gates, and refused to allow American and Commonwealth POWs to leave. Two weeks later a US colonel held a gun to the head of the Russian commandant and threatened to kill him. The POWs were repatriated.

Elsewhere, the roads were strewn with exhausted and starving POWs. The group led by RAF WO Dixie Deans, and which included Australian WOs, Lyle Doust and Jack Garland, had arrived at Stalag 357 at Fallingbostel on the last day of March. Many had died. Doust counted the Australians, the numbers had diminished and there were only 37 left. Survivors were drained and traumatised. Painstakingly they had accumulated a few belongings and attained a small feeling of self. Now they were a pitiful group retaining only the clothes they wore, reminiscent of when they had fallen from fury into hell. As many as 12 men needed to share one towel and 10 a toothbrush. Stalag 357 was not conducive to recovery. Already overcrowded with POWs living in corrugated cardboard sheds no larger than 'big dog kennels', there was no food or supplies.[218] On 6 April the POWs were ordered out of the camp to march north-east to the Baltic. For 12,000 POWs, some retracing the route already endured, the nightmare continued.

Columns split and men dropped by the road. Deans commandeered a bicycle to ride up and down the road encouraging men to look after each other and 'survive'. On 19 April near the village of Gresse, Germany, further rage was released from above. The sound of aircraft caused POWs to turn and look to the sky. Four RAF

(McCleery)[287]

Typhoon fighter bombers came into view. Recognising the RAF insignia, they cheered. The fighters circled, dropped altitude, and attacked. It happened too quickly for weakened men. Cannon fire strafed the lines, red hot shrapnel pierced flesh and destroyed lives. The last Typhoon pilot realised that these were not retreating German soldiers and climbed rapidly, but friendly fire had already lain waste their own and the road was littered with the dead and injured. The irony was not lost on those who now buried their dead in the local church yard: 60 Allied soldiers and airmen who had endured so much as POWs, killed by their own, so close to liberation. The incident and deaths were not included in the official RAF WWII history and families were told no more than 'died as a POW'.

WO Dixie Deans approached the German escort and demanded that he be permitted to cross no-man's-land under a white flag to contact advancing Allies to ensure his men were not attacked again. This he did and, ignoring invitations to remain, returned to his men. The POWs marched for a further 13 days before halting in a village and refusing to go any further. Since 6 February, they had marched between 600 and 700 miles (966 to 1127 km) in 85 days. On 2 May small arms fire and the grinding engine and track noise of British tanks meant they were finally free.

F/O James McCleery (RAAF) had departed his country, as a 20-year-old pilot

(McCleery)

in 1943 with fellow West Australian, 22-year-old WOP Victor Widdup; Victorian 20-year-old navigator Wesley Betts, and South Australian bomb aimer 22-year-old, Henry Long. In England they had teamed up with 20-year-old Western Australian air gunner Donald Dyson. Determined to remain together they were pleased to be posted to RAAF 460 where two Englishmen completed the crew. As aircrew deaths increased, McCleery was appointed leader of 460 'C' flight. He was 21. On the night of 11 May 1944, during an attack on the railway yards at Hasselt, Belgium, McCleery and crew were shot down by a night fighter. Dyson somehow evaded capture. Long found himself shunted into Luft 7. Widdup was sent to Stalag 357. McCleery and Betts were sent to Luft III.

Just before midnight on 27 January 1945, with the Russians less than 16 miles (26 km) away, 11,000 POWs were forced from Luft III in 6 inches (15 cm) of snow and freezing temperatures. After 50 miles (81 km) they arrived at Spremberg. Broken into groups, some marched to Stalag VIIA at Moosburg, others to Stalag XIIID at Nürnberg. The Luft III group which included F/L Peter Kingsford-Smith (RAAF) marched towards Marlag und Milag Nord, a camp of Royal Navy and British Merchant Navy POWs, located 19 miles (30 km) from Bremen. They were overtaken by British forces near Lubeck on 2 May and repatriated to England on 8 May.

James McCleery's group trudged on for a week to Stalag IIIA near Luckenwalde, 50 kilometres from Berlin. During the search at the gates a German soldier took exception to a cartoon in McCleery's diary, which depicted a POW digging a tunnel below a German guard. 'He grabbed the bloody book ... yelling at me and hit me on the back with the rifle butt.'[219] McCleery would not let go of his most precious possession. A German officer appeared to determine what the commotion was about. The soldier ranted and fumed, and the book was opened at the cartoon. The officer burst into laughter and handed the book back to McCleery.

On 21 April heavy artillery, mortar and machine-gun fire surrounded the camp.

It seemed they were under attack by all sides, and at midday the German guards disappeared. F/S Tom Lonergan and his mate F/S Max Staunton-Smith had found themselves in Stalag IIIA and were attempting to remain positive. A flight of United States Marauder medium bombers flew low over the camp, and POWs scattered. A detachment of SS in nearby woods, and local Hitler youth, meant anyone straying outside the wire was likely to be shot. Last stand resistance caused the Russians to shell the town. On 22 April, the Russians assumed charge of Stalag Luft IIIA. On 23 April, a Messerschmidt strafed the POW huts. 'We tumbled out of our three-storey bunks and huddled on the floor.'[220]

Jim McCleery was not yet 22 and found himself senior air force officer, a responsibility which weighed heavily. Days went by and the gates remained locked. There was no food, 'we were worse off than with Germans ... the food situation was grossly inadequate'.[221] A great influx of Italian refugees had added immensely to the overcrowding and severely degraded sanitary conditions. McCleery complained to the Russians that POWs had suffered enough and should be freed – he was ignored. An American representative arrived from Supreme Allied Headquarters with orders to evacuate British and Americans, but Russians refused to accept his credentials. Despite assurances, 'we now saw the Russians actively preventing such repatriation'.[222] Risking physical punishment, McCleery approached the Russian commandant and demanded that he be allowed to communicate with Allied Command. He was pushed aside.

Commonwealth aircrew were separated from other POWs and asked to give personal details. Unclear where this was leading, McCleery advised the Australians not to provide accurate information. Something may have been lost in translation but strangely all the Australians were named, 'Ned Kelly or Glen Rowan pub'.[223] They were then asked to volunteer to fly Russian aircraft. No-one volunteered. The Russians were unimpressed and removed the small amount of food that remained.

How could they keep going? When was this captivity and deprivation going to end? Every POW knew the same questions echoed in the minds of their fellows. Tom Lonergan admitted he was 'getting more and more depressed'.[224] Local village women were now attempting to enter the POW camp to 'save them from the Russian soldiers who were raping every woman in sight'.[225] The mood within camp was very unsettled and confused. The Battle of Berlin had finished on 2 May. On 4 May 1945, British Field Marshal Bernard Montgomery accepted an unconditional surrender of all German forces at Lüneburg, from General Admiral Hans-Georg von Friedeburg, and General Eberhard Kinzel. Yet, POWs attempting to leave Stalag IIIA were forcibly stopped by Russian soldiers.

United States trucks arrived at the gates of Stalag Luft IIIA. Lonergan and others eagerly climbed on board but Russian soldiers surrounded the trucks and at gunpoint POWs were escorted back inside the camp. 'The Americans had no alternative but to leave without us.'[226] Lonergan and his best mate Max Staunton-Smith could take no more and on 11 May they sneaked past the sentries and walked away. Having walked 12kilometres they were stopped by a Russian soldier who pointed back to the camp. The two Australians muttered obscenities and kept walking. The Russian fired over their heads. There was no alternative 'we trudged back to the camp.'[227]

Another day and another American appeared to tell the Russians there were five army trucks waiting to collect POWs. The Russians again refused. As he was leaving the US officer communicated to McCleery that they were waiting down the road among some trees. McCleery gathered as many POWs as he could to sneak through an opening in the barbed wire and into the woods. The two truckloads of Stalag Luft III POWs had only driven a short distance when they were pulled over by Russians on motorcycles and instructed to follow. The American drivers offered a friendly gesture and obliged. As soon as they approached a junction, they swerved the trucks in a different direction, to a former factory that they had commandeered.

The same impatience was occurring in Stalag IVB. WO Keith Skidmore left as soon as he could, accompanied by another Australian. They trudged on to the Elbe River, only to be stopped by Russians. There was much gesticulating and only when they had been searched roughly, stripped of any valuables, including watches, were they allowed to walk gingerly across the bombed bridge. American soldiers waited on the other side and the treatment was entirely different.

Bert Stobart and two mates decided the claustrophobic camp could no longer be tolerated. They walked out of the gates on a food foraging expedition and kept walking. The chaos in the next village was disturbing. Russian soldiers roamed free, looting, and cruelly abusing the inhabitants. A German family approached the Australian aircrew to be guests in their house, indicating that the presence of Allied POWs ensured the family's physical safety. 'Come and stay with us. We will keep you, feed you, everything, come and stay with us.' The family consisted of women and children. The man of the household had been a Luftwaffe Stuka pilot who had been killed. The world had just become even more bizarre. Bert was living in a house to protect the family of a Luftwaffe pilot.

While we were there, we never saw a Russian, you saw the furniture being taken out of other houses in the street. And the big trucks being filled up with stuff, but they never came near this one.

After a couple of days, regardless of the pleas for them to stay, the urge to reach Allied lines could no longer be ignored. Bert felt a confusion of emotions, most of which he could not comprehend, but most prominent was the guilt he felt turning away from the fearful faces of the women in the German household. War was a savage beast, particularly for non-combatants. As they moved through the city of Leipzig, a city now in name only, the confusion did not ease. 'Well and truly bombed, shattered, devastation, a whole big mess of rubble.' He and his fellow Bomber Command aircrew had been complicit, but thoughts of dead crew and mates offered some justification.

CHAPTER EIGHTEEN

'We didn't realise how precarious our situation had been.'

WO Bert Stobart (RAAF)

They had been through trauma and physical deprivation only they could appreciate. They had been surrounded by gunfire, under siege from the enemy and allies, and prayed so long for freedom. It mattered not who stormed through the gates, be it Russian or British, horse or tank; they just wanted it over and to go home. They despaired but were unaware they were cruelly caught up in political posturing.

The Americans became more proactive. At one camp their trucks arrived and POWs quickly boarded. Russian sentries attempted to stop the repatriation. The trucks smashed through the closed gates. The 20th of May was a very good day. Negotiations finally resulted in the Russians agreeing to transport the remaining British and American POWs to the River Elbe for transfer to the Allies on prisoner exchange. The power morass concluded, 1000 for 1000. 'We were counted across the bridge ... an exchange of supposed allies.'[228]

Australian Observer WO Assheton Taylor (413687) hobbled across the bridge, his feet covered in large blisters. His arms were firmly grasped by a burly American, and he was given a hearty welcome before being lifted into a waiting truck. His relief was immense; finally he could relax and no longer was there 'a risk of being shot in the back by an unfriendly German or Russian ... freedom ... wonderful'.[229] The exchange took half a day before trucks transported the weary POWs to a captured German airfield outside Halle, via the city of Leipzig. They marvelled that they could carry on loud conversations without fear of retribution. Australian soldiers had added an AIF brand to their vehicle and the opportunity to ridicule defeated German soldiers was not missed.

There was less frivolity as they drove through Leipzig. Trucks needed to slow and detour to avoid bomb craters. They were astounded at the damage caused by the Allied bombing offensive, buildings reduced to rubble and others Taylor observed as 'blackened and empty skeletons' the result of fire storms.[230] It looked different from ground level. Bert Stobart regarded the 'truly messed up, shattered' city and attempted to justify it but platitudes like 'the so and sos' got what they

Incident on a Journey, painting by Alan Moore (AWM)

asked for … they fought a war and lost' seemed to fall flat and he turned his mind back to, 'I must get home.'

They were shells of the men they once were. 'We were a bunch of tottering skeletons,' admitted WO Jack Liley, lice-ridden and filthy.[231] They were treated with care and reverence. Basic medical attention was administered, blankets were provided, and food supplied. They marvelled at walking into a large mess hall, sitting down at tables covered in clean cloths, with cutlery they had almost forgotten how to use, to be served hot, well-cooked food. Food, glorious food; and yes, they could ask for more, 'until our tummies were full'.[232] Few could resist although they were cautioned to take care with undernourished digestive systems. Jim McCleery could not. 'Sweet corn, eggs, bacon, spinach, pancakes, three biscuits and a cup of tea. Went round again.'[233]

Bert Stobart had lost 40 per cent of his body weight and considered himself lucky. He had always been slight. Larger men looked the worst; or so he thought until he caught sight of himself in a full-length mirror. It was startling: his ribs protruded and his legs and arms were bony. He was uncertain what he enjoyed most in those first hours of glorious freedom, the relief, or the food. 'Treated marvellously, fed the best of food.' He appreciated the gentle manner of those who assisted, so very different to the harsh, strident behaviour of his former captors. It

Delousing, painting by Alan Moore (AWM).

was disquieting to hear that Hitler had demanded that 'all POWs be shot before capitulation'. 'We didn't realise how precarious our situation had been.'

Dakota DC3s ferried Commonwealth POWs to Brussels, Belgium, pilots deviating from the flight plan to circle the German city of Cologne. WO Gordon Stooke (RAAF) was travelling with fellow Stalag IVB POW, Bert Stobart, and they were shocked by the devastation below. 'We could have easily been convinced that we were looking down at a huge treeless cemetery.'[234] The delousing with thick grey powder was necessary but unenjoyable and that is the condition in which they were taken to another airfield for the long-awaited evacuation to England. For aircrew, there was an additional surprise.

RAAF POWs had wondered if they had been abandoned but, 'The Scheme for the Repatriation of RAAF POW ex-Germany', had been carefully planned months previously. Now the three phases were implemented.

Phase 1: The collection from prison camps in Germany and movement to the UK.

Phase 2: Reception holding and embarkation to Australia.

Phase 3: Reception and disposal in Australia.[235]

While much of the population of the United Kingdom were celebrating

A German airfield with Dakotas awaiting, painting by Alan Moore (AWM).

peace in Europe, members of RAAF 463 and RAAF 467 squadrons sat again in briefing rooms. This time the operation was very different. There was no red thread indicating a deadly route through flak and night fighters, no intelligence on which city or military installation was to be targeted. For RAAF F/O Raymond John Kelly (431104) and crew, 'It was great for aircrew as it meant that no longer had one to wake in the morning to see if we had flight duty. We could look to a future and make plans.'236

Kelly had been unable to enlist in the RAAF until May 1943, and join RAAF 463 Squadron until late 1944. He had missed the worst raids conducted by Bomber Command but the service and sacrifice of aircrew who undertook the fury of those operations was to be admired. He and members of his crew eagerly volunteered for operations to bring these survivors, these heroes, to safety. 'We were pleased to have the opportunity to bring our fellow Aussies and others back to safety.'237

As they flew over Europe in daylight the physical devastation of war was blatantly obvious. So much destruction everywhere. Bomb and artillery craters on the Brussels runway had been hastily filled and made for a bumpy landing.

Kelly was unsure what to expect but was shocked by the sight of those he was to fly to England. A sad motley collection of bedraggled men awaited. A few had refused to give up their dirt-encrusted faded remnants of RAAF battle dress. The rest were clothed in a variety of non-matching uniforms not necessarily adhering

Briefing RAAF 463 Squadron to evacuate POWs (AWM).

to the service to which they belonged. They were haggard and stooped but Kelly thought he saw eyes brighten as he disembarked wearing full RAAF battledress and with AUSTRALIA emblazoned on his shoulders. The POWs were 'naturally subdued, and it was difficult to get them to talk'.238 Kelly's crew appreciated how precious their cargo was – it was clear from the solemn expressions and emaciated bodies how savage life as a German POW had been. The mood on board was sombre, 'Very few words were spoken in flight' but clearly 'the released men [were] amazed and delighted to be flying to freedom'.239

When RAAF POWs arrived at Brussels airport, waiting for them were the specially modified Lancaster bombers. Climbing the short steps and smelling the scent of grease and fuel evoked complex emotions. Bert Stobart mounted the short ladder and smelt the scent of grease. He was numb and his hands gripped his knapsack. He had left those makeshift eating utensils, the physical vestiges of POW life. He carried now only the most valuable items from the previous years: the painting of Noel, artwork that had sustained him during his time as a 'kreiger', his diary and the bundle of letters from Noel and his family that had fed his soul and encouraged him to endure. They could never appreciate how nourishing those precious letters had been, how many times they had been read and re-read and shared with mates hungry for news of normal life.

He looked at fellow POW aircrew as they sat again in a Lancaster. They

From Brussels, painting by Alan Moore (AWM).

relished being in the RAAF hands again but there were noticeable twitches as they wrestled with the memory of their last RAF bomber operation. He too had unpleasant flashes, of his own Lancaster crashing into the ground and bursting into flames, knowing that within it life was extinguished, of crew mates who could never return home.

Bert allowed himself to be lulled by the familiar throb of the Merlin engines, and this time no rear gunner hypervigilance was required. Over the intercom came a voice announcing they were approaching the English coastline. Eager eyes peered and moistened. Bert realised a smile creased his face as the Lancaster touched down. No longer was he sitting in a freezing rear turret, feeling the last and first bump as the bomber lifted off and landed. He wouldn't miss that, or the fear. 'England after 21 months, was simply marvellous in fact words cannot express my feelings.'

It was 16 May, and they could not wait to alight, assisted from the aircraft by members of the Women's Auxiliary Air Force (WAAF) – English women, a sight to behold. During the Death March, Australian WO Sam Birtles had wondered if he 'wanted to live or die', now he struggled to hold back the tears when a young English woman helped him from the aircraft saying, 'Welcome home darling, it's good to have you back.'[240] It really was 'the worst feeling I've ever had in my life.'[241] They were walked to the closest hanger, a space no longer full of ground crews feverishly repairing flak and bullet holes in wings and fuselages, so these

Painting by Alan Moore (AWM).

aircraft could fly again at night. The hanger was now occupied by canteen workers who with soothing greetings offered as many biscuits, cups of tea and cigarettes as anyone could wish for.

There was too much to take in during the next days. The first long hot shower with soap was glorious, as was a haircut and proper shave. Debriefing sessions were conducted to assist authorities in authenticating deaths, to catalogue POW treatment to ensure criminal proceedings could be taken against cruel perpetrators. A real bed and clean white sheets would take some getting used to, as would the new Bond Street tailored RAAF blue uniform, with impressive new warrant officer rank insignias and peaked cap. Much anticipated contact with family in Australia was permitted. The words didn't come easily because all Bert could think of was, 'We're back, we're free.'

The United Kingdom was still suffering from food rationing, and it caused some amusement when ex-POW airmen were accorded 'expectant mother' food ration cards, entitling them to twice the normal ration of eggs, milk, fresh fruit, cheese and meat to expedite their return to health. 'Everyone was super, and boy did we appreciate it. At times the old lump would rise in the throat.' The station canteen also provided light meals and snacks and Bert wrote 'I am putting on weight.'

The first POWs were repatriated to England on 4 May. Operation Exodus resulted in Bomber Command conducting around 2900 flights over 23 days to evacuate 72,500 POWs. Australian authorities realised how important it was to ensure everything ran smoothly, and rapidly transported RAAF aircrew to the Brighton transit centre.

There must be some organisation to deal with these chaps as quickly and efficiently as possible ... it needs to be 'perfect' as it will play a big part in the ultimate rehabilitation and assimilation either into service duties again or back into civilian life.[242]

It was so strange to be billeted again on the same coastline to which they had arrived from Australia, young and eager RAAF aircrew, unaware of how little they knew or what the future held. Bert recalled clearly the Canadian officer in charge of the Bournemouth centre, complaining about 'the rotten, crook food'. That bloke didn't know what, 'rotten, crook food' was, least of all no food – he needed to do time as a POW before he could make that complaint. And the other statement with which he greeted Australian aircrew, 'It's a hell of a war but it's better than no war at all.' Bert wished he could run into that Canadian

Far from a German POW camp, enjoying Brighton (AWM).

again. Being in Brighton preparing to return to Australia suited him simply fine. There were pubs to visit, movie theatres and in particular, 'Kriegies Corner'.

Authorities were keen to see that all handling of the 900 or so RAAF personnel was undertaken with complete 'understanding and sympathetic to their needs'.243 It was a challenge never undertaken before. From April, in ever increasing numbers until the middle of May, as many as 150 ex-POW airmen a day arrived. A priority was that they were able to access 'a good meal' regardless of the time, day or night. It was acknowledged that POWs were likely to 'act abnormally to any administrative blunders or hitches' and every effort was required to avoid unsettled situations.244 Fellow RAAF aircrew were assigned to meet and brief the ex-POWs, as it was unlikely that they could relax in the company of civilians or even other service members. While 're-education' was needed, particularly for POWs who had been prisoners for years, there was an awareness that this needed to be undertaken at a calm and easy pace.

The Australian Red Cross had undertaken a popular initiative, 'Kriegies Corner', near Brighton's Metropole Hotel. POWs had been crowded into small rooms, sharing beds, scant rations, and never alone. Now they had their own room, or shared a Metropole Hotel room with one other, as well as the freedom to move where and when they liked. It took getting used to.

Wandering into Kriegies Corner meant the company of others attempting the

'Kriegies Corner' (AWM).

same adjustment, recognising men who had shared their lives, and never needing to explain what medical authorities clinically referred to as 'physical disabilities, psychological disturbances as a result of their confinement harsh treatment and isolation in camps'.[245] Bert, like the other POWs, needed to work on the 'disabilities' and 'disturbances' part but the word 'isolation' was not a camp thing, it was a freedom thing.

Bert Stobart fattening up in Britain (Stobart).

There simply were not enough seats in the Brighton theatre to accommodate all the ex-RAAF POWs being briefed for their trip home. It was essential for their morale and the morale of their families that they return quickly but there simply were not enough ships available. Around 100 RAAF airmen remained in hospitals, too weak to move. The remainder were then medically graded, with those carrying medical conditions given priority. Bert was not in the highest category, which commonly held survivors of the forced marches. He was encouraged to rest and fatten up.

'Really great to be in uniform again,' Bert wrote.

Sitting room only for the briefing of ex-RAAF POWs for homeward journey (AWM).

The urge to return to Australia was strong but he was given leave, and with back pay in his pocket there was plenty to enjoy. Plenty of fresh pads and ink to write letters home. To communicate thoughts and wishes to Noel concerning their future marriage and the life they would lead. Train passes allowed for trips to London and then onto the pastor's house in Cornwall. Again, he was lavished with English hospitality, breakfast in bed, only this time his mate F/S Bob Inglis wasn't there to enjoy the opportunity, having been killed in December 1943. The British clergyman's counsel on this and on the deaths of others was well intended but Bert realised that his relationship with religion and his God had diminished. The avid churchgoer had been lost somewhere in this war.

He was pleased to return to Brighton, and Kriegies Corner – the company of fellow ex-POWs felt more comfortable. But their numbers were dwindling and by August Bert was becoming impatient for his ticket to Australia. The notice to travel to Liverpool came, the last flurry of thankyous and farewells were over and on 8 August, 600 of those who boarded the 22,000-ton troopship *Orion* were the last Australian ex-POWs to sail from Britain.

There had been the euphoria of uninformed youth when Bert had boarded a ship destined for this country on 24 August 1942. He was bulletproof, invincible, determined to fight against evil, prove himself, if not a hero, a defender of his

Finally on the way home (AWM).

family, the British empire and freedom. Watching the landmass disappear allowed time to reflect. It was a seasoned and more subdued RAAF airman who climbed the gangway this time. He looked at the faces of others and realised they reflected his own – men with little youthful resilience remaining. Weathered faces which spoke of the tragedies they had witnessed, the death and destruction that made less sense as the years advanced; yet they were the lucky ones. So many could not climb into this ship or other transports to return home. It was impossible not to think of Robin McPhan, John Spence now buried in foreign graves; Donny Finlayson, other blokes he had trained with, others from 460 Squadron – their faces etched in his mind – or the thousands of other Aussies he never knew. Their families would not await dockside.

The sea voyage was relaxing and annoying. The trip over had seemed to take forever because he was so anxious to be part of the air war. The return trip was far more comfortable, he was much better fed and accommodated, he gained weight and his health improved, but the impatience remained. Perhaps in another life he would bask in this month-long cruise through the Panama Canal, with stops at exotic ports, sunbaking on the deck as the ship passed through the massive Pacific Ocean, but all he could think of was getting home. He doubted that he would actually, leave Australia again. He had his book titled 'My Trip Abroad' – it was full of pictures, just not the sort you purchased in tourist resorts.

He watched the ship's hull cut through the blues and greens of the ocean. He needed to appreciate that Australia and Australians may have changed. His countrymen and women had weathered a war with Japan, which had breached their safety from the air and killed thousands in Indian and Pacific Ocean outposts. Bert had not taken any part in that war – would he be judged for that? Or would he judge himself? If he gave in to the deepest thoughts, he had only fought an enemy for less than four months; all that training, all the hype and just four months of active service. His war had been spent as a prisoner of Germany. Did that make him a fraud? He had suffered physically and mentally but how could others at home appreciate that? There was a huge void between being a hero and being a POW.

CHAPTER NINETEEN

'The most mental and physical deprivation, the memory of which I shall carry to my grave.'

F/L Eric Livingstone Maher (RAAF)

Watching the Australian coast was superb. It was difficult to leave the top deck even for a meal. Passing Sydney Heads and entering Sydney Harbour was breathtaking – never did the harbour look so beautiful. Bert Stobart was not a Sydneysider, but this was Australia.

Families on the dockside were cheering and waving and the reunions brought tears to eyes. He took advantage of quick shore leave to find a telephone to ring Melbourne – he had forgotten the sounds of their voices. His mother had difficulty speaking so his father took hold of the telephone. He too was virtually speechless and could but ask when his son was returning. 'Just a few days' was the answer, as the ship was leaving as soon as it could. There seemed too much to say and no way of saying it: 'See you in just a few days.'

It was difficult to sleep during the short voyage between Australia's largest cities. He would marry Noel as soon as he could. Being a POW had taught Bert much about not wasting any time. Being one of two survivors from his crew had taught him how tenuous and precious life was. He must make the most of every opportunity, find a job, build that house drawn in his POW book, enjoy family life, enjoy.

Orion entering Sydney Harbour (AWM).

Families were not permitted at Station Pier on 10 September, they were gathered at the Melbourne Cricket Ground. The triumphant sounds of an RAAF band welcomed.

There was an urgency in disembarking and filling buses, RAAF ex-POWs hanging out of windows shouting and grinning. The trip through Melbourne city centre

From Station Pier and off to the Melbourne Cricket Ground and their families (AWM).

evoked memories, of quiet times they once deemed as 'mundane' even 'boring'. Their arrival had been announced in the media and the procession of RAAF ex-POWs' buses drew people out of businesses and onto the streets. For Bert, 'I passed the place where I was working before, and they had people out waving' – that 'lump in the throat' again.

There was impatience in completing the RAAF paperwork because relatives awaited outside. 'Noel and the family were all there, to meet me.' The reunion was overwhelming, hugs, kisses, slaps on the back, excited chatter. It barely settled over ensuing days as more family and friends arrived. There was the need to slow down but an urgency to get on with life. 'I was going quicker than I thought I would.' Bert was due to be discharged from the RAAF in January 1946, there was so much to be done, organised, he needed a job, plan a wedding, and Christmas. This Christmas was going to be very different to the last three. Thoughts of the family Christmas had stayed with him during spartan times and there was never going to be another complaint about that hot Christmas roast lunch in the heat of an Australian summer – snow and freezing temperatures were not going to be missed.

Bert was surprised to receive a phone call from the owner of Stott and Hoare, 'Mr Stott himself, who said, "Your job is here".[246] Bert had never had an easy pre-

Robert McPhan (left) and John Spence
(right) (Spence family).

war relationship with the firm's sales manager. The same individual was in the position. The man had not seen active war service and that was now important. Bert travelled into the office to thank Mr Stott and then visited the sales department. The sales manager was less than impressed to hear Bert had been offered his job back. 'He was flattened a bit when I told him I had no intention in coming back.'[247] There needed to be a new start and a job offer with Australian National Airways (later Trans Australian Airways) proved a much better fit and sustained Bert throughout his working life.

Contact with the families of his dead Australian crew proved difficult but was something Bert needed to do. Heather Spence was too young to be a widow and had been left to raise a young son alone. It was no consolation in knowing she was one of many thousands of widows whose lives had been altered irreparably. The letter dated 10 March 1944 had informed her:

The German report of your husband's death has been officially confirmed by the disappearance of his name on a casualty list issued from Berlin, which states that he was buried.[248]

The British Air Ministry had therefore presumed, 'your husband's death for official purposes.'[249] The Minister for Air expressed his 'profound sympathy', well-intended but blunt. It was impossible not to believe they were mistaken, to hold onto that last thread of hope. How, could anything be so categorical in war-torn Europe? John could be a remote hospital or POW camp, there could have been a mistaken identity – the war had not yet ended.

The black bordered RAAF brochure was intended to 'assist you in the present sad occasion' but the typewritten information blurred beneath the tears. She was now permitted to apply for 'a widow's and mother's badge'.[250] A son was supposed to outlive his mother, a widow was supposed to grow old with her husband, a piece of metal to pin on a dress seemed too little, much too little.

John's belongings, including the red leather folder with Heather's portrait, left on his bedside table when he made that last flight over Europe, had been boxed up by personnel with solemn expressions. This duty they had undertaken every day, it was never easy and left a sad lasting impression – so many handsome, youthful men, gone. Photographs and negatives were withheld, sent instead to the Air Ministry in England, to ensure none were images that may compromise the security of the air war. Aircrew logbooks were commonly confiscated for the same reason. Family requests for these continued after the war with varying success.

It was not until July 1947 that those final hopes were extinguished. Another official letter, containing a small black-and-white photo of a stark white cross with the name John Spence in thick black letters. The questions long harboured now answered and the truth was terrible.

> Your husband's aircraft crashed and exploded on impact ... the remains of the five deceased crew members were recovered from the wreckage ... the remains of your husband and three of his comrades are interred in a communal grave.[251]

Another brochure informing her that she could select what was to be engraved on the permanent Imperial War Graves Commission headstone, a headstone shared with a navigator and family she had never met, RAF Sgt Michael Simpson. Suggested phrases included 'For God, King and Country' and 'His Duty Nobly Done'. How could such words express the grief Heather Spence felt?

Robin McPhan and John Spence are buried in Amersfoort in the Netherlands (Spurling).

It was a phrase William and Martha McPhan wrestled with also, for a tombstone and a grave they could never afford to visit. Their son's belongings became especially important, particularly his logbook, which they were denied. The logbook was a record not just of Robin's service and sacrifice but was one of the few items with a strong personal connection. He had carefully handwritten each training flight in black and every operation in red. They discovered that he had collected souvenir coins, no doubt mementos to share with them highlighting his trip around the world to England.

The McPhan family came from the tiny and sparsely settled Kanwal, New South Wales. Sheltered on the central coast north of Wyong they looked over vast spaces of water, lakes and the Pacific Ocean. Their son had crashed 4 miles (7 km) from the village of Benschop, the Netherlands, a place so small it could not be found on their atlas. They were informed Robert was now buried near a town called Amersfoort, the Netherlands, wherever that was, on the other side of the world. Could there be anywhere more different or further away? The graves of pilot Robert McPhan and his bomb aimer John Spence were in a forest, a Dutch forest. The graves seemed out of place, between the trees and undergrowth, Australians buried next to the graves of Polish, Canadian, English and New Zealand aircrew, together in a foreign distant cemetery.

For the families of aircrew, the war did not end in 1945; it never ended but threaded sadly through generations. Families broke and drifted apart. The parents of West Australian PO Leslie 'Jack' Haymes (415082) quickly lost touch with their son's wife Betty, who by 1948 had remarried. As they were not the next-of-kin no direct information from the RAAF was received. They had lost the future as they had imagined it and needed to know how, why and where. From his mother:

> I would be very grateful if you would please send me particulars of the crash of his aircraft, burial, grave etc. We, his parents would value any information you can give us.[252]

It was unclear if the not knowing was worse than the knowing. Jack's 460 Squadron Lancaster was shot out of the sky on 1 September 1943 during an attack on Berlin, one of 47 aircraft and crews destroyed that night. The force of the crash had made it impossible for the remains of Jack to be distinguished from the disintegrated bodies of fellow Australians, PO James Hocking, PO Harold Symons, F/S Trevor Jones, and F/S William Fitzgerald. Could the grief be lessened by the knowledge that the remains of these Australian mates remained together in one grave?

POWs were expected to simply rejoin families and a society that could never understand the horrors and deprivation. The very authorities who had sent them into conflict had little consideration for the damage done – they were not the ones who fought the wars. Physical injuries could be seen, anxiety and depression caused by trauma were not. The war was over, they needed to accept and move on, left to fight the demons themselves. Like so many, WO Assheton Taylor suffered from survival guilt. His good friend and rear gunner never made it out of the Lancaster.

During the intervening years I have often wondered why one young life should have been taken that night whilst the other six were spared. Maybe one day the answer will be revealed.[253]

It never was.

WO Ron MacKenzie (RAAF) admitted there was something 'badly, wrong'. He refused passage back to Australia, remaining in England 'until I had sorted it out, or faced it', because 'I was terribly frightened as frightened of myself as of anyone else'.[254] He had lost faith in humanity and himself. MacKenzie had found himself near Belsen concentration camp. He witnessed the horrors conducted against the Jewish people.

West Australian, WO Raymond Walter Perry (415738) was a bomb aimer with 466 Squadron when shot down in May 1944 while attacking marshalling yards west of Paris. Three of the crew evaded capture, Perry did not. He joined a group of 150 Commonwealth airmen transferred by the Gestapo to Fresnes Prison, Paris, then to Buchenwald concentration camp.

They had heard of the crimes being committed there, and as they were still in the hands of the 'fanatical Gestapo', feared the worst, 'that we had been brought to Buchenwald to be exterminated'.[255] They were taken to a building, stripped and all body hair was shaved. They were then led to a long building, to a totally enclosed room with jets in pipes under the ceiling. Perry was, 'convinced my 21st birthday was going to be cut short'.[256] They expected gas, but it was water which shot out of the jets. They were then given the same blue and white uniforms as the unfortunates they would see disappear into another building to die.

It was impossible to rid oneself of the visions from the German concentration camps. F/S Jim Gwilliam (432355) and F/S Eric Johnston (418957) were members of an RAF 78 Halifax crew when they were shot down on 22 June 1944 en route to bomb Laon, France. They were also with Ray Perry in Buchenwald. The two airmen were photographed before shipping home,

F/S Jim Gwilliam (left) and F/S Eric Johnston (AWM).

but their eyes clearly betrayed what they had witnessed, things 'only monsters could have devised'.257

Ron MacKenzie delayed returning to Australia as long as he could. He struggled with his faith, 'between God, the all-merciful or nothing'.258 He had been told by the Germans when he was captured, 'For you the war is over,' but 'it was never true then; it is never true now. War is a parent.' He could never forget or forgive. 'To any rational being, who studies history, a pragmatic view may well be that it is essentially stupid to start any war'.259 Other POWs could not agree more. Roy Child wrote, 'The audacity and arrogance of the men in high places who draw their people into conflict and sacrifice our young'.260

F/L Eric Maher wrestled with trusting himself and others. He was now shy and embarrassed in company and unable to express his true feelings. 'My once easy flow of small talk and conversation was missing. I felt awkward, clumsy, and out of things'.261 His table manners and ease in company was 'anything but satisfactory. I usually managed to say the wrong thing at the wrong time'.262 When he volunteered to go to war, he never imagined the consequences. 'You can taste war, but cannot savour it, you can smell war, but cannot bask in its flavour, you can see war, but cannot envision yourself in it'.263

There was that remote thought that he may be killed or injured, but never this, not, 'the most agonising mental and physical deprivation, the memory of which I shall carry to my grave'.264

The healing process was ongoing, it was a journey no two ex-POWs took the same. They had lost their youth, deprived of the simple joys of adolescence. They worried relatives and friends thought they were changed, and they wished they could understand why, but these were generations who harboured their emotions, not publicly acknowledging the unusual, but privately condemning it. WO Jack Liley had survived the camps and the marches, for which he was grateful, but the emotions remained close to the surface. Grown men were not supposed to cry but tears came when he approached his home to find his mother waiting at the gate. She later admitted that she never expected him to return.265 He had contracted hepatitis, which weakened his return to good health, and illness persisted throughout the rest of his life. His emotional battle too was ongoing. 'The low mental state I was in when I returned to Australia persisted for a few years'.266

Tom Lonergan had been away from Australia just 17 months. That didn't seem possible, it had to have been longer, but he was about to turn 21. It wasn't easy to just return to his previous life. 'I can't help but think about all the horrible things I witnessed in the past year'.267 Lonergan returned to his pre-war employment as a cost clerk at Australian Paper Manufacturers, in Sydney's Botany, but it was impossible to work behind a desk. Sixteen months were spent as a milk vendor, but the POW experience had weakened his physical stamina. Married to Claire and with a child, they purchased the Gladesville Hotel. His lifeline was phone contact with crew members, his pilot Cy Borsht, navigator, Brian O'Connell and WOP Max Staunton-Smith.

Cy Borsht had returned to Brisbane to work in his father's clothing factory and married Pauline. O'Connell remained in the RAAF and became air commander on board the RAN aircraft carriers HMAS *Sydney* and *Melbourne* and served during the Korean war. Staunton-Smith returned to Hobart and became manager of Tasmania's only radio manufacturer. He died at age 84, two days before O'Connell. Tom Lonergan struggled with ill health and at age 30 was forced to apply for a disability pension, suffering from debilitating headaches, anxiety and gastrointestinal disorders. He was dead at age 60.

Lyle Doust's health was poor on his evacuation to England and he was one of the first 150 RAAF airmen repatriated to Australia. He was sent to a Sydney medical centre to 'fatten up' until 16 October when he returned to Yass, New South Wales. He married Marjory Willis, the Yass station master's daughter, on 17 April 1946 and completed his carpenter's apprenticeship. Unfortunately, the frostbite on

(McCleery)

The wedding day of WO Bert and Noel
Stobart. (Stobart)

his feet that he had suffered during the Long March inhibited his ability and he found employment as a site foreman. Lyle Doust died on 21 February 2005.

Jim McCleery had departed Australian shores on 15 January 1943 as a pilot, not yet 20. He was still 20 when 460 Squadron losses saw him appointed Acting 'C' Flight Commander, and still 20 when shot down and made a POW in Luft III. He was only 21 when he found himself the camp senior British officer at Luft III after surviving a forced march. Injuries required the amputation of his left leg below the knee. In 1952 he applied for Australian Government financial assistance for himself and his family. His reduced income as a 'consequence of wearing an artificial leg' after tax, superannuation and hospital funds caused hardship. The official reply was 'No Hardship'. F/L Jim McCleery died in 1959, he was 35.

Bert and Noel married while he still wore RAAF uniform and they did set up home in Melbourne, close to Brighton Beach. It was easy to be satisfied with a settled married life and three children but contact with ex-POWs brought with it an awareness that so many struggled. Bert too had left Australia imbued with almost naive beliefs but returned with a new caution in his soul concerning the infallibility of his superiors, who directed others into conflict. There were memories he could never divulge to family, and which never needed to be repeated in the company of other POWs. Bert Stobart became heavily involved with the Returned Soldiers League (RSL), assuming many roles within the local Elwood sub-branch and becoming senior Vice President Victorian RSL.

Advocacy for ex-POWs of Germany remained a priority. So many were broken men who never returned to the life Bert enjoyed, too many contended, with debilitating health and died prematurely. They spurned the RSL, and ex-RAAF associations because they believed their experiences could not be and were not shared by members. Bert Stobart realised the importance of establishing ex-POW organisations and a rare space where they felt comfortable, in the company of other aircrew, who had suffered in German camps.

There were fights to ensure successive governments appreciated their service and sacrifice and ongoing battles with the Department of Veteran Affairs. 'I think the government could have done a bit more soon after the war.' While it was acknowledged that Australian POWs of the Japanese suffered inhumane treatment, Australian POWs of Germany were lost to bureaucracy. In time the Australian Government awarded $25,000 to prisoners of the Japanese but nothing to ex-POWs who were interned in Europe.

In a 2001 submission to the government WO Max Staunton-Smith, a member of the Cyril Borsht and Tom Lonergan crew, queried the decision to financially compensate some POWs and not others He was informed that this was because 27 per cent of Japanese POWs died and only 7 per cent of German POWs. Staunton-Smith had nearly died during the Death March and believed that the conditions under which he and his companions had suffered in Europe should not be underestimated. Of his forced march he wrote:

> 1,200 people set out, they were all air force NCOs, only 800 arrived, 400 died on the way through malnutrition, shot, mauled by dogs, TB and pneumonia and also froze to death.[268]

It took six more years before the government readdressed the decision. Although they did not concede that POWs such as Bert Stobart, Max Staunton-Smith and other POWs of Germany were worthy of any financial compensation it was agreed that $25,000 should be paid to the widows of Australian servicemen who died as German POWs.

Bert Stobart was pleased with this small concession although he continued to believe there was a 'good argument that a TPI [Totally and Permanently Incapacitated Pension] should have been awarded automatically to all POWs'. There

Noel and Bert Stobart (Spurling).

was never any official acknowledgement of the suffering of the young Australian men sent into the fury of the skies over Europe and who parachuted into hell. On Australia Day 1988 Bert Stobart was awarded the Order of Australia (OAM) for his services to the veteran community.

Bert and Noel Stobart remained in the same house, and pride of place in their foyer was given to that painting of a young Noel painted in a POW camp in Germany. They died within months of each other. Noel Margaret Georgina Stobart died on 28 January 2015 aged 94. Albert 'Bert' Adrian Stobart OAM died on 16 September 2015 aged 94.

BIBLIOGRAPHY

Australian War Memorial, Canberra

AWM 54	'The scheme for repatriation of RAAF POWs ex-Germany'
1DRL/0428	Australian Red Cross Society, report
PR00423	Abraham, R., papers
SO2773	Bain, R. G., recorded interview
F940.547243 B414	Beecroft, J. M., monogram
PR91/193	Bullock, J. H
AWM2016.392.1	Campbell, K. W., diary
AWM65 927	Currie, A. McG., papers
PR03373	Currie, A. McG., papers
PR05477	Colclough, E. J., papers
AWM 65 983	Davies, R. F.
3DRL/3566	Davies, J. and Welch, J., book
PR04233	Docking, G., papers
PR01451	Farrell, G. W., records of punishment
PR03101	Fraser, C. N., papers
PR85/353	Fordyce, H. S. W., book
PR86/111	Garland, J. D., papers
PR88/132	Garland, J. D., papers
AWM315 419/036/035	Garland, J. D., papers
AWM315 421/011/022	Grinter, A. R. W.
PR04734	Haley, A.A., letter
PR91/092	Holliday, J., papers
AWM 65 2771	Hunter, J. D.
PR03211	Kingsford-Smith, P., book
MSS1436	Liley, J. W. F., 'Jack's War', unpublished manuscript
PR91/116	Lumsden, B. C., papers
PR04658	Lynch, T. J., papers
PR03697	MacDonald, N., letters
AWM315 419/064/057	McCleery, J.

PR88/160   McCleery, J., book
PR00873   Maher, E. F., papers
PR89/129   Mann, R. W., papers
PR05830   Mellor, R. W., papers
PR00506   Morschel, J. R. G., papers
PR85/323   Norton, C. R., papers
3DRL/4164   O'Riordan, C. T., papers
PR03000   Playfair, A., papers
PR86/181   Radke, D. A., papers
PR05422   Shannon, R., papers
AWM315 419/096/017 Smith, W., papers
PR83/165   Thomas, M., papers
PR88/129   Thomson, P. A., papers
PR05478   Wheatley, B. F., papers
PR00918   Woolmer, E., papers

National Archives (Canberra)
A705 166/5/530   Betts, Wesley Hirst
A705 166/6/753   Borsht, Cyril
A705 166/8/145   Conklin, Norman Frank
A705 166/8/695   Cooper, Ronald
A705 166/8/732   Currie, Alister McGregor
A705 166/10/4   Doust, Lyle
A705 166/15/47   Gibbs, William Lionel
A705 163/104/111   Due, Einar Ernest
A705 166/10/186   Dyson, Donald Jeffrey
A705 166/17/293   Haymes, Leslie Jack
A705 166/17/272   Haynes, John Bengough
A705 166/18/133   Hunter, John Dempsey
A705 166/22/362   Kingsford-Smith, Peter
A705 166/25/215   Lonergan, Thomas
A705 166/25/155   Long, Henry Jeffries
A705 166/26/455   McCleery, James
A705 166/26/227   McPhan, Robert Barr
A705 166/27/651   Mayo, Tinbury Alan
A705 166/30/18   Nowlan, Stanley Roderick
A705 166/31/259   O'Connell, Brian
A705 163/50/52   O'Riordan, Clifford Timothy

A705	166/35/64	Ransome, Horace D'Arcy Meadows
A705	166/35/437	Redding, William Frank
A705	166/37/129	Shaw, Frank Bernard
A705	166/38/266	Spence, John Andrew
A705	166/38/745	Staunton-Smith, Maxwell
A705	166/38/267	Stobart, Albert Adrian
A705	166/38/186	Stooke, Gordon
A705	38/1/261	Ulm, AFC
A816	54/301/172	Australian and British prisoners of war interned in Germany, Italy and France – Reports from camps Part 1.
A816	54/301/191	Australian and British prisoners of war interned in Germany, Italy and France – Reports from camps Part 2.
A816	67/301/16	Australian and British prisoners of war interned in Germany, Italy and France – Reports from camps Part 3.
A8231/28		O'Riordan, Clifford Timothy
A9300		Kingsford-Smith, Peter
A9300		McCleery, James
A9300		O'Riordan, Clifford Timothy
A9300		Ransome H. D. M.
A9301 412184		Redding William Frank
A9301 408934		Stobart, Albert Adrian
A1539 1942/W/498		Correspondence with Officers of the Commission who are Prisoners of War in Germany.
A1539 1942/W/498		Correspondence with Officers of the Commission who are Prisoners of War in Germany.
A1608 AT20/1/1		War Records – Prisoner of War. Shooting of Air Force Personnel in Germany.
A2939 SC 104		POW Treatment of POW and interned civilians in Austria and German.
A5954 670/3		POWs. Lists of Locations and Numbers of British and Belgium POWs in camps in Germany. Provided by German High Command.
A5954 670/4		POWs arrangements for exchange of POWs.
A5954 670/5		POW exchange.
A9652 Box 35		RAAF Sqn narrative reports – 460 Sqn – 11 June 1943 to 30 June 1944.
AA1969/100 Box 1		RAAF POWs Original German identity cards RAAF airmen includes photos of airmen.

B1535 715/1/36	Flying training
B3856 144/4/34	Deceased POWs
B3856 144/1/152	Exchange of sick POWs
B3856 144/4/36	Australian POWs location Germany
B3856 144/4/38	Date of deaths of POWs Germany
B3856 144/4/39	Camp transfers
B3856 144/4/42	Camp transfers
B3856 144/4/43	Camp Transfers
B3856 144/4/45	Camp transfers
B3856 144/4/47	Camp transfers
B3856 144/4/52	Transfers and exchange
B3856 144/11/4	POW exchange
M1416 66	Personal papers of Prime Minister Curtin 'Handcuffing of POWs in Germany'.
MT1384/3 221	Aust. Flying Corps

National Archives (Melbourne)

MP16/1 1918/159	Boberski
MP98/1/1 556/201/1743	Pay for POWs in Germany
MP367/1 415/1/1213	Air Force Bill
MP367/1 559/26/41	Hinkler and Little
MP367/1 559/28/334	AFC
MP367/1 567/9/52	'The treatment of British Prisoners of War in German and Turkish Camps'.
MP508/1 284/750/46	Letter from Aust. POW relatives Association re repatriation from Germany of members of the 2/5th AGH
MP742/1 336/1/852	POW ill-treatment
MP742/1 255/18/191	Repatriation of POWs
MP742/1 336/1/929	Part 20 Ill-treatment of POWs
MP1049/14 1915/9443	Aust. RN Flying Corps candidates

Secondary Sources

Air Ministry, *Bomber Command*, 1941.

Bates, H. E. *Fair Stood the Wind for France*, Michael Joseph, 1949.

Beede, J. *They Hosed Them Out*, Australasian Book Society, 1965.

Brickhill, P. *Escape or Die: True Stories of Heroic Escapes*, Cassell, 2003.

Brickhill, P. *The Dam Busters*, Evans Bros., 1952.

Champ, J and Burgess, C., (eds) *The Diggers of Colditz*, Allen and Unwin, 1988.

Charlswood, D. *No Moon Tonight*, Angus and Robertson, 1979.

Child, R. *A Wartime Log: of a young RAF Air Gunner POW 1944–1945*, self published, 1985.

Christiansen, C. *Seven Years Among Prisoners of War*, translated by Winther, E., 1994, Ohio University Press.

Enright, M. *Flyers Far Away*, Longueville Books, 2009.

Green, P. *The March East 1945: The Final Days of Of Stalag IX A/H and A/Z*, Spellmount, 2012.

Holliday, J. E. and Radke. D. A. (eds) *Stories of the RAAF POWs of Lamsdorf, Including Chronicles of their 500-MileTrek*, Lamsdorf RAAF POWs Association, 1992.

Hoyle, A. *Into the Darkness: A Personal Memoir*, self-published 1989.

Kelly, R. *Tail of a Gunner: a WOAG from Wagga Wagga*, Triple D Books, 2013.

Krentz, H. *To Hell in a Halifax: The story of an RCAF Pilot and His Fellow POWs*, self-published, 2006.

Lewis, B. *Aircrew: The Story of the Men who Flew the Bombers*, Cassell, 2000.

Mounteath, P. *POW: Australian POWs in Hitler's Reich*, Pan MacMillan, 2011.

Munro, R. *Holidaying on the Continent: The Journey of an RAAF Volunteer 1940–45 460 RAAF Squadron*, Australian Military History Publications, 2009.

Odd Bods at War 1939-1945, Vol.1, Odd Bods U.K. Association, 1988.

Pearson, R. *Australians at War in the Air 1939–1945*, Vol.1, Kangaroo Press, 1995.

Pearson, S. *The Great Escaper: The Life and Death of Roger Bushell*, Hodder & Stoughton, 2014.

Reid, P. R. *Colditz The Full Story*, Pan, 1984.

Reid, P. R. *The Latter Days at Colditz*, Cassell, 2003.

Spurling, K. *A Grave Too Far Away: A Tribute to Australians in Bomber Command Europe*, New Holland, 2012.

Stephens, A. *The Royal Australian Air Force*, The Australian Centenary History of Defence, Vol. II, Oxford University Press, 2001.

Stooke, G. *Flak and Barbed Wire*, Australian Military History Publications, 1997.

Taylor, A. F. *One way Flight to Munich: Memoir of a 460 Squadron (RAAF) Navigator*, Australian Military History Publications, 2000.

Taylor, G. *Piece of Cake*, Corgi, 1980.

The Australian Women's Weekly, 19 January 1935.

Walley, B (ed.). *Silk and Barbed Wire*, RAF ex-POWs Association (Australia Division), Sage Pages, 2000.

Wilkins, L. *Artists in Action: From the Collection of the Australian War Memorial*, AWM, 2003.

Websites

www.ozatwar.com/460sqdn/lanclosses.htm

www.abc.net.au/news/2019-03-24/the-great-escape-film-was-fiction-but-paul-brickhill-left-a-mark/10911138#:~:text=It%20was%20a%20dog%2Deared,camp%20in%20World%20War%20II.&text=It%20was%20a%20shattering%20end%20to%20the%20ultimate%20boy's%20own%20tale

www.thisdayinaviation.com/24-march-1944/

s.telegraph.co.uk/graphics/projects/great-escape/index.htm

kenfentonswar.com/stalag-luft-vi/

Endnotes

1   Stephens, A. *The Royal Australian Air Force*, The Australian Centenary History of Defence, Vol. II, Oxford University Press, 2001, p. 67.
2   ibid., p. 68.
3   Pearson, Ross. A. *Australians at War in the Air 1939–1945*, Kangaroo Press, 1995, p. 21.
4   After World War II, this became the RAAF School of Radio until the school was moved in 1961, to RAAF Laverton, Victoria.
5   Stephens, op. cit., p. 72.
6   3DRL/4164, O'Riordan, Clifford Timothy, Australian War Memorial, Canberra.
7   Kelly, R. *Tail of a Gunner: a WOAG from Wagga Wagga*, Triple D Books, 2013, p. 174.
8   126 squadrons served with Bomber Command. On paper, 32 were non-British, 15 RCAF, 8 RAAF (4 Polish, 1 Czechoslovakian, two NZ two French. Canada supplied a total of 94,000 aircrew.
9   Hoyle, A. *Into the Darkness*, self-published, 1989, p. 32.
10 Pearson, op. cit., p. 57.
11 A9652 Box 35: RAAF Sqn narrative reports – 460 Sqn – 11 June 1943 to 30 June 1944, National Archives, Canberra.
12 ibid.
13 Pearson, op. cit., p. 58.
14 ibid.
15 A9652, Box 35.
16 3DRL/4164 O'Riordan, C. T., AWM, Canberra.
17 ibid.
18 ibid.
19 ibid.
20 ibid.
21 ibid.
22 ibid.
23 ibid.
24 ibid.
25 ibid.
26 ibid.
27 Pearson, op. cit., p. 60.
28 ibid., p. 62.
29 ibid.
30 A9652 Box 35 RAAF Squadron narrative reports – 460 Squadron – 11 June 1943 to 30 June 1944.
31 W/O Edwin Garth Carthew (407963); F/O Sidney Milton Forrester (416558); W/O Cyril Augustine Walsh (401605). RAF Sgt John Cresswell Coombes (1388894); Sgt Herbert Freeman Jowett (1685619) Sgt Ernest Albert Cecil Thirkettle (1217817) and Sgt Arthur Rolfe (1681963).
32 Author's father.
33 Walley, B. (ed.), *Flak and Barbed Wire*, Military History Books, 2000, p. vii.
34 Munro, R. *Holidaying on the Continent: The Journey of an RAAF Volunteer: 1940–45 460 RAAF Squadron*, Australian Military History Publications, 2009, p. 105.
35 ibid., p. 117.
36 F/O Maxwell Alton Norris (author's father).
37 *Odd Bods at War 1939–1945*, vol.1, Odd Bods U.K. Association, 1988, p. 54.
38 Middlebrook quoted in Munro, R. *Holidaying on the Continent*, p. 100.
39 A9652 Box 35 RAAF Squadron narrative reports – 460 Squadron – 11 June 1943 to 30 June 1944.
40 The night fighter has been cited differently, as a: Bf 110 or Ju 88, and as a ME110. Another report says a Heinkel 219 piloted by Hauptmann Hans-Dieter Frank.
41 AWM 64 (1/293) AWM (1/294) AWM 237 (63). NAA: A705, 166/26/227.

42 A705 166/26/227, McPhan, Robert
Barr, National Archives, Canberra.

43 A1608 A1608/1 446 11 277 6 2 5
(B567642); National Archives, Canberra.

44 AWM65 2771, Hunter, J.D., AWM.

45 AWM54 Part 1 779/3/126.

46 ibid.

47 Walley, B. (ed.) *Silk and Barbed Wire*,
RAF ex-POW Association (Aust), 2000,
p. 149.

48 PR88/160, McCleery, James, 'A wartime
log', AWM.

49 Wilkins, *Artists in Action: From the
Collection of the Australian War Memorial*,
AWM, 2003.

50 Three years later Esther Gwendolyn
'Stella' Bowen died of breast and liver
cancer having been unable to return to
Australia. She was 54.

51 McCleery, op. cit.

52 ibid.

53 MP367/1, 567/9/52. 'The treatment
of British Prisoners of War in German
and Turkish Camps', National Archives,
Melbourne.

54 ibid.

55 PR03000, Playfair, A., papers, AWM,
Canberra.

56 ibid.

57 PR05477, Colclough, E. J. P., papers.

58 ibid.

59 MSS1436, Liley, J. W. F., 'Jack's War',
AWM, Canberra.

60 ibid.

61 ibid.

62 ibid.

63 ibid.

64 Beede, J. *They Hosed Them Out*,
Australasian Book Society, 1965, p. 26.

65 www.ozatwar.com/460sqdn/lanclosses.
htm.

66 PR04658, Lynch, T., diary, log book,
service papers, AWM, Canberra.

67 ibid.

68 ibid.

69 ibid.

70 ibid.

71 ibid.

72 PR88/132, Garland, Jack. 'On the
Wings Like Eagles', manuscript, AWM,
Canberra.

73 ibid.

74 ibid.

75 ibid.

76 Augenstein was believed to have shot
down 46 Allied aircraft before he was
shot down and killed in December 1944
by F/L Edward Hedgecoe (RAF) in a
Mosquito Mk XXX N/F. Hedgecoe was
killed on 1 January 1945.

77 Waller, D. 'Navigating the War', privately
published 15 copies, Canberra, 2010,
p. 32.

78 PR04658, Lynch, T.

79 A705 166/10/4, Doust, L., National
Archives, Canberra.

80 Waller, D., op. cit., p. 39.

81 Garland, J. op. cit.

82 Garland, J. op. cit.

83 A705 166/35/437; A9301 412184,
Redding, W. F., National Archives,
Canberra.

84 AWM54 Part 1 779/3/126 statements
by RAAF POWs in Germany.

85 ibid.

86 ibid.

87 PRO1451, Farrell, G. T. W., AWM,
Canberra.

88 Garland, J. op. cit.

89 A9300, Kingsford-Smith, P., National
Archives, Canberra.

90 A705 166/22/362, National Archives,
Canberra.

91 AWM65 3031, Kingsford-Smith, P.,
AWM, Canberra.

92 A705, 163/64/183, Williams, J.E.A,
National Archives, Canberra.

93 A9300, Kierath, R.V., National Archives,
Canberra.

94 ibid.

95 Catanach, James, A9300, National
Archives, Canberra.

96 A9301 403218, Hake, A. H., National
Archives, Canberra.

97 AWM65 3031, Kingsford-Smith, P.

98 ibid.

99 AWM54 Part 1 779/3/126 statements
by RAAF POWs in Germany.

100 Following the end of the war, a three-year
investigation, resulted in 18 Nazi soldiers
being found guilty of war crimes for the

murder of the recaptured POWs and 13 were executed.

101 AWM54, Part 1 779/3/126, statements by RAAF POWs in Germany.

102 ibid.

103 ibid.

104 Clutton-Brock, O. *Footprints on the Sands of Time: RAF Bomber Command Prisoners of War in Germany 1939–1945*, 2003, p. 471.

105 A9301 425186, Mirfin, Roy William, National Archives, Canberra.

106 ibid.

107 kenfentonswar.com/stalag-luft-vi/

108 Garland, J., op. cit.

109 ibid.

110 AWM54, Part 1 779/3/126, statements by RAAF POWs in Germany.

111 PR03000, Playfair, A., papers, AWM, Canberra.

112 MSS1441, MacKenzie, R. C., 'An Ordinary War', AWM, Canberra.

113 ibid.

114 ibid.

115 ibid.

116 AWM54, Part 1 779/3/126, Statements by RAAF POWs in Germany.

117 ibid.

118 PR88/132, Garland, J., AWM, Canberra.

119 ibid.

120 ibid.

121 ibid.

122 PR00873, Maher, E., 'My Experiences as a POW in Germany', AWM, Canberra.

123 Garland, J., op. cit.

124 PR01451, Farrell, G., private record, AWM.

125 ibid.

126 Taylor, A.F. *One Way Flight to Munich*, Australian Military History, 2000, p. 175.

127 There is little consensus concerning numbers. One report suggested 89,500 US and 1408 British casualties. It is believed there were between 63,222 and 98,000 German casualties.

128 Lonergan, 'The War Diary of Thomas Patrick Lonergan: The Missing Years', unpublished.

129 ibid.

130 ibid.

131 Spurling, K. *A Grave Too Far Away: A Tribute to Australians in RAF Bomber Command, Europe*; New Holland, 2012.

132 Lonergan, op. cit., p. 11.

133 ibid., p. 15.

134 AWM64 1/342 – [RAAF formation and unit records] Operational Record Book, No. 463 Squadron, December 1943 – September 1945, AWM.

135 ibid.

136 Lonergan, op. cit., p. 20.

137 Not to be confused with RAAF 460 Lancaster by the same code name which ultimately was brought out to remain in the Australian War Memorial.

138 Lonergan, op. cit., p. 20.

139 ibid., p. 24.

140 ibid., p. 27.

141 ibid., p. 28.

142 ibid.

143 ibid., p. 29.

144 ibid., p. 32.

145 ibid.

146 ibid., p. 33.

147 ibid., p. 39.

148 ibid., p. 40.

149 AWM 64 1/342(3) 1/343 AWM 54 779/3/129 Part 26, AWM.

150 Lonergan, op. cit., p. 41.

151 ibid.

152 There is some discrepancy and confusion in the naming of the lufts (officers) and stalags (non-commissioned officers), particularly towards the end of the war when the two appeared to merge. Luft 7 appears as well as Stalag VII. A combination of both is also used (as when McCleery later takes charge of Stalag Luft III).

153 A9300, Holliday, J. E., National Archives, Canberra.

154 api.parliament.uk/historic-hansard/commons/1942/dec/01/chained-prisoners-of-war.

155 Holliday, op. cit.

156 ibid.

157 ibid.

158 AWM54 Part 1 779/3/126 statements by RAAF POWs in Germany, AWM, Canberra.

159 May, M. 'As it Happened: Oh, To Be in
     Aircrew', Australian Gold Coast Branch
     of Air Crew Association.
160 ibid.
161 ibid.
162 ibid.
163 ibid.
164 ibid.
165 ibid.
166 Holliday, op. cit.
167 AWM54 Part 1 779/3/126 statements
     by RAAF POWs in Germany.
168 Shannon, R. PR05422, diary, papers,
     AWM, Canberra.
169 ibid.
170 ibid.
171 ibid.
172 ibid.
173 *The Australian Women's Weekly*,
     19 January 1935, p. 7.
174 PR03000, Playfair, A., papers, AWM.
175 ibid.
176 AWM54 Part 1 779/3/126 statements
     by RAAF POWs in Germany.
177 Child, R., op. cit., p. 32.
178 Walley, B. (ed.), op. cit., p. 11.
179 AWM54 Part 1 779/3/126 statements
     by RAAF POWs in Germany.
180 A705 166/39/233 and A9301 418711,
     Terrett, L. J., National Archives,
     Canberra.
181 AWM54 Part 1 779/3/126 statements
     by RAAF POWs in Germany.
182 ibid.
183 ibid.
184 PRO1451, Farrell, G. T. W., AWM,
     Canberra.
185 AWM54 Part 1 779/3/126 statements
     by RAAF POWs in Germany.
186 A9301, 407822, National Archives,
     Canberra.
187 PR01451, Farrell, G., private record,
     AWM, Canberra.
188 Thomson, P. 'The Ides of March 1944',
     in Walley, B. (ed.) *Silk and Barbed Wire*,
     RAF ex-POW Association (Aust), 2000,
     pp. 203–21
189 ibid., p. 217.
190 Lonergan, op. cit., p. 55.
191 Lonergan, op. cit., p. 55.
192 ibid.
193 Thomson, op. cit., p. 219.
194 Lonergan, op. cit., p. 58.
195 Thomson, op. cit., p. 219.
196 ibid., p. 218.
197 ibid.
198 Lonergan, op. cit., p. 59.
199 Lonergan, op. cit., p. 57.
200 Pearson, op. cit., p. 121.
201 Lonergan, op. cit., p. 60.
202 Thomson, op. cit., p. 221.
203 Lonergan, op. cit., p. 66.
204 ibid.
205 AWM54 Part 1 779/3/126 statements
     by RAAF POWs in Germany, AWM.
206 ibid.
207 Garland, J., op. cit.
208 ibid.
209 ibid.
210 ibid.
211 ibid.
212 ibid.
213 ibid.
214 Christiansen, C. *Seven Years Among
     Prisoners of War*, translated by Winther,
     E., 1994, Ohio University Press.
215 Stooke, G. *Flak and Barbed Wire*,
     Australian Military History, 1997, p. 110.
216 AWM 27 424/22-424/26.
217 ibid.
218 Waller, D., op. cit.
219 ibid.
220 Lonergan., op. cit., p. 71.
221 McCleery, op. cit.
222 ibid.
223 ibid.
224 Lonergan., op. cit., p. 73.
225 ibid.
226 ibid., p. 75.
227 ibid., p. 76.
228 AWM54 Part1 779/3/126 statements by
     RAAF personnel from Prisoner of War
     camps.
229 Taylor, A. F., *One Way Flight to Munich*,
     Australian Military History Publications,
     2000, p. 232.
230 ibid., p. 233.
231 MSS1436, Liley, J.; 'Jack's War',
     AWM Canberra.
232 ibid.
233 McCleery, op. cit.
234 Stooke, op. cit., p. 118.

235 AWM 54, 'The Scheme for the Repatriation of RAAF POW ex-Germany', AWM.

236 Kelly, op. cit., p. 248.

237 ibid., p. 247.

238 ibid.

239 ibid.

240 Pearson, op. cit., p. 123.

241 ibid., p. 121.

242 AWM 54, 'The Scheme for the Repatriation of RAAF POW ex-Germany', AWM, Canberra.

243 ibid.

244 ibid.

245 ibid.

246 ibid.

247 ibid.

248 A705 166/38/266, Spence, John Andrew, National Archives, Canberra.

249 ibid.

250 ibid.

251 ibid.

252 A705 166/17/293, Haymes, Leslie Jack, National Archives, Canberra.

253 Taylor, A. F., op. cit., p. 103.

254 MSS1441, MacKenzie, R. C., 'A Ordinary War', AWM, Canberra.

255 Walley, B. (ed.), op. cit., p. 253.

256 ibid., p. 255.

257 MacKenzie, R.C., op. cit.

258 ibid.

259 ibid.

260 Child, op. cit., p. 33.

261 PR00873, Maher, Eric, 'My Experiences as a POW in Germany', AWM, Canberra.

262 ibid.

263 ibid.

264 ibid.

265 PR89/162, Liley, J., AWM, Canberra.

266 ibid.

267 Lonergan, op. cit., p. 80.

268 A705 166/38/745, Staunton-Smith, M. R., National Archives, Canberra.

269 Stooke, G. *Flak and Barbed Wire*, Australian Military History Publications, 1997, p. 21.

270 Outdoor group portrait of members of No. 460 Squadron RAAF, based at an RAF Station that has been newly formed and equipped with Wellington bomber aircraft. Identified from left to right: 404539 Sergeant (Sgt) (later Flight Lieutenant (Flt Lt)) William John Chaplain from Brisbane Queensland; 402600 Sgt Trevor Hopetoun McIlveen from Sydney, NSW (killed on flying operations over Germany on 29 April 1942); 400337 Sgt (later Pilot Officer) Stuart Wood from Victoria in front (accidentally killed in the UK on 15 February 1943); next two at back are unidentified; 404256 Sgt (later Flt Lt) Francis Joseph Nugent from Queensland, in front (later awarded DFC); 407828 Sgt (later Flying Officer) Arrol Ainslie Penglase from South Australia; 407531 Sgt (later Flt Lt) Allan Francis McKinnon from South Australia (later awarded DFC) (killed on flying operations over Germany on 5 March 1944); 408122 Sgt John Percival Cosgrove from South Australia (killed on flying operations over Germany on 29 April 1942); 404684 Sgt (later Flight Sergeant (F/S) Alexander Clive Johnston from Queensland (killed on flying operations over Germany on 13 May 1943); 400524 Sgt (later F/S) Hugh Rowell Brodie from Melbourne, Victoria (killed on flying operations over Germany on 3 June 1942); 400335 Sgt John Robert Shearer from Victoria, in front (killed on flying operations over Germany on 7 May 1942); and 404705 Sgt Reginald Henry Murphy from Queensland (killed on flying operations over Germany on 7 May 1942).

271 PR03211, Kingsford-Smith, P., AWM.

272 McCleery, J. PR88/160. Private record, AWM.

273 ibid., p. 229.

274 wallyswar.files.wordpress.com/2012/07/ferrets.jpg.

275 Walley, B. (ed.), op. cit., p. 45.

276 www.historyextra.com/period/second-world-war/five-myths-of-the-ww2-great-escape.

277 ibid.

278 www.abc.net.au/news/2019-03-24/the-great-escape-film-was-fiction-but-paul-brickhill-left-a-

mark/10911138#:~:text=It%20was%20
a%20dog%2Deared,camp%20in%20
World%20War%20II.&text=It%20
was%20a%20shattering%20end%20
to%20the%20ultimate%20boy's%20
own%20tale.

279 www.thisdayinaviation.com/
24-march-1944/.

280 s.telegraph.co.uk/graphics/projects/
great-escape/index.html.

281 www.abc.net.au/news/2019-03-
24/the-great-escape-film-was-
fiction-but-paul-brickhill-left-a-
mark/10911138#:~:text=It%20was%20
a%20dog%2Deared,camp%20in%20
World%20War%20II.&text=It%20
was%20a%20shattering%20end%20
to%20the%20ultimate%20boy's%20
own%20tale.

282 In 1948 it was found that the memorial
had been broken into. Urns had been
damaged with their ashes missing.
The memorial was reconstructed and
continues to stand.

283 Walley, B. (ed.), op. cit. p. 234.

284 Child, R. A Wartime Log: of a Young
RAF Air Gunner POW 1944–1945,
self-published, 1985.

285 Walley, B. (ed.), op. cit., p. XV.

286 PR03000, Playfair, A., papers, AWM,
Canberra.

287 PR88/160, McCleery, James, F. O.,
'A wartime log', AWM, Canberra.

ACKNOWLEDGEMENTS

I owe the motivation for the book to the late, Warrant Officer (WO) Albert 'Bert' Stobart (RAAF), and other amazing Australians who fought with RAF Bomber Command during World War II and who survived not only the fury of the air war, but life as prisoners of war of Nazi Germany.

During my research for an earlier book, *A Grave too Far Away: A Tribute to Australians in Bomber Command Europe* (2012) I was privileged to interview veterans, ex-POWs and their families. Their stories were extraordinary; men who believed themselves regular Australian boys forced too rapidly into manhood. The stories were grim but riveting, and highlighted bravery and the indomitable human spirit. They deserved a book of their own.

During my interview with the wonderful Bert Stobart, he produced a book titled 'My Trip Abroad'. I must admit the title did not immediately inspire, but the contents did. Each page offered a story, a painting, a poem, a cartoon, drawn and penned by Bert's fellow POWs in Stalag IVB, providing a rare insight into the lives of incarcerated Australian aircrew. The time I spent with Bert is a wonderful memory, as is the painting of his then fiancée Noel, completed in Stalag IVB and which returned to Melbourne, Australia, to take pride of place in their home throughout their long marriage.

Kathryn Spurling

Dr Kathryn Spurling

Served with the Women's Royal Australian Naval Service (WRANS). Her late father F/O Maxwell Norris (RAAF) served with RAF Bomber Command during WWII. After securing her PhD in military history Dr Spurling tutored history and strategic studies and guest lectured in history at the University of New South Wales, Australian Defence Force Academy, Canberra. In 2012 she was appointed a Visiting Fellow at the Australian National University, Canberra and in 2014 became an Adjunct Visiting Research Associate with Flinders University. She has lectured extensively overseas on military issues. Most significant: First Australian invited to speak at NATO HQ, Brussels, on women in the military; First Australian Summer Military History Fellow, United States Military Academy, West Point; Guest lecturer at the Dutch Defence College, Amsterdam, the Netherlands. Keynote speaker at the Women's Research and Education Institute 'Women in Uniform Conference', Washington DC, four times. Keynote speaker, Australian Women of the Year National Congress, Canberra. Keynote speaker 'Women in the Australian Defence Force', Chief of Defence Force Conference on Women in Security and the ADF. Speaker at Crime and Justice Challenges for the Contemporary Military Conference, Onati School of Sociology, Spain. Commemorative address, RAN Centenary Ceremony for the Loss of AE1 and Crew, Rabaul, New Guinea. Appearances include *The Drum, Four Corners* and *Insight*.

Books:

Women in Uniform: Perceptions and Pathways, eds., K. Spurling and E. Greenhalgh, UNSW@ADFA, 2014.

Cruel Conflict: The Triumph and Tragedy of HMAS Perth I, New Holland, 2008.

A Grave Too Far Away: A Tribute to Australians in Bomber Command Europe, New Holland, 2012.

Inspiring Australian Women, Missing Pages Books, 2013.

The Mystery of AE1: Australia's Lost Submarine and Crew, Missing Pages Books, 2014.

HMAS Canberra: Casualty of Circumstance, New Holland, 2016.

Abandoned and Sacrificed: The Tragedy of the Montevideo Maru, New Holland, 2017.

Fire at Sea: HMAS Westralia 1998, Elephant Tree Publishing, 2019.

Bureaucracy, Bankers and Bastards: A Farmer's Story, Ginninderra Press, 2020.

kathrynspurling.com